Rachael Mogan McIntosh is a mum of three, crisis counsellor and community trainer from the south coast of New South Wales. Her writing has appeared in publications across Australia, France and the USA. Rachael loves books, baths, coffee, podcasts, TV and Terry's Chocolate Orange, consuming them simultaneously whenever possible. *Pardon My French* is her first book.

Pardon My French

RACHAEL MOGAN MCINTOSH

affirm
press

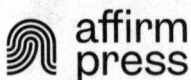

affirm
press

First published by Affirm Press in 2023
Boon Wurrung Country
28 Thistlethwaite Street
South Melbourne VIC 3205
affirmpress.com.au

10 9 8 7 6 5 4 3 2

Parts of the following chapters are edited versions of articles previously published
in media outlets: 'Schedule unfolding', first published in *Good Weekend* magazine;
'The Calade', first published in *The Saturday Paper*; 'Sommières market', first
published in *Sunday Life* magazine; 'French food', first published in *News.com.au*
and the *New York Post*; 'Snow and pierogis', first published in *Sunday Life* magazine;
'Grand tour', first published in *Sunday Life* magazine.

A catalogue record for this
book is available from the
National Library of Australia

ISBN: 9781922848390 (paperback)

Cover design and illustration by Louisa Maggio © Affirm Press
Typeset in 12/17 pt Garamond Premier Pro by Post Pre-press Group
Proudly printed and bound in Australia by McPherson's Printing Group

MIX
Paper | Supporting
responsible forestry
FSC® C001695

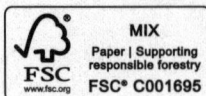

For my darling Keith

Contents

The worst life a child has ever had

'All landscapes ask the same question in the same whisper:
I am watching you – are you watching yourself in me?'

Lawrence Durrell

It's lunchtime in the south of France and my family and I are enjoying some wholesome and educational together-time, making fun of pigeon sex. It's become something of a ritual. Terracotta-tint rooftops sprawl down the hill below our sunroom and most days we sit at the table and watch a bird we call Larry hop across them as he clumsily attempts and fails to mount his uninterested partners.

'Go, Larry!' cries my six-year-old daughter, Mabel, as the poor bastard hops about awkwardly, trying to get purchase. After a time his partner shakes him off and flies away to sit, unmolested, on another rooftop. Larry looks sad, we agree. Sweet little avian incel. But is Larry sad? I don't know. More likely pigeon sex is often this awkward and unsuccessful, and we're just wrongly ascribing character traits and motivations for Larry, like we do for every aspect of our strange and confusing new life.

When we planned this family adventure in France I didn't imagine us sitting around cracking gags about the saddo sex lives of animals, but then again, nothing so far has unfolded exactly as expected. Go to France, they said! Life will be sophisticated, they said!

Sophisticated? *Non*. But it is splendid. The bright sunroom from which we poke fun at Larry sits at the very top of our narrow terrace house in Sommières, a small village in southern France halfway between the large cities of Nîmes and Montpellier. Just over the border from Provence, it's a town marinated in history. Settlement dates back to Roman times, and behind our house on Rue Canard, or 'Duck Street', soars a twelfth-century tower. Long ago, unruly women were denounced as prostitutes and locked up in its damp stone rooms.

The River Vidourle is visible in glimpses between the plane trees, which now, as autumn begins, are starting to shed golden leaves, and somewhere on it is the pair of swans we call Charles and Camilla. Between the buildings, a higgledy-piggledy tapestry of narrow lanes weave in and out of tunnels and archways and overhangs. They are paved with uneven cobbles that get slippery with pigeon shit in the rain.

The five of us sit in mismatched chairs around the battered old wooden dining table. It's littered with lunchtime debris, and we're all a bit shattered. The midday break is here – two hours off school for the children and a welcome pause for my husband, Keith, who's been working since 5am, catching the end of the Australian business day. For me, it's a break from my full-time occupation: making a tit of myself in public as I scramble my way through the cultural and social norms of small-town France.

Flaky crumbs are everywhere. On our walk home from school we picked up baguettes at the *boulangerie* called Farine. With these I made our standard lunch: long open sandwiches of fresh mozzarella, tomatoes, baby spinach, mustard and mayonnaise. These are always followed by lunch dessert, where almond croissants, *pain au chocolat* or custardy Paris–Brest are fished out of their warm paper bags and shared. We drink gallons of lemon *sirop* (cordial) and fizzy water.

Mabel is in kindergarten here at École Albert Camus, her nine-year-old brother Alex (we call him 'Biggles') in *CM-un* or Year 4, and ten-year old Tabitha in *CM-deux* or Year 5, the final class of the primary-school system. They'll spend the European school year there, and then we'll all return to real life back on the south coast of New South Wales in Australia.

Larry flies away, having failed, again, to get lucky at lunchtime. I look at my phone to check the time. The school run requires me to set several daily alarms. Many children stay at school for the midday meal at the *cantine*, but our kids are far from being able to cope with a three-course sit-down lunch. We need that two-hour break to put them together emotionally for their afternoon shift in class, so we must trek back and forth to school four times a day.

The only English spoken by their classmates comes at break time in the lively schoolyard, when they sing 'Allo dakness my ol' frenn ...' to any child who cries, drawing an imaginary tear down their cheek with a finger. Folk sarcasm, it burns. Home in Rue Canard at lunch is the only part of the day in which the children can talk.

It's one way that this year-long French adventure is proving more difficult than we had anticipated. Like Larry, we're just giving things an awkward, hopeful go, and it's quite possible that strangers are laughing behind their hands at us, the very same way we mock Larry. That optimistic, horny little loser.

The screen-time debate commences. Usually we allow the children little access to soul-sucking blue lights, but here in these early weeks of our France life we are all about trying to ease the transition. After a morning at school the children need to decompress. Distribution of screens between the three, however, is a finely tuned negotiation. One child scores my laptop, another the slow and glitchy 'kids computer' and the last gets the TV with the French cartoon channel. Mabel is not happy with today's outcome.

'But I want to watch the gymnastics girl!' she says. Mabel loves talent-show clips on YouTube. Biggles and Tabitha are unwavering. Biggles is playing the world-building game *Civilization* with Dad, and it's Tabitha's turn for Netflix sitcoms. It's *Mr. Bean* in French for Mabel today, and no arguments. This latest indignity lands on top of her stresses of the morning. It's all just too much.

'This is the worst life a child has ever had!' wails Mabel. I look at her. She has half a chocolate croissant in one grubby little fist and the remnants of the other half smeared across her face. Above, swallows dive and soar in the cloudless sky, while scraps of music and French conversation float up to us from the streets beneath the window.

Parenting. You can't win. 'Sorry, Mabel,' I tell her. 'It's just for a year. You'll have to find a way to endure.'

The bath in the bedroom

Six months earlier, it is a bath in a tiny attic bedroom that first sells me on Sommières. Searching online for a rental in France, Keith and I ponder listings featuring images of mountains and farmhouses and cities. We discuss our selection criteria: small local school, cheap price, warm weather and that elusive X factor. It's hard to find listings in English but one day Rue Canard appears, like a perfect little jewel. I peer at the thumbnail photos of the small stone terrace and the iron bed with a claw-foot tub squatting at its end.

The picture of the bath grabs me by the goolies. I'm a bath aficionado. I spend an hour in my watery chapel every day – the tub is my happiest of happy places, second only to my bed. To have one within three steps of the other? Dream come true. On the couch, I nudge Keith and pass him the laptop.

He sets his work aside to inspect my discovery. Quickly, he realises that my bathtub is in the medieval stone village where he and his sister lived for a few months when they were very young travellers. The romance of it seizes him immediately, and I'm even more sold when I find that English writer Lawrence Durrell lived in Sommières for thirty years. It feels like kismet. Like it's meant for us. Heading to France for a year of adventure is perhaps not the most original of ideas, but we'll wash away the shame of being bougie clichés with buttery pastries as big as our heads, I decide. And I'll eat mine in the bath.

This is our plan: Keith will work from home, I will write and run the house, and the children will go to the village school for a year. Although they don't speak French, we decide to drop them in headfirst, 'immersion learning' style. It's romantic in theory, but there is a tight knot in my chest in anticipation of how tricky and painful their adjustment might be. It can take up to four months, I'm told, for the babble surrounding the kids to coalesce into recognisable sentences, at which point they will have 'functional' French. After this, I think, it will be only a short period until they can share Australian fart jokes, the champagne comedy of their culture.

At the start, though, we know the children will face an unfamiliar world, a situation that will take all their courage and intestinal fortitude. They will surely feel stupid and misunderstood, like outsiders and weirdos, and they will undoubtedly grapple with difficult schoolyard politics and complex communication issues. The payoff is that at the end of the year the children will, to some degree, speak a new language, which will be a great treasure to their adult selves. We also comfort ourselves with the notion that even the thorniest and most distressing aspects of adjustment will hold hidden gifts. Strength of character through adversity and all that crap. Keith himself spent a year in Paris as a child, a year that was, although difficult, a monumental and formative part of his childhood.

At times I find myself wrestling with these kinds of worries and must pause to deliver a metaphorical spanking to my brain, as a reminder that our whole plan is outrageously, fabulously luxurious. Check (spank!) your (spank!) privilege! (Spank, spank!)

The ability to embark on this epic adventure makes Keith and I incredibly wealthy by any reasonable standard, free to indulge in worries about our kids' emotional adjustment to their year abroad. (Won't somebody think of the children?!) But although we are rich in wild dreams, fart jokes and portability, we are not flush with cash. We live a frugal life on a tight budget, dreaming of updates to our ramshackle house, avoiding credit and keeping our luxuries edible (cheese and chocolate, mainly). It's not going to be a flashy vacay. We think of this year as more of an opportunity to sink roots into fresh soil and see what sprouts.

Still, I feel sick at the thought that we are taking the trusting little hands of our babies, dropping them into a surging ocean and shouting, 'Save yourselves!' Can we withdraw routine, comfort and stability from the lives of these very small people in the hope of a future deposit of memories and skills? Is it a fair transaction? Time will tell.

Ours is a type of baby-raising you might call Best-Guess Parenting, if we were required to give it a BuzzFeedy title. We try not to Helicopter, where parents anxiously hover, or Snowplough, where they remove all difficulties from a child's path. At times we do both, of course. Mostly, Keith and I figure out how to raise these children one mistake at a time, and we really love being parents, even when we get it wrong. School will be challenging, Keith and I tell each other, but home life will run as usual (lost hats, *Harry Potter*, little arms and legs in strong warm cuddles). We will endeavour to keep things as safe and familiar as we possibly can.

This family adventure marks an end to a certain chapter of family life, as our biggest girl is soon to turn eleven – sometimes called the 'old age of childhood'. Right now, we are a solid team, Mum and Dad still the suns around which our small planets circle, but life will not be this way forever. Adolescence, with all its charms and challenges, is just around the corner. But it is not here yet. This year the children still need us to be their soft place to fall.

I am sold, gone, drunk in love with that bath in the bedroom. By the time we learn that the house with the tub is no longer available, I have fallen for Sommières itself – watching, over and over, a shaky drone video of its alleyways on YouTube. When we are offered the house next door we leap at the chance and take it. Maybe I can make friends with the neighbours and pop in to eat a croissant in their bathtub occasionally? *Pas de problème!*

I show the kids my Sommières drone footage, but our day-to-day routine for the next year is impossible to imagine. At home, we live in a small town tucked between the escarpment and the sea on the south coast of Australia, on the land of the Wodi Wodi people, who are a part of the Dharawal nation.

Our house features a composting dunny and a rope swing (located on different parts of the property, I hasten to add). There are wallabies, deer, possums and innumerable birds: from tiny finches to the kookaburra we call Kevin Rudd (he's been popping up for years) to huge tropical parrots. Miniature donkeys gallop about comedically in the paddocks along our unpaved street, and at the bottom of the hill we swim in powerful, thundering Pacific surf. In Sommières, our new home will be a tall, narrow stone house built in the 1700s, I tell the children, positioned underneath a castle and overlooking a Roman bridge. They blink at me.

The place isn't renovated yet, so we can't send you photos, the English owners say. We just bought it, and actually it's ... well ... a derelict wreck. But we can have it ready for August when you get here. Probably. We're pretty sure.

For us, it's a no-brainer. Renting a ruin, sight unseen, on the other side of the world? What could possibly go wrong? We sign on the dotted line. Our lease on Rue Canard will begin on 1 September 2017, and the French school year starts just two days later. Right now, it's March. Deep breath. Stomach in. Tits out. Time to get organised!

Nitty-gritty details

Over the next six months, we must pack up, repair and rent out our house in Australia, negotiate our ruin in France, find a school and enrol the children, gather a metric ton of paperwork and navigate the bureaucratic portal to hell that is the French consulate. The first thing I do is tack up five huge posters in my hallway and turn them into to-do lists, separated into sections: Visa, Houses (France/Australia), School, Packing, Medical/Health, To Sell, To Buy, To Fix, To Take (a couple of Panadol, for a start, along with a good lie-down).

Early on, we rule out shipping, which is massively expensive, so we decide to only pack what we can carry, filling our suitcases with a year's worth of clothes, books, toys and electronics. All our other possessions are crated up and packed in the shed or donated to the Salvation Army. It's a little emotional. This house has been, for ten years, a place of babies and breastfeeding and pregnancy, of *1-2-3 Magic* and don't-make-me-come-in-there and *Play School* and pureed pumpkin found in places pumpkin should never go. But when we come home again, our youngest will be seven. It's the end of an era.

Our dealings with the French consulate are epically, comedically difficult. There is no chance of arriving without accommodation for our full length of stay, a school registration, a hefty bank deposit and the blood of a unicorn slaughtered at midnight, decanted into three

9

different vials and signed in triplicate. The bureaucracy is hidden-camera-level outrageous, but I have made a vow to myself to focus on the funny side of all the preparation. I need to remind myself of this vow often as I grapple with what I come to think of as Frogtape.

Making contact is our first hurdle. An appointment is near-impossible to make. The consulate website, which functions spasmodically, gives no phone number, but eventually – through a seizure-inducing process of administrative acrobatics – we manage to secure an appointment at a desperately inconvenient time at an office two hours' travel time from home. At this meeting, in which we ask questions about the process of a bored public servant from the 'computer says no' school of corporate robots, we are advised of the paperwork we will need for our next appointment, which is set at a time even less convenient than the first. It's ... progress? Ha ha! See the lady smile! See the smile not reach the lady's eyes! See the lady cry and smile! See the French man laugh! See him throw his baguette in the air!

All our visa, school and rental arrangements require a sea of documents. Keith manages most of the paperwork, gathering and sorting complex piles of material into various manila folders. When the type of visa we need changes, he must generate a whole new set. I constantly run text back and forth through Google Translate, and as I wait in various buildings and government offices, I poke at my phone nonstop, messaging and emailing, writing notes to self and managing the endless off-shoots of my Master List. Keith is overseas for a fortnight on business and his return home marks six weeks before we leave.

In these ridiculous final weeks, there are birthdays for Keith, my mum and two of the kids as well as a complex weekend away to plan for my parents' fiftieth wedding anniversary. Every square on the calendar is booked solid and the to-do lists in the hall are starting to look like the scribbled-over ravings of a lunatic. Whenever I feel my cortisol rising, I remind myself of the comedy vow and deliver the Spanking.

I film a series of Instagram Stories advertising our house for rent, shamelessly exploiting the miniature donkeys in the background, and post an ad in the local cafe window. My flyer joins ads for the group Surfing Mums, the course 'Honouring the Feminine Womb Journey' for those who feel 'disconnected to their menstrual cycle', and toy poodle puppies for the eye-watering price of four grand each.

Our place, nestled in the bush, is not an easy sell: though it's on the market for a much cheaper rent than the rest of the neighbourhood (plus), you'll have to haul your bins along the ungraded road and flip your own faeces into a pit every couple of months (minus). Eventually we find a wonderful tenant. Hattie is excited to move in, although she does drink two large wines in swift succession after her lesson in emptying the composting dunny is over.

The kids need lots of attention. Nervous about what is to come, they are absorbing the elevated air in the house and reacting to it, like finely tuned emotional barometers. I squeeze a big combined birthday/farewell party for all three at the trampoline place into the heaving calendar and in the meantime try to meet their varying parental needs.

I organise extra play dates for Tabitha with her friends Beth and Sandy. The three of them call their gang the Nerd University of Unicornia, and they like to march about the backyard singing their anthem ('Oh Pizza Pie!'). As a trio, they are sweeter than a hatful of kittens.

Biggles needs a lot of physical affection. Specifically, he needs to cuddle up with me on the couch so I can read to him from his book *1000 Fantastic Facts* and help him to regulate his body with my own. Mabel, too, needs a lot of physical mothering, but her comfort comes with a macabre twist: obsessed with all things medical, she is most becalmed when discussing blood, gore and surgery.

For her fifth birthday last year, Mabel asked for a wheelchair, a set of crutches and a medical boot. I found a second-hand chair, bedazzled it a little, tied a bow around it and rested the crutches jauntily beside. When Mabel saw her gift on the morning of her birthday, she screamed like we had presented her with the Hope Diamond.

Before going to sleep at night, especially if Mabel is feeling a little frazzled, we discuss what she calls her Secret Dream.

'I'm in hospital, Mumma,' Mabel says, excited. 'And then what?'

'You're going to have surgery tomorrow,' I say.

'Ten operations,' Mabel says. 'No, twelve. Go on.'

'Yes, twelve,' I say in my most soothing tones. I go deep Mullumbimby Hypnotherapist. 'You have a broken leg, and your liver needs resecting, and your spleen has been lacerated *very badly*.'

'And I have diabetes,' Mabel adds. For some reason, she is very taken with diabetes. Eyes closed, Mabel drops happily into sleep.

A nasty virus is going around school. It takes down the kids, one by one. In this pre-Covid era, a cold is just a cold, not the complex, emotionally triggering experience it will become in the future. Still, it messes with my system: for our last few weeks I have, every day, at least one snuffling patient home from school as I empty cupboards, clean a decade's worth of fly carcasses from windowsills and paint and scrub all the corners of the house that have needed attention for years. Keith's 'outdoor' to-do list is equally epic (deal with a crumbling retaining wall, concrete the drains, empty the grease trap, repair the grey-water system) but he and I occasionally meet on the couch to watch a few minutes of TV together before we pass out, dribbling, in a deeply erotic scene.

Our Sommières landlords helpfully put us in touch with Vanessa, their 'fixer'. It's our first encounter with the force of nature who I will come to know as The French Woman. To my eternal gratitude, Vanessa takes over the school enrolment for us and makes arrangements to meet us at the Montpellier train station with our bags after we get the TGV from Paris. She will bring us to Sommières and take us through the admin of the house and the car we're also renting from our landlords for the year.

Getting Vanessa on board makes things feel real. I am nervous. We are not only from Australia, we are from the coastal suburb of Coledale, in Wollongong. Don't get me wrong, I *love* Wollongong: there is a thriving art and music scene here, the living is easy and our beaches are spectacular. Still, it's also true that a man was recently arrested outside local pub Dicey Riley's for performing the 'helicopter' with his penis. I feel a certain amount of hometown pride for this, but while I'm sure that Sommières will have its own cultural idiosyncrasies, I'm not sure that public dick-swinging is one of them.

I know how to handle an unexpected helicopter ('Call that a penis?' 'Does your mother know that's out?' etc.) but I have no idea what the French equivalent might be, or how one might deal with it. I practise the phrase 'Sorry! We are Australian!' I fear we'll need it. *Je suis désolée! Nous sommes australiens!*

I may have to raise my standards. French women are famous for their sartorial flair, while at the school drop-off I often look as though I have been shagged through a hedge backwards. Modern grooming is the worst. It's like painting the Harbour Bridge: once you get through the waxing, plucking, colouring and moisturising involved, it's time to start all over again. I try to get myself a full service before we leave. I have a haircut and a leg wax and even book in a spray tan for just before departure, reminding myself with glee that even though I am currently spending eighteen hours a day scrubbing floors, texting the French consulate and rocking in corners, moaning, I will, in mere moments, be kicking back in the Parisian high summer.

One day, it's Biggles's turn to be home from school sick so, rugged up with a hot water bottle and a hanky, he keeps me company on my endless errands.

'What are we doing now, Mum?' he asks.

'Well, yesterday this lady ripped all the hair out of my legs. And today she's going to paint me brown with a little spray gun.'

'Why?' he asks. My very logical child is confused, and I have no reasonable answer.

'Think of Paris,' I remind myself while I stand in the small bathroom of a local beauty salon. Wearing nothing but a paper G-string while a young woman with a spray gun tries to draw contours on one's exposed flesh is humiliating at the best of times. There's always the possibility ahead of leaving the store in a shameful shade of Trump-pumpkin (Trumpkin?) no matter how much you yelp, 'Not too dark! Not too dark!'

'Turn around,' the young, flawless beautician instructs me, 'and I'll do your back.' She speaks with the even tones students are surely taught in beauty school to avoid expressing even a hint of the horror felt at seeing middle-aged women in all our glory: caesarean scars, overgrown winter bushes and beards that grow more lustrous year on year. We must be like a terrifying 'ghost of Christmas future' type scenario.

At least in France they celebrate the older woman, I remind myself. I mean, everybody says that. I hope it's true. Perhaps I might even develop some of that famous 'French Girl Poise', a quality that has always eluded me.

How will my style – perhaps kindly called *derelicte* – fly in small-town France? I used to be a fashionable creature, once. Ten years of being a stay-at-home mum and writer have turned me into a sort of relaxed mole-person, all about the elasticated waist and the 'good' tracksuit pants for special occasions. But in a galaxy far, far away (that hazy past before children) I was a city gal, a night owl, a butterfly in search of a party, and always had a great outfit to make an entrance in.

Somehow, this year in France feels like a step into another incarnation. The intense work of shepherding little ones through early childhood is waning and I can, perhaps, strike out on my own a little again. But who will this new me be? And what the hell will she wear?

In the last week, I begin the task of trying to actually transfer all the piles I have gathered in the lounge room into our suitcases. I'm facing more *stuff* than there is *case*, so I must edit and adjust endlessly. There are so many variables to consider.

For instance, the children are all obsessed with their stuffed animals The Friendys. Great gangs of them spill over every bed, and they have complex kinship systems and backstories. Our rule: the kids are allowed to bring just four Friendys each to France, and they must choose who to leave at home. This is a wrenching task for them, but it still leaves me with twelve stuffed animals to pack. When I put the Friendys into a space-saving bag and suck all the air out with a vacuum cleaner, Mabel bursts into tears. That's her nightmares sorted for the next little while, I realise, as we both gaze upon the Friendys contorted into unearthly positions and squeezed against the plastic, eyes bulging out and staring into space.

The winter gear – puffy coats for everybody! – is squeezed into another space-saving bag. I am besotted with these vacuum-shrinking bags and thrilled at how much I can fit into each case, once all the oxygen is removed. But when I try to lift a bag, I just about pop a vertebra. My dodgy back is not going to let me carry these bags far. Apologies, but that's a problem for Future Keith, I decide, heaving the cases off the table and stacking them by the door.

Even my beloved space-saving bags can't help with the book issue. We are all voracious readers, and even though I've bought a Kindle, there remains a huge pile of books to pack. The Harry Potters alone practically fill a carry-on. Friends are horrified by the books we plan to take and cannot understand why we wouldn't buy them anew when we arrive, but – the budget! Every dollar counts. The idea of being without books fills me with nervous anxiety. We'll find room.

Leaving Mum and Dad is very sad. They moved to Coledale when Mabel was a baby and are very close to their grandchildren. Mum has a degenerative lung condition called bronchiectasis and she won't be able to fly, so there will be no European visit for them. Saying goodbye to my parents feels heavy. This farewell, even though just for a year, has a shadow about it of something more permanent – just a smudge, a mist that will later harden into a sinister shape. My mother-in-law, along with Keith's older brother, plans to farewell us at the airport, a lovely moment to share but another bittersweet reminder of the family we are leaving behind.

Our visas arrive mere days before we leave (see the French man wink!) and the final desperate last-minute house cleaning and packing is performed on just a few hours of sleep and with shaky, queasy hangovers thanks to a big farewell party the night before departure.

As a parting gift, my girlfriends present me with a huge pair of granny knickers.

'For you, Rach,' says my friend Sarah. 'All the hard work is over. Now you can get on that plane, put on an adult nappy, take a Valium and piss yourself all the way to Paris.'

I give Sarah a big hug.

'Living the dream, Sarzy,' I say.

'Do it for all of us,' she replies.

Head lice in Paris

The phrase 'Wherever you go, there you are' floats through my mind. We are in Paris trying to ask a pharmacist for head-lice treatment. Biggles is both sniffling and scratching his head like a rhesus monkey and an email from school entitled 'The bugs are back!' (why so jovial, office? why?) tells me that not only did we transport the vestiges of the Wollongong Plague to the other side of the globe, but also, it seems, a scattering of good old Aussie nits. I dread to think that we might bring some heinous combination flu/lice epidemic to Europe. Would my passport photo (in which I look like a halfwit criminal) be the image used to identify patient zero of the outbreak?

It's at times like this that I am no longer frustrated by the length of time it took the French consulate to issue us a visa. I'm relieved they allowed us in at all.

'*Excusez-moi*,' I say to the pharmacist. '*Mon fisse, il est ... il est ... le poux avec le tête. Avez-vous le médicine pour le ...* situay-shon?'

He narrows his eyes at me. I am mortified. Tabitha and I have just spent five minutes outside the pharmacy in the bustling Gare du Nord train station while I composed my inquiry: 'My son has nits on his head. Do you have medicine for the problem?'

French-language practice did not go well in the lead-up to our trip. I have an internal stockpile of French words and phrases, but barely any of the French grammar that would allow me to string them into a coherent sentence. I can't understand a word anybody says to me, and the children have no French at all, so we are all relying heavily on Keith.

My intentions are noble but my internal dial is set to low comedy and so, despite myself, the only things that stick are stupid. For instance, when I come across a French lesson book full of ridiculous sample sentences, I find them so delightful that I am compelled to commit them to memory. 'He has retained his vigour throughout the years.' 'I buy only beige stockings.' 'Poor little thing. She is cross-eyed.' Also, I come across a wonderful French tongue twister that we all learn, and even set to music: *'Didon dîna, dit-on, du dos dodu d'un dodu dindon,'* or 'Dido dined, they say, on the enormous back of an enormous turkey.' It's hard to see where any of this will be helpful. In the end, I find that 'Frenching' up English words has a moderate success rate, so I lean into the accent harder than an episode of *'Allo 'Allo!*

'What's the French for "nits", do you think?' I ask Tabitha, in the pharmacy.

'It's "*poux*",' she says. 'Dad told me.'

I look at her carefully for signs of trickery, but she nods enthusiastically.

'So I'm saying, "Help me, my son has poo on his head"? Are you pranking me, miss?' I peer intently into Tabitha's eyes.

She holds her ground.

'I'm going for it, either way.'

Tabitha is right. Nits is '*poux*' – a French word I'll become terribly familiar with over the coming months. In the Gare du Nord, I shell out a squillion euros for chemical shampoo and resign myself to the fact that our first night in the new house will involve holding squealing children between my thighs as I drag a fine-toothed comb through their ratty locks. Wherever you go, there you are.

School starts in just a few days, but we're not in Sommières yet. We've been tramping the summer streets of Paris for a week, poleaxed by jetlag, eating crêpes and trailing through museums and parks, all three kids sleeping on a fold-out couch in an apartment belonging to the friend of a friend in the sixteenth arrondissement.

We struggle through the surging crowds of the train station, head-counting at intervals – fifteen bags, three children; fifteen bags, three children – before we find our train and settle in for the four-hour journey south. I'm absolutely rooted, as we say in the old country. I don't know if I am Arthur or Martha, or Claudette, or Jean-Pierre, or Lady Fanny of Omaha. But I'm delighted to be on this train, and I cannot believe that this is the final leg. At Montpellier, we meet up with Vanessa the fixer, who manages to fit fifteen bags, three children and two exhausted parents into and on top of her small car, the first of many acts of practical magic she will perform over the coming months.

The scenery passes in a blur as Vanessa takes us to Rue Canard, and just like that, we end the mode of perpetual motion that we have been in for the last six months. No more moving, packing and planning. No more Master List. Just a home.

That night, we order pizza in a little Sommières restaurant and balance it on a rickety plastic table by the river. Keith and I are intro-duced to the *pichet*, a little carafe of wine, and the children are thrilled to be allowed Coke and iced tea. They don't get the gravity of this meal. But Keith and I can't wipe the smiles off our faces. This simple supper is the manifestation of a years-long dream.

Street lanterns glow yellow on the unassuming, astonishing Roman bridge behind us, ordered by the emperor Tiberius in the first century CE and still taking Sommièrois from one side of town to the other two thousand years on. Time folds here, under these trees, where the late-summer air is thick and spicy, the brackish tang of the mud-slow river ringing a note below the damp, mouldy comfort of old stone and red wine. Here we are. Here we are.

I exhale a long, heavy breath as an old man cycles past in a flat cap and a couple nearby argue vociferously, waving cigarettes to punctuate their points, and then I reach across the table to hold my beloved Keith's hand, for the touchstone of its reliable steadiness.

'Chops,' he says. This is his pet name for me. Embarrassing but true. 'Chops. We made it.'

'Cakes,' I reply. (My name for Keith is just as odd.) 'Let the games begin.'

New home, who dis

Waking up on our first morning in Rue Canard, I stretch like a cat, luxuriating in the fact that this will be my room for the next twelve months. From our bed I can see our cases on the cement floor, unspooling their contents with relief. Lie there for a year, you bastards, I think with a thrill. The pressure is off! Shifting on the hard mattress, I inspect the bedroom.

This self-contained little space is right at the base of the house. Below us lies only the *cave* – the sprawling underground cellar and storage space. Our bedroom features a startlingly uncomfortable double bed, complete with solid, square European pillows. The wardrobe consists of open shelving and rails strung across the far wall, and the open-plan ensuite contains a shower cannily positioned so as to leave the toilet consistently wet. I rarely use it after a few late-night bottom-soaking incidents. This bathroom will become Keith's territory.

The buttery stone walls are thick, roughly plastered and cool to the touch. They feel as though they hold the ghosts of a hundred inhabitants. The house was built in 1791, just two years after the French Revolution began, and later, when I ponder this, it makes me smile; here in this southern village, we are far from the action in Paris, immersed in our small-town dramas and crises, and I feel sure that it must have felt much the same two hundred years ago: Marie Antoinn-*who*? Let them eat *what*?

The house has been through unknowable iterations since those days and a year ago it was a derelict shell. Our landlords made it habitable before we moved in – just *barely* before, from the looks of some of the fittings and fixtures. The house is full of odd quirks. I leave Keith sleeping peacefully and head out to check on the children.

From our basement bedroom doorway I pass the tucked-away hatch that opens up to the *cave* and walk into the lounge room, which gives onto the street. This compact room has three couches, a tall desk and a TV squeezed into its corners, and a large square coffee table fills the centre of the room. The colour palette features gentle Provençal pastels of blue and cream, but it's crammed like a Victorian parlour, and I immediately realise that I'm going to have to cover the couches – twelve months, small children and three pale couches is a bad combination. It's a lovely space, though. As soon as we walked in yesterday afternoon, I breathed a sigh of relief that the decorator has an aesthetic that I like, even if there's a tiny bit too much of a good thing.

A narrow spiral staircase winds like a mobius strip up the next two floors and feels like the most medieval part of the house. The stairs are wooden, washed in gunmetal blue paint, and carting Friendys and laundry up and down them multiple times every day will become my exercise program. French buns! French buns! I will remind myself when feeling defeated by the stairs. One flight up, the stairs open onto the main bathroom, narrow and tall, with a beautiful chandelier strung high above the bathtub and a tiny window, inexplicably placed near the ceiling, that opens with a chain. I will spend many hours in this bath musing on what the room could have been used for two centuries ago.

I stop to do a quick wee and am disconcerted when the seat slides beneath me. What is this madness? A detachable plastic seat? I grip the sides and hold on. The experience is unpleasant.

To the right of the bathroom is a bedroom that will become Keith's office. He'll perch his laptop and papers on a small dressing table squeezed between two single beds, while billowing curtains at the window let in snatches of blaring television from the terrace next door, where a rotund old lady sits in her armchair, hour after hour, an immobile silhouette. 'Is the TV lady dead?' the children will sometimes check. It's not a great office, but Keith can concentrate anywhere.

Back when he first left academia and started the company I like to call Egghead Enterprises, Keith worked out of a derelict caravan on the driveway. We'd bought it from a neighbour for a case of beer, and Keith huddled in it all day, rain, hail and shine. During the searing summer it was an oven, and in the winter he froze. Insects crawled about and spiders shimmied down threaded ropes to slip inside his shirt, but Keith was oblivious, on another plane thinking through the physics of complex problems. In fact, the rougher, more decrepit and ridiculous his punk/ monk office got, the more he seemed to like it. He would wander out to start work in the morning wearing a sarong, reluctantly putting on a shirt only to Skype clients and loving every minute of life. Keith can handle the minor inconveniences of this French office.

On the other side of the bathroom is the kids' bedroom, a huge room with a bunk bed, a single bed facing it from the opposite wall, and a zebra-print chaise longue. The walls are washed white, but a rough scar across one side marks a break in the paint where the stone underneath is allowed to shine through. The children were delighted to find new stuffed animals on all their beds. Friendys! French cousins! These animals – in particular a giant leopard called Muscles and a small panda called Pandora – were immediately incorporated into the complex family history of their beloved Friendy gang. A furry animal-print blanket, soft as a cloud, was pounced upon and named Big Bertha. Sprawled across their beds this morning in their new room, the children are dead to the world. I can hear hooting and hollering, and I open the window and lean out, surveying the street below. To my astonishment, a man hops along the cobblestones beneath my window on pogo-stick shoes as a group of fellow acrobats applauds his progress.

'Kids, wake up!' I say. 'You won't believe what's going on out here!'

The acrobats take it in turn to bounce along the narrow street, catapulting metres in the air off the uneven stone. They are dressed in tight leotards, their bodies sculpted. They are clearly gifted athletes. The kids and I have no idea what they are shouting to each other, but we lean out the window and cheer them along in our basic French.

'*Bravo! Superbe!*'

They look up and wave. I am thrilled at the absurdity of the whole spectacle. It has the unexpected, ridiculous charm of a French rom-com. This dream scenario is interrupted by real life.

'I'm hungry, Mum,' says Biggles, who is always driven by his stomach. He's wrapped himself in Big Bertha and is curled around Muscles on the chaise longue.

'Let's go see what we can find, Bigsy,' I say. 'You lead the way.'

Biggles runs ahead of me out the door and up the spiral staircase. The sound of his thundering feet on these wooden stairs will become very familiar over the next months. The girls and I traipse after him.

At the entrance to the top-floor kitchen is a tiny toilet. Having all these toilets is a bit of a treat, actually. At home, we have one bathroom for our family of five, which contains a waterless environmental toilet. Three flush loos! It's quite the luxury, even if one wets your arse, one is something of a carnival ride and one has a tiny chain lock on the outside, so that using it leaves you open to being locked in by a mischievous child.

The kitchen itself is small and charming, filled to bursting with a large square wooden table and a set of six mismatched wooden chairs. Stacked in a corner are the leaves that allow the table to expand to seat ten or twelve with extra chairs and stools gathered from all corners of the house. This extendable dining table will become our central gathering hub.

The walls are full of sweet vignettes of stacked plates and teacups, still in those Provençal pastels. We are thrilled to discover a bookshelf full of English-language books, and a dishwasher – another appliance we don't have at home. No food, though. Breakfast will have to wait.

In the corner, a wooden ladder leads to a bricked-in alcove with a tiny mezzanine balcony overlooking the kitchen table. Tabitha scrambles up the ladder like a mountain goat. We all follow. The owners had intended this little space to lead out onto the rooftop terrace, but in renovating they found that it was impossible to build the doorway. Their failed idea has produced a tiny secret chamber, a timber-floored, stone-bricked, windowless hideaway that an adult cannot stand upright in. In short: the perfect bedroom for a privacy-craving ten-year-old Harry Potter fan. Tabitha moves a mattress, a small bedside table and all her books up here. She's as happy as a clam, my independent soul, even though her parents are sleeping three full floors below in an entirely unfamiliar country.

A wide stone step marks a level up from the kitchen to the sunroom. Here we find more white couches and botanical IKEA posters, but the star of this room is that view across the terracotta rooftops and down to the river. It is breathtaking, a postcard brought to life, and once we move the dining table up there, it becomes the place where we will gather to watch poor Larry the Hapless Sex Pigeon make his unfortunate moves.

Outside the sunroom is a tiny terrace just large enough to hold a laundry rack. There is another spiral staircase here, winding precariously up to the roof. It looks straight down into the dusty hole between the terraces and visiting friends with vertigo will never brave it. But strong hearts and stomachs take the winding path. The stairs lead up to a small, bare concrete terrace; in the summer, it is unbearably open to the elements, and in the winter way too cold to stand around on, but with the most jaw-dropping view: behind, to the ancient tower, and below, to those beautiful rooftops, in all their sunset shades. In the distance looms the shape of Mont Aigoual, and to the south, the marshland of Aigues-Mortes.

Keith appears as the children and I hang on the banisters and take it all in.

'Serenity now!' he says. We lean our shoulders companionably together.

'Just through those trees is the restaurant from last night,' Keith says, pointing. 'And there are about a dozen different ways to get there. Look at all the alleyways!'

From this vantage – we are, it seems, actually at the highest point in this part of the town – we can see the straggling streets below, a Roman quadrillage overlaid through the centuries with offshoots like afterthoughts.

'You'll have a mental map of this place in about five minutes,' I tell Keith, 'and I'll never get there.'

'Well, it's lucky we have complementary skill sets,' says Keith. I am already bubbling over with ideas on how we could make this place our own, but first things first: I need a coffee.

Misfits and marginaux

Tabitha and I head out. My hope is to find a coffee shop but, failing that, I'll settle for milk. Our landlords have left us some tea and sugar, and a cup of tea will sort me out until we head to the supermarket later today to stock the cupboards.

'There must be a little shop, right?' I ask Tabitha.

'Of course, Mum,' she assures me. 'Every place has a little shop!' She's such a comforting person, this first mate of mine, sunny and adventurous, always rising to a challenge.

We turn left at the door, making our way down a slight slope deep into the *centre historique*. Terraces loom above us, admitting slices of sky, while arched windows with pale-blue shutters and the occasional pot of geraniums bring a splash of colour to the muted stone palette. Alleys sprout their tendrils off the narrow street, giving glimpses of vaulted passages, ancient tunnels and arches reaching between buildings. The streets feel scrappy and suggestive and rich with secrets, rumpled and sexy as an unmade bed.

We pass a tiny junk store where a svelte woman with red hair in a turban is arranging trinkets on a display table and chatting to an elderly lady perched on a stool beside the door. Behind the seated lady's generous rump I can just see the face of a tiny dog. Tabitha and I walk between them.

'*Bonjour*,' we say softly and '*Bonjour!*' they both answer with gusto. The elderly lady removes her small cigar to give us a broad smile. Tabitha and I have learned the importance of *politesse* during our week in Paris. '*Bonjour*' is the key marker of polite respect, necessary in all social encounters, no matter how minor.

We continue on past an art gallery. A slight man with a rollie hanging out of the side of his mouth is sitting at an easel in the sun, working on a large portrait of Tupac Shakur.

'*Bonjour*,' we say as we pass, and he looks up with a grin. '*Bonjour!*' he chirps.

Although Tab won't often hold my hand, she clutches it today, the feel of each other's paws anchoring us, somehow, in this out-of-body moment. At the end of our street, an archway leads onto the small square of the Place Jean Jaurès. There are boutiques and restaurants here, but I can't see a coffee machine or anything resembling a 'little shop'. We walk through to the narrow street at the far side, passing a *boulangerie* where I pause to watch an aproned man, wiry with muscle, preparing a tray of baguettes for an enormous, ancient woodstove. The hot fragrance wafting from his doorway smells unbelievably delicious. On the steps opposite, a woman with a raw, uneven neck tattoo and a huge pregnant belly smokes as she laughs with a group of teenage boys in pristine activewear.

We pass some high-end clothes stores, an old-lady hairdresser, a fish shop and a string of junky antique stores, but no little shops. On the steps of each premise stands a shop assistant watching the passing parade.

'*Bonjour, bonjour*,' we nod to them all until we reach the end of the road. There's a classic French bistro on this corner, and a proper street with cars. We turn left and walk until we reach the Vidourle. In the daytime, this is a wide, shallow and mud-green waterway, its banks lined with plane trees. Cars are crossing the Roman bridge, and there is a foot crossing too, at the end of which a bunch of kids are jumping, squealing, into the water.

There are a few bars here along the river. But still no sign of a little shop.

Tabitha and I turn and retrace our steps up the cobblestones. Eventually we spy a *tabac*, a tobacconist. It's the closest thing we've seen to a general store. There are a bunch of men hanging around at the door, laughing and talking animatedly.

'*Excusez-moi*,' I say as I squeeze past them to get inside.

'*Bonjour!*' says the portly man behind the counter.

'*Bonjour*,' I reply, bracing myself for the next bit where I must communicate past 'hello'.

'*Avez-vous le lait, s'il vous plait?*' – 'Do you have milk, please?'

'*Hein?*' he says.

Bugger.

'*Avez-vous le lait*, er, *pour le café? Et ... le ...* tea?' I stammer. I make drinky-drinky motions, daintily lifting my pinkie.

'*Le lait!*' shouts a man from the doorway.

'*Le lait?*' the tobacconist says. He is totally confused as to why I'm asking for milk in a cigar shop. To me, it's reasonable. I'm thinking of him as something like a 7-Eleven. But to him, it's as random as if I were requesting an electric sander or the morning-after pill.

'*Le lait!*' the group at the doorway shout, and then they launch into an exuberant discussion, hands flying everywhere as they debate. Eventually one of them claps his hands decisively.

'Come!' he says. Tabitha and I look at each other in confusion, but the group of men nods encouragingly and waves us out of the shop. The milk-man is trotting at a good pace and Tabitha and I follow behind.

'I guess he's going to show us a shop?' I say, and Tabitha shrugs. Following the man, we leave the square and make our way up an alleyway before veering right into a small passage. The sounds of the square are fading. These back lanes are calm and deserted but for the occasional prowling cat. I clutch Tabitha's hand and try to quell my panic. Why am I taking my child to follow a strange man through a town we don't know? Is this Best-Guess Parenting gone bad?

As he trots, the man talks to us over his shoulder in very broken English. 'Jus' a little further! Is my house!'

His house? What?

The man stops in front of a doorway and grins.

'*Et voilà!*' he says, before gesturing us to go inside.

I shake my head wildly. '*Non, merci,*' I say.

'*C'est bon!*' he smiles, before running inside, tossing, '*Cinq minutes!*' over his shoulder.

Tabitha and I wait on the street. I smile brightly at her to show I'm not freaked out, but she looks at me askance. I think I am baring every single one of my teeth.

Soon the man reappears with a carton of long-life milk in his hand. It's for his children, he explains. He is divorced, and he keeps milk for when they visit. He is pleased to give it to us.

I feel a wash of relief that Tabitha and I have escaped being chopped into small pieces. The kind stranger walks us back down to the *tabac*, explaining that there is no little shop in the village. Fresh milk is not a big thing here, we learn later, unlike in Australia, where we go through two litres a day. Long-life milk is the standard.

Tabitha and I make our way back up Rue Canard. As we pass the art gallery, we pause to inspect the Tupac painting. Tupac's expression is hard to read, his eyes slightly skewiff.

'*Ça va?*' the artist says.

'*Oui, ça va,*' I answer. All good so far! Sadly, the string of French that follows is beyond my understanding.

'*Je ne parle pas français,*' I say, sadly, and the artist switches to halting English. His demeanour totally shifts when he learns that we are not passing through, but that we will be his neighbours on Rue Canard for a year. It's the first of many such conversations. Why Sommières? people ask with astonishment. Why here?

'I am Cédric!' our neighbour says. 'Tonight I 'ave music in the street. Is my party. You will come? Is my friends and neighbours, we make the art and music. You are welcome, please, the children also.'

'*Merci*,' I say to Cédric, deeply touched. '*Oui! Superbe.*'

We say farewell – *à bientôt*, at least – and Tabitha and I make our way home, clutching our strange treasure, to the new house we have taken to calling the Wormhole. I'm thrilled that we have made a friend on this first foray into town, and Tabitha is in heaven, having during this sojourn acquainted herself with – and named – a half-dozen cats that she will adore over the coming year.

This first walk down Rue Canard is an apt introduction to Sommières: its kindness, its oddness and its utterly idiosyncratic charm. For me, it's love at first sight. Later I will hear the town described as a land of 'misfits and *marginaux*' (fringe dwellers) and I will wonder if this is why I felt so immediately at home.

Still, it's *not* home. All my familiar cues and markers are missing, and making sense of this place takes an enormous amount of trust. Who is good? Who is dangerous? What is normal? What should set off my alarms? In our early days, we will notice that Sommières does have a slightly lawless vibe, but we will dismiss these fears. We need to rely on the kindness of strangers and we are not disappointed.

Later that evening, we make our way back down the street to Cédric's party. He has set up his easels outside and about twenty people are sitting around on crates and chairs, jamming to Amy Winehouse with guitars and drums. Cédric pours us a rough red from a cask, somebody slips me a sneaky cigarette, and I join in on 'Valerie'. I can't translate a word anybody says to me, but I'm as happy as a pig in *merde*.

Keith talks to a thin, jovial friend of Cédric's who cannot understand why we have come to Sommières.

'This is crazy town, man!' he says. 'It's crazy town of crazy people!'

'Oh, everybody seems very nice,' says Keith, taking a chip out of a packet resting on a drum stand.

'No, you don't get,' the man says excitedly. He moves closer to Keith. 'To your face, they are good, sure, but when you not looking, they stab you in the belly!' He illustrates his point with a short, sharp poke in the midsection.

Keith chokes slightly on his chip and laughs weakly. The man winks at Keith.

'Be careful, friend,' he says.

Later that night, up in Tabitha's mezzanine, there is a painful argument. Eagle-eyed Tabby spotted my sneaky fag and she is horrified, with the earnest self-righteousness of the very young.

'How could you, Mum?' she wails. 'Smoking kills! You are my only mother!'

I try to reassure her, but she won't be placated. I too am stubborn, and I won't be railroaded by Tabitha into promising that I will never have a cheeky cig again.

'It's such a rare thing, Tabs,' I say. 'Every blue moon I have a party ciggie. And I agree with you, smoking is very dangerous. But this is not something you have to worry about.'

'Promise me you will never do it again!' she begs, with all the passion of her intense nature.

I'm in a quandary.

'Look, I just don't want to lie to you, mate!' I say. 'Smoking's bad, but lying's worse. Let's just leave it at this: I'm sorry you saw Mum do something that upset you, but it hardly ever happens and we really don't need to make it into a massive drama.'

'Promise me!' she demands.

It's late up here in the mezzanine. We're going in circles. This debate feels like a new boundary, a line in the sand. The cracks are showing to my sharp young daughter: a fallible, flawed mother appearing beneath the shell of the all-knowing Madonna of her early childhood. These children are so much a part of me that I hardly know sometimes where they end and I begin. What right have I to a private life? Where do our separate adventures intersect?

I'm too tired, and France is weird enough for my little friend here.

'Okay, Tabby,' I concede. 'You're right. Smoking is a health hazard. I won't do it again.'

Smile lines bisect the tears on Tabitha's face. She hugs me tightly.

'Thank you, Mum,' she says. 'You won't regret this decision!'

I hug my earnest, determined child, descend the mezzanine ladder and make my way down the mobius staircase to the bedroom, where Keith is googling Sommières crime statistics. The battle when Tabitha next catches me with a fag? That's a problem for Future Rachael.

The big bed

Down in the uncomfortable dungeon bed, I am reading my book when Keith suddenly turns his back, rustles in his drawer for a notebook and begins scribbling furiously.

'What are you doing?' I ask.

'Just filling in my Bitterness Log,' he replies.

I'm stunned. What is this?

'Are you okay?' I ask.

'I think so,' he replies. 'There's a bit of a problem and I'm just trying to map it. I'll tell you later if there's anything in it.'

I lie back on the spartan pillow, contemplating. I know I married a scientist, but this is taking things too far. I think back on the day we've had. Did something happen to upset Keith? I made fun of the holes in his underpants, I recall. Was that it? Usually, he can take a joke. In fact, he's inexplicably proud of the holes in his underpants. Is it about the crime stats? Did I say something embarrassing at the party? What's happening?

'Is it your underpants?' I ask in a quiet voice.

Keith tucks his pencil in to mark the page and turns to face me.

'I'm sorry?' he says.

'What bitterness are you logging, Cakes? Is something going on?' My voice goes up an octave. 'Do we need to talk?'

Here's the story: Keith has an unusual sharp, bitter taste in his mouth that comes and goes and, ever the scientist, he is keeping track of how and when it occurs so he can map it. I am relieved. He's just a weirdo. Not an unhappy husband.

During our years together, Keith and I will share many beds. There are romantic early days, awake until dawn in the bed we call White Heaven, where we drink champagne from the bottle and sing Nina Simone, and I smoke cigarettes out the window. There's Dee Why Beach, a flat on the cliffs above the Pacific Ocean, where our only problem is the difficult choice between going back to bed or out for eggs Benedict. There's our first shared flat in inner-city Sydney, where we wallpaper our bedroom with golden monkeys and palm trees and bring home our first baby.

There's a bed in a fantastically mad pre-baby adventure in Borneo, where we arrange to stay overnight in the long house of a remote village halfway down the Rajang River in Sarawak. We've been ripped off by an unscrupulous small-town travel agent, and after a hairy canoe trip with a drunken guide waving a machete, we end up passing a sleepless night on the floor. The long-house host does not want us there, the guide has made it clear he has sexual designs on Keith and the whimpers of a monkey in a tiny cage outside the kitchen penetrate my dreams.

On a backpacking trip across the outer islands of Vanuatu with all three children in tow, our bed is in a rickety treehouse perched three storeys high and overlooking an active volcano. We must put the children in the middle of the bed and curve our bodies protectively around them when a rat starts chewing on our bags in the middle of the night.

This is life with Keith. The longer we are together, the more I trust him and the safer I feel. This mild-mannered scientist contains multitudes. Over time he proves himself to be the greatest dad and husband I could hope for: an intrepid companion for a life's journey. At our wedding his two oldest friends make a speech about how annoying it can be to have a friend so accomplished. He's hard-working and kind, a gentle soul who can switch the gears of his wonderful brain from astronomy to some mad flower-fairy fancy of Mabel's, and be just as happy in either discussion. He's flawed, too, of course, thank God. That handsome exterior houses issues and flaws, like all the rest of us. But together, Keith and I are, I hope, more than the sum of our parts. This is perhaps the purest beauty of partnership: we cover each other's failings.

Here we are in this dungeon, in another bed, on another adventure. Wherever we are, the bed that brings us the most joy, the most peace and the most uncomfortable sleep of our lives, is the family bed.

There is almost never just two of us in there. There are often five, and once we're all wedged in, there's not a lot of room to move. It's the season of parenthood where the children crave physical proximity to us. As time goes on, one by one, the children will drift away to their own spaces, but at this age they are still drawn, like homing pigeons, constantly back to the warmth and comfort of Mum and Dad, a lovely habit that comes at a price. We are sometimes woken suddenly with a kick in the kidneys from a child lying sideways across the bed or pinned under youngsters whose dead sleeping weight has inexplicably tripled.

I'm relieved that the Bitterness Log Keith is keeping is not a marriage Burn Book listing the failings of his wife, and the bitterness passes without any medical intervention. But the log, for a while, is one of the rituals that Keith keeps at night, along with strapping his legs together to help with back pain (on the advice of his osteopath) and flipping an eye trainer back and forth in front of his face at speed in order to avoid needing spectacles as long as possible. Arousing! Who knew that that buff young nerd who kissed me outside a wedding marquee in the Kangaroo Valley would end up being this farting middle-aged man in threadbare underpants, logging his ailments in a notebook and strapping his knees together? And that along with him would come three magical children, taking up all the room in the bed and breathing their hot little dreams into my face? Or that the whole motley crew of us would end up in this ancient house, embarking together on a mad adventure? I guess I just got lucky.

La rentrée

The night before school starts, I nervously try to pull 'first-day' outfits together. The children I've spied in Sommières look pretty snappy. Their shoes are clean, their clothes well ironed, their short hair pomaded into place. Generally, they are turned out with care and precision.

I look at my three. One child is wearing two odd shoes, another is wearing nothing but a single sock and Mabel looks as though she has survived some kind of charity-shop explosion. They are playing Farting Rainbows with the Friendys. This is a game in which the Friendys compete for the crown of Queen of Farts. The highly complicated rules of the game are too disgusting to outline in mixed company, but there is an overarching storyline that involves eating magic beans that allow Friendys to fly using bottom propulsion. The falsetto voices that all the Friendys use to speak are painfully headache-inducing. They even fart in falsetto, and Muscles the Leopard farts the loudest of all.

I am nervous. Will Farting Rainbows translate? Will it – in some international language of comedy, perhaps – bridge the gap between my scruffy surf-rat trio and the small, wily local children darting through alleyways on their oversized bikes?

On Monday morning, it's show time. The first day of school. We're all jangling with nerves, but Keith and I try our best to hide our anxiety with brio. Down the cobbles of Rue Canard we go, through the square, down the far street, under the archway, along the alley and around the corner to École Albert Camus. The building itself is a small two-storey structure curved around a dusty cement yard dotted with a few stunted, dehydrated trees. The building is encircled by a high steel fence and the gates are decisively bolted shut.

There are small groups milling about outside and the parent committee has set up a trestle table serving welcome-back coffee for *la rentrée*, the return to school. We stand awkwardly about for a while before I decide to brave the P & C.

'*Bonjour*,' I say brightly.

'*Bonjour*,' the elfin brunette behind the table replies.

'*Ça va?*' I ask, and she blinks at me suspiciously.

'*Ça va*,' she spits out, and turns to fiddle with her urn.

I smile weakly. The awkward silence burns between us. Eventually I help myself to a small paper cup of black coffee. There are masses of sugar packets but no milk in sight, of course.

'*Merci*,' I say.

She nods and I retreat, burning my tongue on the first sip of the bitter brew. It's the worst coffee I've ever had, and after a few weeks in France, I've had some shockers. The coffee problem of this country is hard to come to terms with, considering its wonderful food. Here in France, the cheese is delectable, the pastries divine, but the coffee is like the piss of a necrotic wolfhound. It's not only bitter, but often it's actually served cold. The barista might as well just swish it around his mouth and spit it in your face. Coffee forms the most critical segment of my food pyramid, but breakfast culture, my favourite thing, doesn't exist here, and I have not yet clapped eyes on a coffee machine in Sommières.

Looking around, I feel a long way from Coledale. Cigarette smoke, a fragrance that will become a Proustian sense-memory of this place, winds through the air. I am no longer in the land of turmeric lattes and sourdough, I realise. The markers of this place are baguettes and cigarettes, and, in perhaps the most jarring culture shock of all, none of the women are sporting activewear.

Other parents shoot side eye and children encircle us curiously but nobody approaches until a buxom woman with a long plait, clearly an envoy from the group by the fence, comes over, her intimidating rack reaching us moments before the rest of her.

'*Bonjour*,' she says. It's a question.

Keith takes on the conversation. Hello, he says, we are from Australia and the children will be going to École Albert Camus this year. She asks a couple of probing enquiries before nodding a sober goodbye and returning to the watching group to relay the information. There's a burst of chatter from them, but we still stand alone.

Biggles and Mabel clutch my hands tightly. Tabitha holds on to Keith. I feel a little sick as I watch a woman with a short dark bob and a beautiful scarf unlock the front gate, and there's a burst of activity as children kiss their parents goodbye and stream through. We make our way over, and Keith explains to the teacher at the door that we're here to enrol.

Looking astonished, she gestures to us to head inside and up the stairs. Children stare as we go through a corridor hung with posters until we find an office where a red-headed woman sits behind a large, untidy desk. This is our first encounter with Madame Montagne, the principal, or *Directrice*.

'*Oui?*' she asks, looking slightly affronted. Her desk is strewn with paperwork and she is clearly busy.

'*Bonjour*,' I say, before launching into the standard speech I am starting to think of as The Spiel: 'We are from Australia and we are living in Sommières for a year, and the children will go to École Albert Camus ...'

'*Nous sommes les Australiens, et nous habitons à Sommières pour un an et mes enfants attendant École Albert Camus cette année ...*'

Madame Montagne removes her glasses and levels her piercing gaze upon me. The children press closer. I trail off. I've run out of French anyway. Keith takes over. Soon comprehension passes over Madame Montagne's expressive face and she breaks into an enormous smile.

'Ah! The Australians!' she says. I sigh with relief at her English. She inspects the children.

'*Parlez-vous français?*' she says. They shake their heads.

'Well, I speak English,' she says. 'I worked in California for three years. But I will not speak English to the children. They will not learn French if I do this.'

She asks their names one by one and they answer in soft voices. Shy and overwhelmed, Biggles is unable to answer her at all. He opens and closes his mouth like a fish.

'Speak up!' she says. 'It is your responsibility to make yourself understood.'

Then she directs a flurry of French at me.

'*Désolée*,' I say. '*Je parle français juste un petit peu.*' – 'Sorry, I speak only a little bit of French.'

'A little bit' is a vast overestimation of my capabilities, but I feel it's not the time to mention beige stockings and I can see no cross-eyed babies nearby to comment upon.

'This is no good,' Madame Montagne says. 'You must get a job, in a French office, otherwise you will not learn.'

I am too scared to go into any kind of explanation as to our strict visa conditions, let alone my inability to think of what French office this small town might hold that would employ a non-French-speaking donkey who will leave work three times a day to walk children to and from school.

Despite her fluent English, Madame Montagne then reverts to French, addressing rapid-fire instructions to Keith for ten minutes before standing to dismiss us.

I realise this is the end of our interview and my heart sinks. I have no idea of the details of school life and this is my only chance to find out.

'Madame Montagne, what school supplies do the children need?'

'I have no idea. That's not my department,' she says. She is more confused than scornful.

'And lunch, do they pack food and snacks for the morning, or ...'

'Well, if they want to, I suppose,' she says. 'I really could not tell you.'

She ushers us to the door. The interview is over.

'Welcome to École Albert Camus,' she says. 'I am very busy, as I'm sure you understand. If you like you can make an appointment to come back in six months and discuss the children's progress. But for now, I will take them to their appropriate classrooms.'

We are dismissed. We give the children hard hugs and leave the room. Heading back down the stairs, my throat has a large painful lump in it. This school culture is very unfamiliar, and I have a sneaking suspicion that our 'challenge to build the children's resilience' may in fact be a massive crock of shit.

Holding hands, largely silent, Keith and I walk back up Rue Canard. Keith goes to his office to work, and I sit at the kitchen table and spend a while tinkering with my phone, setting four alarms for the school run that I am coming to realise will utterly define our days. And then I take a deep breath and turn my attention to other things.

I'm delighted to have some alone time, but I can't relax. I wander about for a while, picking things up and putting them down again, and then I decide that I'd better start trying to establish a routine like everybody else. I'll head out to find somewhere to write.

Since Tab was a baby I've worked as a freelance writer, scribbling in pockets of time among the gentle chaos of family life. I've written many articles for magazines and newspapers, and for seven fun years I wrote a parenting column for an Australian magazine, but mostly I write 'on spec', which means I come up with an idea, write an essay and then try to sell it. My pieces usually sell (eventually) but it's a lot of work pitching things around, and it's ... let's call it 'emotionally bracing', to be frequently rejected. The steady decline in print publishing means that there are fewer pages and more freelancers to fill them with every passing year, and writing 'content' online pays so terribly it's barely worth the time.

I am, at this point, deep into the first draft of a memoir about motherhood. *Mothering Heights* is not commissioned, sold or agented. Nobody asked me to write the bastard. Trying to finish the manuscript is a gruelling exercise in discipline and I don't know if I have what it takes to anchor the boat, to be honest. But being a writer, especially a memoirist, is a kind of madness, a somewhat humiliating, show-offy hobby that requires steadfast pushing on in the face of all messages to the contrary. I feel, at this stage, somehow unable to stop picking at the scab. When I am not writing, I feel untethered and irritated. It grounds me to examine my world and sculpt it into words, these quiet, internal wrestlings fuelling me for all the other parts of my life.

I like working outside the house, and in Wollongong I have a few favourite cafes and libraries with good coffee and comfortable chairs for my pesky bad back. It's time to find my writing spot in Sommières. The only place with potential seems to be the cafe in the square run by a tall man with a thin ponytail snaking down his back. Small clutches of people are sitting at tables in the sunshine. I wander inside to find a room largely filled with boxes and shelves. Clearly, customers only sit outside. I park myself at an empty table and boot up my laptop.

Everything is wrong. The sun is shining on my computer screen so I can't see it properly, my stool is backless and uncomfortable, and the stereo is inexplicably belting out Samantha Fox's 80s hit '(Hurt Me! Hurt Me!) But the Pants Stay On'.

Working on a laptop in public is normal behaviour at home, but it feels weirdly performative here. People are staring like I am doing kundalini yoga or plucking my bikini line. Ponytail, who is wearing a shoelace as a necklace, raises an eyebrow at me in what I am coming to think of as 'resting suspicious face' – the 'resting bitch face' of France. I order and he brings me a bitter black coffee, my second disgusting brew of the morning.

It will be months before I learn to order a *'noisette'* or 'hazelnut' coffee, and in the meantime I'll get used to drinking my coffee black.

Suddenly a cat jumps onto my shoulders. I yelp loudly in my cool, laidback way, and the waitress hurries over, apologising and lifting the creature off. *'C'est ça! C'est ça!'* I babble. She looks at me askance. I'm trying to say, 'It's fine,' but in fact, I realise later, I'm saying, 'That's it! That's it!'

It's not an auspicious start. I go home to set up at the kitchen table, where the wooden chairs are epically uncomfortable, but I am safe, at least, from flying cats, the judgement of strangers and 80s BDSM-lite pop music. I make a plunger coffee and open my manuscript on the computer.

Soon, my phone alarm beeps. We're due for the lunchtime pick-up.

Other parents are again watching us as we wait outside the school. The bell rings and the children begin to pour through the gate. Tabitha has her game face on but Biggles has his head down, and when he spots us he runs at me and buries his face in my belly, hard. Mabel is holding the hand of a small girl in a red dress. The little girl runs off to her mother and I can see her talking animatedly and pointing at us.

The woman approaches us, smiling. She is tall and lovely, with dark skin and a cascade of braids.

'Bonjour,' she says in a warm, kind voice.

'Bonjour,' we say.

Mabel tugs my hand. 'That's Clementine,' she says, and then adds proudly, 'my friend.'

'Je m'appelle Rachael,' I say to the woman.

'Je m'appelle Chloé,' she replies. She shakes my hand, smiling, and I feel a comfort that settles into my fizzing stomach like a flannel blanket on cold feet.

'Nous sommes australiens ...' I begin. I run through my lines, delivering The Spiel, and the predictable happens: Chloé answers me in a stream of incomprehensible French. I turn to Keith. He takes over.

Mabel and Clémentine are holding hands and smiling up at us, proud to have found each other. One of the three children is happy? Feels like an excellent start. I'll take it.

After lunch – more *pain au chocolat*? a little screen time? See, kids, life in France is amazing! – we make our way back to École Albert Camus for afternoon class. The children are brave. We promise them that the afternoon session will be short, and then Keith and I retrace our steps again. Neighbours and shopkeepers are beginning to recognise us. *Bonjour! Salut! Ça va?*

I'm starting to feel overwhelmed at the prospect of this relentless school run. Every day, this walk? Four times? Exercise and I don't play well together, and although I can be socially enthusiastic, exuberant and chatty, I desperately crave time alone to recharge my batteries. The older I get, the more my introverted inner hermit is taking over the show. School-gate culture is going to take some managing.

Keith disappears back into the office and I clean the kitchen of lunch debris and make a grocery list for the afternoon. We are in dire need of a proper weekly shop. After pick-up today, it will be time to brave the supermarket.

Off goes the alarm again. We'll need the car today, so instead of turning down Rue Canard this afternoon, we climb the stone stairs opposite our house, next to the Ursuline Convent, built in 1666. A large tree presides over these stairs, notable for being one of the only splashes of green, other than the plane trees by the river, in this monochromatic land of stone and cobbles. Above the winding steps a tunnelled exit gives onto to the street winding beneath the château tower, which leads to a carpark where our little rented Peugeot is waiting. Although it belongs to our landlords, we must park it some distance from the house. Cars can squeeze through some of the narrow lanes of the *centre historique*, but there's certainly no room to park them.

We loop downhill and around the river to drive to school.

At the gates, word has spread. Kids have told their parents over lunch about the family of kangaroos who have joined the school. I can see Chloé waiting by a tree. As we approach, she beckons, and we go to stand with her small group. We do *la bise*, a triple-cheek affair in this part of southern France.

Cigarette smoke wafts past as usual, but there's a particular top note today: somebody is smoking weed behind a tree. Chloé introduces us to Esmé, who is shy and pregnant, with a sweet, heart-shaped face, and Gigi, loud and sporty with a cheeky spark in her eye. As we stand around waiting for the gate to open, Keith manages the conversation. I stand silently beside him. I can't understand his French, but I try hard to keep up with the emotional flow of the conversation – smile when people smile, laugh when they laugh and look serious when the conversation takes a tone. It is emotionally and physically tiring, and I can feel the first twinges of what I will come to think of as the Migraine of Stupidity. Keith looks slightly panicked. The women speak fast, one over the top of the other, and he's struggling to keep up.

The gates open. Children pour out. Our kids look a little shell-shocked and we brace ourselves as they barrel into our midsections for violent hugs. There's no time to process their day right now, however. We're off to the supermarket to fill the pantry.

Bonjour Intermarché

When we get to the Intermarché, the large supermarket on the other side of town, I'm pretty excited. I love to cook, but more than anything I crave a sense of confidence, and this place is where I hope I will find it. I'm going to normalise our Sommières life, one meal at a time.

Before the food, however, we must tackle the long list of stationery requirements that the children have been given. We find the right section easily. *La rentrée* is big business in France and there are rows and rows of supplies. The problem is that the lists themselves, all in French of course, are utterly incomprehensible. What the hell is a *trousse*? Is it used to tie a chicken? To lift a sagging scrotum? What?

'What's a *trousse*?' I ask Tabitha. She shrugs helplessly. 'What about a *règle*?'

Keith pores over the printed document. He doesn't recognise any of the words either. Our decision not to bother with French sim cards means that we don't have translation apps for situations like these. After a gruelling afternoon in a phone shop, we learned that a French bank account is required for a French phone account and – still traumatised by our experiences with the consulate – we just couldn't face the paperwork. We'll use roaming when travelling, we conclude, and leave our phones to function basically as cameras outside the house. At home in the Wormhole, I can access the wi-fi for podcasts, Instagram and WhatsApp. The decision has benefits as well as drawbacks. There's a sharp immediacy to living life without a phone, but today I would give my left nip for five minutes with Google Translate.

'Okay, we'll just guess,' I say. 'We'll just get all the stuff that seems right.'

The kids are wound up: taut and twitchy.

'Mum, we have to get the exact right things!' says Tabitha. 'The teacher yells! I'll get in trouble!'

'We'll sort it out, Tabs,' I say.

'You don't understand, Mum,' she insists. 'It's super specific, and their stuff is weird. The teachers aren't like at home.'

'That's true,' Biggles chips in. 'My teacher shouted a lot. She was like AFAFAFAFAFOOFOOFAFATA!'

A customer turns to look at us.

'Yes!' says Mabel. 'But it's more like AFAFAFAFOOO-FATATATATA!'

'Mabey!' Keith says. 'Please! Anyway, I'm sure they're not that bad.'

The children round on us in a pack and give a series of examples, talking over the top of each other as they try to demonstrate the sound of an angry French woman. It's all stuff they need to process, to explain, to release. I understand this. But there are so many of them. They are all pretending to be enraged teachers. And the Migraine of Stupidity is kicking in.

'Look, guys, we'll just do our best,' I say.

We spend twenty minutes picking through the aisles. We manage to buy pencil cases and pens and highlighters and rubbers, and then we call an end to proceedings. Nobody is happy. The children remain worried. One is crying. But we still need to do the food shopping, the most critical part of this outing, and I can see that the children have reached their limits and Keith still needs to get back to his workday.

I wheel the trolley around and around. Trying to tune out the squabbling kids, I search for the basics that will keep us going for the next few days.

We need laundry powder and dish detergent and Nurofen and head-lice treatment and pasta and fruit and breakfast stuff and coffee and milk and wine. We need a mountain of potatoes. Keith pushes the trolley and soothes the children while I rework mental menus and lists. Every product is unusual and messes with my sense of order. They are kept in strange places, given strange names, paired with strange companions. The layout of this large store is counterintuitive, and my back hurts. I try to stay calm, but stress is aerating my bloodstream.

I've done all I can. We head for the checkout. Piling our first load on to the strangely short conveyor belt, I say, '*Bonjour!*' to the cashier.

'*Bonjour*,' she allows, guardedly, but when I follow up with a hopeful '*Ça va?*' she glares at me with an expression I've come to think of as the Withering Parisian.

'*Le sac?*' she says.

'*Pardon?*' I squeak.

'*Le. Sac.*' she spits, following this up with a series of mouth sounds that in any other country would represent a significant episode of tics, if not a full Tourette's diagnosis. The woman in the queue behind me adds a few tuts of her own.

'Bag,' Keith translates, looking around for where they might be.

It turns out that in a French supermarket you must bring your own totes. Keith grabs a handful of them from a nearby rack, and when the cashier starts scanning and shooting items down the countertop, we realise that we are supposed to pack them as well. The conveyor belt is too short for all the shopping. Keith and I are slow and clumsy at managing the system, and the woman in the queue behind us is tutting so hard that I am tempted to ask her if her pacemaker is malfunctioning. If only I had snark-level French.

The cashier pauses when she can't find a price on the cherry tomatoes.

I know they were sixty-nine cents, and I search my mind for how to translate the number. French maths is awful – the word for ninety, for instance, is *quatre-vingt-dix* or 'four twenties and ten'. Sixty-nine, sixty-nine, I muse, and the answer suddenly appears. Of course! It's a favourite Jilly Cooper racy French-ism! The Cotswolds Casanova Rupert Campbell-Black suggests (and performs) *soixante-neuf* frequently, often while reading a copy of *Horse & Hound*.

I practise internally: '*Excusez-moi, Madame, soixante-neuf, oui? D'accord?*' At the last minute, I think better of it. If the conversation goes wrong, I have no way of explaining to the Intermarché teller why I am propositioning her sexually. The cashier mumbles out an incomprehensible number. Keith translates for me, and I fumble through my euros, looking for correct change.

'*Désolée,*' I say. '*Je viens d'Australie!*' And then I try to add a little self-deprecating flourish: '*Je suis un con!*' Later, I find out that I'd got 'I'm from Australia' right but instead of 'I am a dork', I'd said something closer to 'I am a cunt', which may be true but is, regardless, something I had hoped to keep a secret from the supermarket teller for a while. Thank God I didn't suggest a sixty-nine.

We pack the boot and head home, parking up on the hill and hauling the numerous bags down the road, past the tower, down the stairs beside the convent, across the cobbles, into the house, and up those endless spiralling stairs. After carrying all the shopping upstairs, Keith heads back to his office and the kids and I collapse at the kitchen table, exhausted. My back and my head are throbbing, and the poor children are wrung out like wet dishcloths.

Tomorrow, heaven help us, we'll get up and do it all again.

Schedule unfolding

L ife is taking shape. Mornings start early for Keith, the rest of the house sleeping as he begins his day with meetings: at this time of year, 6am in France is 2pm in Sydney. Keith's job is incomprehensible to me. He has a background in solar physics and engineering, creates computer programs for photovoltaic research and writes award-winning academic papers with titles like 'Mismatch loss in bifacial modules due to non-uniform illumination in 1D tracking systems'. He and his two mates run a small software company and sometimes, after a few wines, I try to explain Keith's work to our friends. It usually ends in him looking pained and hiding my drink.

Sometimes I get up early too, to start my writing day at the kitchen table, but more often I languish in the dungeon for another hour before cajoling the kids up the stairs so that I can try to prepare them for their difficult school days with a good breakfast and encouraging chats around the table.

School starts at 8.30. Walking down Rue Canard, Keith and I decide which child looks to be most in need of support from which parent. We divide and conquer, and treat the walk as something of a therapeutic exercise. Often, it is a beautiful time of chatting about life and learning the town, but some days are harder than others and getting our trio through those gates can be a gut-wrenching process. Four times a day we tramp the same kilometre-long loop, past Cédric's art gallery and the hole-in-the-wall *brocante* (bric-a-brac shop) owned by the old lady. We know her now. She is an Algerian ex–burlesque dancer called Lucie, and her beautiful witchy daughter, Juliette, has become a friend.

We pass an old house and examine the keystone, the wedge of stone locking the arch into position, which bears an inscription reading 1598. This dwelling was built not long after the siege of 1573, when locals poured boiling oil on their Catholic attackers below. We pass the markings that show the 2002 water levels when the River Vidourle flooded as high as the second storey of the terraces, inspiring locals to row boats along the streets and throw cigarette packets into the apartment windows of stranded residents. We pass the *tabac*, the fishmonger and the old-lady hairdresser, and we keep an eye out for the man who brings his boa constrictor out for an occasional sunbath on the front step and will allow us to stroke its smooth, dry skin.

'*Bonjour*,' we say to the locals, who we are coming to know. When we meet again, on our next pass along the cobblestones, we say '*Rebonjour*', or '*Salut*' or – my favourite – the sweet slang '*Coucou*'.

On the third morning of school, Keith and I hide behind a fence and watch the children. They sit nervously on a bench in the dusty concrete yard while kids frolic around them twittering in French, incomprehensible as birds. My heart twists in my chest when I see a small girl with wildly curly pigtails approach small Mabel. The two little folk gaze at each other. The will is there to play, but the method eludes them.

I have a sudden brainwave.

'Mabel!' I call, emerging from my hidey-hole. Keith looks at me aghast (I have blown our cover forever) but Mabel runs over, thrilled.

'I have a game for you, honey! Say this to your friend! "*Qu'est-ce que c'est?*" And then you point to your nose!' I tell her through the fence. 'And she will tell you what it is! It is your nose!'

I demonstrate.

'It's like, "What is this?" The nose! *"Qu'est-ce que c'est?"* The hair! *"Qu'est-ce que c'est?"* The tree!'

Mabel looks confused.

'It's fun!' I say enthusiastically. 'It's how to play with your little friend there! What's her name?'

'Élodie, I think,' says Mabel. We both turn to look at the little curly-haired girl.

'Yoo-hoo!' I call to her. She looks at me warily.

'It's okay!' I shout brightly. 'Come here! Élodie! *Élodie!*'

Keith is looking at me, horrified. He takes a step back.

'Qu'est-ce que c'est?' I call out to her. *'Qu'est-ce que c'est?* The nose! The nose!'

I am beckoning frantically through the fence. Élodie is shaking her head. It dawns on me, terribly, painfully slowly, that I look like a creep. The bell rings, Mabel and her little friend run inside, and Keith and I begin the walk of shame home along the cobblestones.

'Sorry,' I say to him in a small voice. 'I was just trying to—'

'It's fine,' he says. 'I understand.'

We cannot quite make eye contact. I'm no longer in Australia, I realise, no longer at our little beachside primary school where parents wander in and out of offices and classrooms, where I comprehend the rules and where I belong. This creepy-lady episode forms just one of the endless faux pas I feel that I am making every day.

Once home, Keith goes back into his office and I often take a long bath, reading, thinking and staring up at that tiny, mysterious window. Sometimes I write, but mostly I spend the morning cleaning, washing and cooking while listening to French-lesson podcasts, the bulletin from Radio France Internationale and the BBC *Daily Commute* on my head-phones. Up and down the stairs I go. French buns! French buns!

I spend a lot of time in my kitchen. When my pocket vibrates, I pull out my phone to see that the cooking-timer app is telling me to check the cake in the oven. On the stove, last night's chicken carcass is alchemising into gelatinous stock, a saucepan of eggs simmers for lunch and a big pot of bolognese sauce reduces into sticky rich deliciousness. I'm in my happiest state here, in the flow zone, juggling burners and recipes, cooking up a storm. I open the oven and the sweet spicy fragrance of cinnamon and ginger wafts into my nostrils. I shut the door again. The cake could use a few more minutes to get a beautifully darkened crust, but it already smells divine.

When my alarm pings for the midday pick-up, we retrace our steps along Rue Canard. At the gate, we struggle through the parent chat before we walk the kids home and put their psyches back together over baguettes and games. At 2pm, we drop them off again, a task that is sometimes an emotional roller-coaster for the second time that day, depending how the morning went.

During the afternoon break I write. Pick-up time is 2.45pm, and after school the children are ratty and starving. I make snacks, read books, play games, cook the dinner and manage the emotional weather. Dinner is at about six, when Keith clocks off for the day and heads upstairs to begin his next Dad shift. It's here, around the kitchen table, that we all process our experiences, reaching for the comedy of each day's minor crises.

After the meal we tackle homework and school paperwork. The schoolwork here has a retro vibe, with a focus on times tables and penmanship. The children are expected to conjugate verbs and learn poetry and songs by heart. Mabel, with arguably the easiest transition of all, is starting kindy by learning the French alphabet. With six months of Australian kindergarten under her belt, she can read already, and only needs to transfer those skills to a different accent and grammatical structure. Keith and I sign off on homework every night in the children's little exercise books. It's very hard, and Google Translate is often unhelpful. One night it tells me that the P & C is 'an association of volunteer parents who organise abductions for children'.

Then comes bathtime for whoever is most stinky, and a couple of episodes of *Friends*, curled up on the squashy sofas under Big Bertha, the softest blanket in the world. Sometimes we read a chapter or two of a book out loud; at the moment, we're alternating Agatha Christie's *Death on the Nile* with Andy Griffiths's *The Day My Bum Went Psycho*. The children need to be encircled, enclosed and comforted. They need us to make this strange place safe.

In these early days, Keith and I do most of the school runs together. Any conversation with French adults that extends past The Spiel is up to him. (I'm having no luck yet with the beige stockings or cross-eyed babies.) Usually I stand beside Keith, simpering like a moron Stepford wife, while he handles the chat. Keith is a handsome guy, with a sandy-brown mop, a Roman nose, olive skin and an easy smile. He looks a little like a central-casting Aussie surfer, and the school mums love him.

'We are so proud of you,' we tell the children. 'You are doing an incredible job!' A week into term, the children are rolling with the punches. They are, to my great relief, making friends, despite the language gap. Mabel writes phrases down to practise with her pals.

'J'adore le film La Reine des Neiges. *Et toi?'* – 'I love *Frozen*. And you?'
'Tu joues le Loup Touche-Touche avec moi?' – 'Will you play Catch the Wolf with me?'

She immediately builds a gang – Clémentine of course, and Ari and Hari, a set of boy/girl twins with pristine, immaculate outfits, bossy Éloïse with an exuberant afro and quiet, gentle Élodie.

Tabitha and Biggles have picked up a couple of boys who will become, by the end of the year, like our bonus sons. Franc, who also lives on Rue Canard, is small and dark, with a sharp undercut, poor teeth and a disposition sweeter than the lollies he loves, while Alain, full of swagger, is the only other blond at school. He and Biggles have matching shaggy golden manes. Franc and Alain are fascinated by Biggles's thick Harry Potter books, and they like to ruffle his hair and run off, so that he chases them back. We call the game 'Ruffles'. Alain, Franc and a boy named Luc are quickly besotted with Tabitha. They write her love letters and give her gifts of candy and cheap jewellery. She has bonded with two girls called Amélie and Sabine, who run up to her at the gate every morning. They pull Tabitha inside protectively and shout at the boys to leave her alone.

A group forms around Tabitha and Biggles. These children – Amélie and Sabine and Franc and Alain and Luc – are all, like us, misfits and *marginaux*. There are other kids at École Albert Camus who seem steadier, less eccentric, but they make no effort to connect with the new kangaroos. In fact, the arrival of the little Australians seems to be the impetus for this collection of outsiders to coalesce into a gang. These rapscallions are all a bit spiky, odd and unpredictable. But they are also sweet, open and funny, and I will come to love them all very much.

Socialising is intense for Tabitha and excruciating for introverted Biggles. For a few days, he and Tab hide in the toilets and comfort-read Harry Potter, but the teachers put a stop to this. The children cannot communicate in words, so odd sign-language games develop, like pretending to catch and eat insects off each other's heads.

Overall, the children are embraced by their little gang at École Albert Camus, just as we are welcomed by the parents at the gate. These children are polite and mature, affectionate and warm. They are just beautiful kids. But they are also, it must be said, as mad as a bag of snakes. There are declarations of love, tears and recriminations, letters of accusation followed by letters of abject apology. They are a lot, this gang, even before factoring in the language barrier. Luc in particular will, over the months to come, become the bane of Tabitha's life.

I hang at the gate with Chloé, Gigi and Esmé. My relationships with the school mums are blossoming, and they are very kind and patient with my terrible French. Whenever we meet there is a frenzy of triple-cheek kissing, the choreography of which I never, ever get completely right. Once I accidentally kiss another mum tenderly on the nose. (This is less embarrassing than the incident months later when I'm told that the phrase I use constantly – 'I'm so excited!' – actually means, 'I'm so aroused!' I imagine a text going around: *Beware the horny Australian lady. She's into noses.*)

Behind those formidable school gates, the children are really on their own. Anti-terrorism protocols mean that we can't enter the school without an appointment. This is hard. We are very grateful to France and the teachers at École Albert Camus for taking on the time and administration required to transform three small feral platypuses from Wollongong into global citizens. But while the teachers are sweet to our three, treating them, on the whole, more gently than their classmates, and even organising a special weekly French lesson, it's mostly up to the kids to sink or swim on that *Lord of the Flies* playground. There, children wildly release the energy they've contained in those tightly managed classrooms, and Tab, Biggles and Mabel learn the rules of engagement as best they can.

It's busy. All our ideas about what life would be like have crumbled, and there's no space to reflect. We scramble to manage the issues of every day, catching and examining and solving each problem one at a time, like so many objects thrown at a sweating juggler. Here, a ball! Now, a watermelon! Look smart, a chainsaw! A flaming torch! A bag of rats! A cross-eyed baby!

Life is harder than we could have imagined: more exhausting, more complicated. And yet, we are so captured by it that, from the first, Keith and I start discussing how we could possibly stay longer than a year. We peruse bewitchingly cheap ruins in real-estate windows and muse on possibilities, talking late into the darkness of our cosy dungeon. The sights, the smells and the sounds of Sommières have pierced our insides. The very air seems to vibrate at a different intensity, and the five of us grow closer every day, a small platoon startled by the emotional punch of our new posting.

Australia's Highest Husky

Washing up at the kitchen sink, I gaze at the corpse of a decomposing pigeon in a small alcove of the stone wall opposite. The pigeon has been there since we arrived, and every day it grows more desiccated. I know the feeling.

The kids have finished lunch and scarpered off to make the most of their free time before the afternoon school session, leaving me to clear up the lunch chaos strewn across the table. All three of them have runny noses and a slightly manic frisson, and I can feel that they are about to get sick. Alert the media: good times ahead.

Mabel crawls in on her hands and knees and gives me an apple. 'Roo roo roo!' she barks expectantly. This is my cue to hold the apple up high for Mabel to jump and grab. It's her latest game: her name is Henry and she's the champion dog on a TV show she's invented called *Australia's Highest Huskies*.

I dry my hands on a tea towel and hold the apple in the air.

'Aroo!' Mabel cries as she leaps. The athletics are poorly judged and she lands badly, scraping her knee on the flagstones. There are tears. I feel a wave of frustration, followed by a wave of guilt. Like everything Mabel does, *Australia's Highest Huskies* is both hilarious and exhausting. It's hard to keep up with her flights of fancy. Biggles arrives to ask if he can use my laptop to look up Ancient Greek lessons on YouTube.

'Why don't you learn French, Biggs?' I ask. 'Considering that, you know, you are currently living in France, and Ancient Greek is a dead language.'

He shakes his head stubbornly. He's making a point. I sit, give him a hug, find him a tutorial and leave him to it. Tabitha is silently reading *The Hunger Games* in her mezzanine. She hasn't said much since we got home at lunch. Resentment and shame bubble up in a twist as I realise that my small girl probably needs me to climb the ladder for a private talk. The thought of it is exhausting. I am out of parent juice.

Three kids need three different types of mum, and right now, all of them need more Mum than I have to give. Apart from operating as their executive assistant for the admin of life, there is a lot of mental gymnastics involved in shifting emotional gears to meet various needs: this child needs cuddles, this child needs deep-and-meaningful chats, this child needs to be jollied out of her funk, this child needs to run off their energy, this one needs to rest ... on and on it goes, in an endless loop.

I am so grateful to Keith for his patience and commitment to dadding. He's always there to play Highest Huskies with Mabel, to discuss maths and sci-fi with Biggles, to talk Tabitha through her worries, but in the final reckoning, there's a limit to how much Keith and I can help the children adjust to life in France.

We're out of food. I badly need to get to the Intermarché today, and Keith will have to drive. I'm still too scared to drive on the other side of the road, along the daunting narrow passages and across the bridge over the river. I imagine getting into some kind of accident and babbling nonsense to the police about my beige stockings.

I know I will have to brave this drive sooner rather than later. Keith is scrambling to fit everything in. He needs to log eight hours a day at the company around school runs, morning cajoling, lunch rallying, dinner processing, homework and family time. In order to fit his hours in, he starts early, finishes late and pivots constantly to work around the endless distractions. Being my taxi is an extra gig he could afford to lose.

But my role in the family – making plans and arrangements, sorting admin and appointments, keeping the machine running – is hobbled by my lack of language. I am dependent on Keith for a lot at the moment, far more than we both would like.

Keith and I have a solid, easy bond. Most of the time we form a symbiotic pair, acting as each other's sounding board, hype person, champion and defender. We take on different portfolios to manage the complex business of the family, and we value and appreciate the work of the other. In normal times, that is. Right now, like the children, both of us are struggling. Neither of us have set up yet the systems that we need to operate at our best. I start to fray in times of chaos, and need calm, structure and solitude to reboot. Keith, hardworking and sporty, requires lots of exercise to keep on an even keel. He's an energiser bunny and I'm a panda bear who needs rest and recovery time to kick back and chew on my bamboo.

My pesky bad back is part of this. As a teenager I had spinal-fusion surgery to correct a serious scoliosis in my spine; and two years later a second surgery to repair the first, after a broken screw and a problem called 'pseudoarthrosis' meant that the fusion didn't take. This second surgery extended the series of rods and bolts that were straightening my back, and also meant that I'd had four intervertebral discs, by this stage, replaced with hip and rib bone tissue. A few years followed in which I became used to managing chronic pain.

Then, aged twenty-four, I was involved in a speedboat accident in which I broke the vertebra underneath the fused sections. An accident like this after a loss of discs can be terribly painful, and I struggled with my back for a long time, particularly during the baby-wrangling years, when three pregnancies took their toll. The shlepping around of small people and all their paraphernalia was tough. Sometimes I was impaired, sometimes incapacitated. Sometimes it was just a question of glamour: even apart from my back, I broke a rib breastfeeding (a story for another time) and a toe slipping in a puddle of toddler wee on the bathroom floor. It was a dignified, elegant era.

Having a chronic illness or injury is actually a lot like having a really shitty part-time job, one where your boss can suddenly call you in with no notice and refuse to tell you when your shift ends. A job that requires hacks, workarounds and compromises, that compels the whole family to fall in around its unpredictable, unreasonable demands. It's all work: taking care of my physical body and my emotional responses to it, striking a balance between ignoring the pain and attending to it, acknowledging and managing the knock-on impacts that chronic pain can have on the rest of the family. Pain makes all parts of life more difficult.

Pain is a third person in our marriage, too. It's like being in a polyamorous set-up with a bitch of a sister-wife. I find myself in a fight against my own physicality, feeling like my own body is my enemy. Pain is a secret subtext, the intimacy-destroying strategy of an evil bot, a wickedly clever algorithm that defies all attempts to tame it. Sometimes I am stoic, trying to deny pain its power – a coping mechanism that means I operate at a distance, through a glass. And sometimes I need to whinge and offload so that I am not so alone in my reality.

It's hard on Keith, who must manage his annoyance and distress and frustration too. It's easy, of course, to see from the outside exactly how another person should solve their problems, and it's impossible, from the inside, to make your lived experience understood by another. It comes down, sometimes, to energy. People in the disability community some-times talk about 'spoons' as a metaphor for the amount of energy one has in a day. Keith has many, many more spoons than I do in any given day; sometimes I must borrow 'spoons' from the next day, and then I burn out, with nothing left in the cutlery drawer.

There are upsides. I think having chronic back problems has helped me to develop the skill of zoning out to another place in order to escape an uncomfortable reality. It's been a surprisingly helpful mothering tool. I think the art of Not Being Present in the Moment has underrated virtues. Children may be dragging at my legs, wailing about whose Friendy failed to share their imaginary sausages, but in my mind, I am on the shores of Lake Como while an Italian manservant hands me an espresso martini and winks sensually. (Gianni is extremely handsome but completely smooth between the legs like a Ken doll. He wants only to worship me and makes no sexual demands whatsoever.)

By the time we are in France, my back is as stable as it has been for a long time. Mabel is six now, and the intensively athletic mothering required with very small children is finished. Still, the relentless activity of this big move and the physicality of our first weeks here has sparked a lot of pain for me. So much walking on uneven cobblestones, so much traipsing up and down the mobius staircase. All of these things will be positive in the big picture, strengthening my back over the coming year, but in this early period, pain grinds away at my energy and good humour like a relentless, constant sandpaper.

At night, after we get the children to sleep, a final tiring task of the day, Keith and I sit together in the overcrowded lounge room, where nothing is quite set up to our own style of living yet. Sometimes we watch our shows or have a glass of wine and chat about Donald Trump or the children, but poor Keith almost always still has work to do to finish his day. My brain is too fried to write by now, and so I mindlessly wander the internet, watching YouTube documentaries and doomscrolling while Keith taps away on the other couch. We are distant, emotionally as well as physically, in our shared new reality and the disconnection between us foments and grows, quiet as moss.

Keith and I rarely fight. This works for us: along with deteriorating eyesight, we share the failing memory of early middle age, so that after we put resentments on a simmering backburner rather than giving them a healthy airing, we often forget what they were in the first place. But this approach means that when we do argue, maybe once every couple of years, it is painful and raw. We are unpractised, terrible, clumsy fighters. I rail and weep. *Emotionally: this!* He shuts down. *Logically:*

this. Disagreements are so rare that they feel epic, like the veil covering our everyday life from some awful underlying truth is being lifted and so that with every argument, divorce is on the table. 'Well, we've had a fine run, but it's clear we are utterly unsuited to continuing this charade.'

When stress turns my dial a couple of clicks to the right I lean to panic and spikiness. Keith combats this with a near-comatose calm. When channelled and trained right, the combination of these energies can make us a powerful unit, but when we are off-piste it's a trainwreck. There's a battle brewing today, a sour bubble in a giant's stomach. Our separate, silent internal narratives are showering invisible sparks into the air, and it all kicks off over the supermarket.

Foundation argument

I head downstairs and knock on Keith's office door.

'Hey, Cakes,' I say, opening it halfway. Canned laughter from the television next door greets me. Keith swivels on his chair to face me, raising an eyebrow.

'I hate to ask, but can you take me to the Intermarché after we drop the kids back after lunch? We've got no laundry powder and nothing for dinner. And I need to go to the chemist.'

'Fine,' Keith says tightly. My hackles rise slightly. I don't want to go to the bloody supermarket either. I'm not asking for a lift to the beauty parlour.

'Shouldn't take long,' I say. 'I'll give you the warning when it's five minutes to go.'

Disharmony curls its faint poison between us as I close the door.

Soon, the alarm beeps. It's time to gather the children and herd everybody up to the car for the school run. The children are downcast and resigned as they return through the gate. Biggles and Tab are angry at us; Mabel is blinking back tears.

Some of it is theatre, I know – of course you play the Dying Swan as hard as you can if there's a chance you might be allowed to stay home – but the immense difficulty of their school day is real. I know how hard the Migraine of Stupidity kicks in for me after a few minutes of trying to keep up with French conversation, and the children are in this position for hours every day.

Seeing them like this, a new layer of angst settles, like powdery snow, on top of my already overloaded system. What the fuck are we doing here? Keith and I get back in the car and ride to the Intermarché in silence, immersed in our own thoughts. Keith is in work mode and I am running menus and lists in my head so that I can complete my errands and get out as fast as possible.

At the carpark, Keith decides that he will work in the car rather than at the noisy Intermarché cafe.

'Can you get cash out on your account?' he asks.

'Yep,' I say. 'There's an ATM at the entrance.'

We've been using a special bank card for the last couple of weeks, and it's good to get back in the usual swing of things, but when I get to the machine I discover that my PIN, unused for a while now, has utterly disappeared from my memory. I try all sorts of mental tricks to access the number, but it's no good – the tsunami of new information flooding my brain over the last fortnight has completely eliminated it.

I head back to the car and try to make light.

'You'll never believe this,' I say jauntily as I open the passenger door. Keith is crammed uncomfortably into the hatchback, his laptop perched against the steering wheel and open to a complicated, colourful spreadsheet. I force out a breezy laugh. 'I can't remember my PIN!'

It's the final straw for mild-mannered Keith.

'Are you kidding me?' he says. He's not smiling. I step back.

'What?'

'Are. You. Joking,' he says.

My fake breeziness evaporates.

'No,' I say coldly. 'I'm not joking. Did you bring the other card?'

'No,' he says. 'I can't deal with this. You're going to have to sort this one out on your own.'

It stings like a slap. This is far from Keith's normal demeanour, a shocking departure, and I feel a hot lump rise in my throat as I slam the door, hard. I have some euros in my wallet. I'll just do my best to scramble dinner for tonight and forget the chemist. I'll figure out the card later.

I rage-wheel my trolley around the Intermarché, managing vegetables and pasta and washing powder and fruit and bread, enough to get us by. Back at the car, I load the bags into the back, shut the boot and climb back in. Keith starts the car silently and we head home.

'I don't know what to tell you,' I say through gritted teeth. 'I don't know how I forgot the number. I am doing my best.'

Keith is silent. He changes gears forcefully.

'Your best,' he says, 'is underwhelming right now.'

Oh, it's on.

We carry the shopping down the steps and into the house and sit in the bottom room, where the terrain between our two couches feels uneven and treacherous and strange. Then we embark on our clunky, terrible method of conflict resolution, like participants in some awful live-action roleplay of *Men Are from Mars, Women Are from Venus*.

'Things are really hard for me.' I open with a strong defensive manoeuvre. 'I am fried. I am fucking frazzled! But I feel like I can't mention it to you, like you think I should have no response to this stress at all, like a bloody robot! Who else am I going to whinge to? Madame Montagne? Ponytail, the waiter from the bloody cafe? Am I not allowed to have a whinge, for God's sake?'

'Please,' Keith says. 'I just want you to be one less thing for me to worry about.'

'Oh, for fuck's sake!' I say. 'Don't patronise me!'

I start to riff. As I heat up I use ten words where two would do, and I refine and extend my argument as I go, so that by the end I'm not always arguing the same position as I was at the beginning of my rant, although I maintain the same level of feverish confidence.

Keith, meanwhile, withdraws from the emotional onslaught into silence, so that I must start guessing what he's thinking so I can verbalise his side of the piece as well. The ugly-crying begins. My pitch rises to that level only dogs can hear.

'I worked' – *gulp* – 'incredibly hard to get us here, Cakes! And I'm running this house! Just because' – *gulp* – 'right now I need you to drive and my French is terrible – I hate that, don't you get that? I don't want to be dependent on you!' – *hic! hic!* – 'And I won't be! I want to be in charge of my own shit! But you have to give me some bloody time!'

My 'thinking' brain is no longer in the picture. My overwrought amygdala, my 'feeling' brain, has taken over. Regrettably Joan Collins is in charge of this organ. I've become as dramatic as the French gang at École Albert Camus. Luckily there is no pool in sight, or I might have thrown Keith in after slapping his face with one hand and tossing a pina colada at it with the other.

'I feel like you think that if you were handling all my house stuff, you'd be doing a better job, but you don't know the half of what it takes to be thinking about all the shit I think about. You don't see all the machinations behind it, the duck-duck-paddling … the feet … the paddling feet under the water! You just see where you think you could do better. You just … Duck feet!' I conclude, wiping my nose.

Keith suddenly explodes into explanation.

'Rach! Just because you think something, doesn't make it the truth. I don't think any of that, and I do see all your hard work. Look, it's like today – you forget your number and I'm expected to laugh and go home and get the card and have no problem with the fact that I'll be up until eleven, and you don't have to say sorry, or acknowledge any of it—'

'I did!' I say. 'I do!'

'Let me speak!' he begs. I crush my lips together and sit on my hands. The urge to defend myself is visceral. Once she's broken out, it's very hard to put Joan Collins back in her box.

'I don't think you understand how much pressure I am under,' Keith says. 'I can't do my work without time and peace to think, and the interruptions are just fucking with me so badly. I need you to help me make more space and I just don't think you get it.'

'I do get it!' I say hotly. 'I do!' (I don't.) The truth stings. I lean on Keith for a lot of practical help here in Sommières, asking his advice first before I try to figure stuff out on my own. The thing is, Keith is so capable and he never makes a fuss. He's made this bed for himself, frankly.

I go on. 'I feel like I can't talk to you about my worries because you're trying to be so positive and optimistic. Like, I have to process that part on my own, and that just makes me feel more distant. Right now I feel like I am in service to everybody's needs but my own, and on days like today, that sucks, but I can't do any of the things that help me to cope with it, and I can't talk to you about it because you feel like then I'm asking you to fix my problem, which makes it your problem. But I just need to vent! I've lost all my strategies, you know? Having coffee with my friends, driving around getting shit done, writing in the cafe or the library. The stuff that makes me feel like *me*.'

'Like my soccer,' Keith says. 'I am going nuts not being able to exercise.'

I'm built for leisure. I cannot relate to this whatsoever. Still, I sympathise.

'I'm out of juice, too,' says Keith. 'I am trying so hard not to drop any of these bloody balls, and you keep asking more and more and more. Can you move this table? Do you know where the scissors are? You can chill – take a bath, watch a show – but I don't have time for any of that. And then today it was just like the last straw, when you were like "I'm so zany! I forgot my PIN! Rescue me!"'

I snort. I can't help it. The air shifts a little.

'I feel alone,' Keith says.

'God, you're not,' I say. 'Of course you aren't! Just let me be sore and tired and stressed out, and don't try to rescue me. Just fake some sympathetic noises. Say "*naw*". That's it. "*Naw*."'

'*Naw*,' tries Keith. It's fake, but I'll take it.

'We have to keep it together for the children,' I say, 'but surely we can let the cracks show to each other. It's all fine, right? Everything is fine. We're just at, you know, peak stress.'

I know the clouds on the terrible afternoon are beginning to lift when we are able to make a joke.

'I see you,' Keith says, in his best Mullumbimby Hypnotherapist.

'Cakes,' I reply, 'there's no need to get hysterical.'

As our elevated nerves calm, we haltingly choke out our truths and, having quieted the noise in our own minds, we try to hear the other. I explain my mental load. Keith shares his own. We talk about the anxieties of being the breadwinner and the low-status humiliation of being the 'trailing spouse', and we explore our different amounts of battery life for socialising and physical activity. We talk about the isolation and frustration of pain, and the complex emotional experience of being the observer of that pain. We talk about the intensity of the last few weeks, and conclude that right now, pushed past our window of tolerance, we've stopped doing all the small things that keep us feeling cared for. We've lost that critical aspect of appreciating the work of the other. It's a sure road to Resentment Town.

Days like these are awful. It's both the blessing and the curse of the whole institution of marriage: there is nowhere to run and nowhere to hide. You must work through the sometimes-impossible task of explaining yourself to another person, and you must face the shame of your pale, soft underbelly on show. Marriage makes gods and monsters of us all.

Keith and I renew a commitment to kindness, set our compasses back in the same direction and reach the end of the talk just in time for the afternoon school pick-up. It takes a week or so for the emotional residue of the fight to fade, and for us to move into our standard relationship zone, which is one of 'positivity bias', the state in which you are ready to attribute good thoughts and feelings to your partner's behaviour, rather than the opposite: that they are *deliberately* doing things *just* to piss you off. Keith is my North Star, my touchstone, and our marriage is my safe harbour. He tells me that I am his fountain of humour, the architect of our family and the source of his happiness. Here in France, where the sands are constantly shifting beneath our feet, we need that connection and support more than ever.

I resolve to learn to drive myself to the Intermarché as quickly as possible. And a day or two later when I am staring at the dead pigeon in the alcove again, out of nowhere a little neural pathway in my brain reanimates – *pop!* – to deliver, like a talisman for a brighter, more stable future, my PIN. Things are looking up.

Village donkey

Day by day we are growing to know our neighbours, and they are almost all very friendly to us. But on the morning school run Rue Canard is not yet awake, and we share the cobbled streets with only the cats and the other local children.

'*Coucou!*' pipes sweet Franc from his upstairs window, his neat dark cap of hair just visible under a row of flapping washing.

'*Coucou!*' we call back, the five of us all holding hands as we troop along the cobbles past posters warning about chemtrails and advertising jazz events.

By the midday and afternoon school runs in the warm months, the streets are lively. Shoppers mill about, their carts *chock-chock*ing along the cobbles and inconveniencing seniors on walking tours who, in turn, stop to take pictures of the ancient doorways and get in the way of the young men in shiny athleisure trying to get to the *tabac*, where clutches of older men hang about, shouting, gesticulating and laughing. Everybody smokes. Cats wind their way through the throng.

'*Bonjour! Bonjour!*' we say, stopping to exchange triple-cheeked kisses with the people we know. It can be a busy process, the summertime school run, and on some days we feel unable to face the social obligations of the street. In these moods we duck down Rue Flamande, a steep back alley that leads directly to the river, stepping carefully across the uneven path, then treading the stone pathway parallel to the Vidourle, before taking a side-street shortcut back up to École Albert Camus.

After lunch, heading to school we pass the house of Madame Fanny, our chic Swiss septuagenarian neighbour. An Amazonian ex-model with an imposing bosom, she drops some great names from her wild 60s modelling days (which include descriptions of Lawrence Durrell as, rather insultingly, a 'toad') and occasionally throws unusual parties in her empty bottom room that gives onto the street. An exhibition of her grandchildren's art, for instance, or a clothes-swapping sale, all of which seem a thinly veiled excuse for her and her linen-clad friends to get stonkingly pissed. (At one gathering, where the children are all horrified by the taste of caviar, a glamorous seventy-something tries to light a cigarette the wrong way round and kicks over a pot plant, giving me immediate senior-life goals.)

We pass Juliette and Lucie's *brocante*. 'Ah!' calls Juliette as we arrive. 'How is my beautiful Australian family?'

Juliette leans on unexpected syllables with her gravelly voice. Her English is lilting and musical, and with her slanting eyes and dyed red hair, she looks very Celtic. She was born in Brittany, that land far west, full of Neolithic menhirs and dolmens and ancient, mysterious magic, and her mother, Lucie, is a *Pied-Noir*, born during the period of French rule in Algeria, who left after the country gained independence in the 1950s.

Lucie passes the days moving her stool about the narrow street to catch the sun. It's only when she stands up that her tiny dog is visible. He will snarl and show teeth if you reach out a hand to him. He loves only Lucie, and spends his happy days squashed behind her rump.

My girls inspect the ever-changing '€2' box of treasures at the door of Lucie's shop. A neighbour in a shiny tracksuit slams out of the doorway aggressively, every careful comb line visible on his hair. Juliette narrows her eyes at him and he returns her glance coolly.

'*Nous sommes en retard!*' we say to Juliette. 'We are late!' We continue past Cédric's art gallery on the corner, where Cédric is set up at his outside easel. While the sun is out, Rue Canard is a street to linger in. There are three kisses for Cédric and a quick inspection of his current work.

We hurry through the square, where people sit with coffee and wine – *Bonjour! Bonjour!* – before pausing, despite our lateness, to admire the pastries in the window of Catherine's bakery. These are works of art. There are brownies oozing chocolate from their centres and tiny wrapped bundles of chocolate twigs shot through with flecks of orange. There are glistening fruit tarts, delicately layered mille-feuille, buttery almond croissants, fat éclairs and chocolate muffins, the children's firm favourite. Every pastry looks more delicious than the one before.

Directly opposite Catherine's patisserie is our favourite *boulangerie*, Farine, where the young ropy-muscled baker clad in a long grimy-white apron stands at the open maw of a woodfired oven, the ceiling of the medieval room pressing down close upon him, and shapes loaves of baguette dough on a long paddle. He takes the metal tool he is holding with his lips, deftly slices stripes across the top of the baguettes and replaces the tool in his mouth. Then he smoothly sweeps the loaves into the oven, where any residual bacteria from his body will be nicely baked away in the heat. Only the occasional tourist is upset by his technique.

We like to buy our baguettes here, joining the queue every day at lunchtime. The girl behind the counter, young and jet-haired, is grouchy and has very little patience for our terrible French. Every once in a while, there is an unpleasant batch of bread and cake, an anomaly we put down to the baker being drunk.

A delicious little creature on the daily route has caught my eye. She's a sexy snack with the unmistakably curved, generous, zaftig Italian shape of a coffee machine. My precious! She's tucked into the back of an odd little organic vegetable shop that lies at the end of Rue Canard. The shop itself is not particularly inviting. The veggies are piled out the front and the few small tables inside are blocked by a large silver scale and random crates of produce. The industrial-sized coffee machine says 'come in' but the interiors say 'not so fast'.

This coffee machine calls to me like a siren from a rock. If the machine took human form, it would not be safe around me, sexually. But I'm not yet ready to interact with the owner of the shop, a rangy, dark-haired gentleman with a militant vegan sniff about him. The children and I call him Scary Cool Guy.

One day on our afternoon walk home, Tabitha, who is learning to cook, describes to me a recipe she has in mind for dessert. She needs figs. I decide to test the waters with Scary Cool Guy. I'll open with the figs and then I'll ask about the coffee, I decide. I practise the sentence in my head a number of times before I say it.

'*Je voudrais des figues pour le dessert ce soir, s'il vous plaît. Juste une petite boite – six, peut-être?*' – 'I would like some figs for tonight, please. Just a little box – maybe six?'

'Feeg?' says Scary Cool Guy, staring at me and tapping his forefinger on his beaky nose. The silence drags and then he suddenly says '*Figues! Un moment!*' and dashes out of the door of his shop.

I am disconcerted. '*Non, non, c'est bon!*' I call after him as he disappears down the end of the street. 'Don't worry! Please!' I don't know what is happening but I fear it will not end well. A memory flashes into my mind of our first day in Sommières, when Tabitha and I followed the man from the *tabac* on his search for milk. Five minutes later, Scary Cool Guy returns, from God knows where, with a basket full of figs. I smile weakly and pluck out the top six. His jaw drops, infuriated.

'*C'est tout?*' he says. 'That's all?'

I stand my ground. I'm on a budget, I've been charged eye-watering amounts for organic produce in France before and I'm not going to be shamed into buying a bag of expensive fruit by this guy. No matter how scary and cool he is.

Biggles has a phrase he uses to describe a stream of French. He calls it a 'Bloopy Bloopy Blah'. Scary Cool Guy unfurls a long-winded Bloopy Blah at me. I have no idea what he is saying.

'*Désolée*,' I say. '*Je suis australienne. Je ne comprends pas.*'

Scary Cool Guy takes a step towards me, rolls his eyes and repeats himself, louder than before. '*BLOOPY BLAH. BLOOPY BLOOPY BLOOPY BLAH.*'

I get my wallet out of my bag. '*Juste les six figues, s'il vous plaît*,' I say. My voice is shaking. My hands, too. '*Combien?*'

How much, fuck-knuckle?

Scary Cool Guy rocks back on his feet, crosses his arms on his chest and settles into a rant. He's playing to the crowd, and there are quite a number of people around at this time in the afternoon. He calls to the shopkeeper standing in the doorway opposite. I can't understand the words he is using but his tone is clear as a bell.

Get a load of this muppet! he's saying. She asks for figs, I go all the way to my place, and then she only wants six! And she can't speak a word of French. What a fucking liberty.

I am mute. All the comebacks in my head are in English and I have no idea how to handle this particularly French brand of dickhead. He finds himself delightful. At one point during his monologue, he breaks into song: 'Yasterday. Owl my Trupples Sim So Fah Haway.'

The children draw closer to my legs. They are confused and unsure what's happening. I am humiliated but need to maintain my equilibrium for their sake.

'*Combien?*' I say loudly, interrupting Scary Cool Guy's one-man show.

'*Trois euro*,' he spits at me, dropping the figs into a bag. I place the coins on a table and leave without saying '*merci*', which, in the codified French system of *politesse*, falls under 'extreme fuck you'. The adrenaline seeps slowly away as the children and I make our way home. By the time we get to the Wormhole, I just feel tired.

Scary Cool Guy is a grade-A nob, but he's an outlier. We are, against all odds, starting to make friends. The next day I'm at the gates watching a French mum with wonderfully expressive wide-set eyes call instructions to her children as they come running to her. I am wondering if I will ever understand a word anybody says when she suddenly turns to me and says, in perfect Queen's English, 'So, are you one of these Aussies I've heard about?'

My mouth drops open as she laughs. This is Alex, ukulele-playing anthropologist, specialist in the Mesopotamian era, fluent speaker of three languages and soon to become my favourite person in Sommières. Alex grew up in the village with an English dad and a mother from New Zealand and is now married to a Spaniard. She invites us all to her house on the weekend.

I am accepting with delight when another woman approaches us. She's wearing cut-off denim shorts and a sexy little camisole, and has a satchel slung over her shoulder. Her red hair glints in the light and her smile holds the promise of naughtiness. This is Kat. She kisses Alex and then turns to me.

'You,' she says, 'Australia, yes? The kangaroo?' She hops around me in a circle. Other parents look on, nonplussed.

'*Oui*', I say. '*Le* pouch.' I give my stomach a wobble. Kat slaps me on the back, howling with laughter.

'You have the French?' she asks.

'*Non*,' I say sadly. '*Petit, petit peu.*'

'You know this place? The Calade?' She points to a rundown-looking building across a patchy park where men are playing boules and holding glasses of cloudy Ricard.

I shake my head.

'Okay. This good place for you. French lesson, *oui*? French language?'

'*Oui*,' I say enthusiastically.

'I take you tomorrow. When school begin. Okay? I will go you Calade. Okay?'

I just nod, grinning. Kat slaps my shoulder and barks her glorious laugh.

'Okay!' she says. '*Le* pouch!' And then she screams for her child and takes off at speed across the carpark, red hair swinging. I'm a little stunned at the tornado, the life force of Kat, and not for the last time.

I may be starting to make friends, but I'm also making enemies. I guess I've really arrived. I turn my head to peer with great interest in the shop opposite every time I pass Scary Cool Guy from now on, and down the track, when I'm in a bind and need to grab fruit or veggies from his shop, I give him the full Withering Parisian and make a point of cutting dead his attempts to befriend me. When Scary Cool Guy thought I was a dunderhead tourist, he took his chance to make fun of me. And when he realises after some months that I am still living in his town and, in fact, friends with many of his neighbours, I still don't forgive him for taking the chance to be an arsehole when he thought the stakes were low. I lose my chance at that coffee machine when I make Scary Cool Guy my nemesis, but I come to terms with that.

In this new place I have been given the challenge and the gift of rein-venting myself. I don't have a choice. Adapt or perish. Oddly enough, Keith and I are match fit for this task. A family with children is constantly in flux, re-forming, shifting and changing itself to fit the needs of its growing members, so we are adept at adjusting our ways to take on new variables of changed behaviour, routine or developmental stage. Right now, we must reshape, re-carve and pour the stuff of ourselves into new, Sommières-shaped vessels. It's true that I am, at this point, the village donkey. But it may not be a permanent position.

The Calade

Next morning, as promised, there is Kat in all her glory. Today she wears a cream bodysuit with lace detail and a pair of skin-tight jeans. '*Allo!*' she cries, grasping me by the shoulders and giving me the triple-cheeked *bise*. '*Le pouch*!'

Kat leads me across the dusty boules court and into a shabby three-storey building with a sweeping staircase, at the bottom of which is a large bulletin board advertising classes and community events. I spot the poster I am coming to see everywhere around town, a dense block of text about chemtrails peppered with aggressive caps (I suspect it is the work of Scary Cool Guy).

On the second floor, Kat takes me past several classrooms into a small office and introduces me to the French teacher, Nanette. She is toothy and warm, with a mane of strawberry-blonde hair and not a word of English. Together we limp through a conversation, as Kat explains that the Calade is a volunteer-run association that helps migrants settle into France, and Nanette offers to slot me into her Tuesday- and Thursday-morning classes, asking me to pay only a fee of €10 to join the organisation. I worry that I am just a year-long adventurer taking up the place of a needier participant, but Nanette assures me that I am welcome. I accept with gratitude.

Soon, the Calade becomes an anchor. Even though we are only here for a year it is important to Keith and me that we make this place home for the children, and around my classroom table, with all the other new Sommièrois, I start to put flesh on the bones of my new life.

Twice a week, my *maîtresse* Nanette gathers students from Finland, Russia, Morocco, Spain, Brazil, Senegal, Thailand, Madagascar, Ecuador, Iraq and more in a simple, utilitarian room. We are an eclectic bunch around the table, with varying levels of French. It is rather formal, and very funny. Quickly I fall into the routine of it all.

After 'conversation practice' we pause for morning tea, often with cakes we've made. One day, generously built Asha from Morocco breaks out into a glorious hip-shimmy as she delivers a tray of sweets, at which all the Arabic women start ululating and the rest of us hoot and applaud wildly. The Middle Eastern women stir their tea with sprigs of mint they carry wrapped in foil, and I put the sugar cubes (brand 'Daddy') into the coffee I am learning to take black.

Mimi and Josephine help Nanette by translating tasks into English for me. Mimi is French, a local volunteer, sophisticated in her chic bob and twinsets, and her husband, Maurice, is a retired fashion designer. They live in the same building as Josephine near the river and keep a vacuum cleaner on the landing between their apartments. I adore sharp-witted, kind Brazilian Josephine immediately. She will become a close friend.

The outfits of Moroccan Fatima, an older woman with Berber chin tattoos, bring me enormous joy. In winter she favours a beanie with a giant bobble on top of her headscarf, and generally she devotes herself to taking the concept of pattern-clashing to the limit, as in the very edge of visual stress that precedes an actual epileptic fit. Fatima often rocks a velour leopard-print bathrobe, and she is partial to more cocktail rings than she has fingers.

There is a lot of ad hoc communication in the Calade classroom. With the clarity of language stripped from us, we are forced to find subtle alternatives and mainly we fall back on kindness and humour. It is a safe space to be stupid, this room. A safe space in which to slowly work things out. Most bonding of all, it is a room full of laughter.

It is so personally enriching to be forced outside my comfort zone. Normally I am all about words, but here I cannot talk. I am finding profound benefits in being made mute. Being forced just to listen is humbling and infuriating and illuminating. It is ego-busting to be stripped of the practised performance of my personality.

On Tuesday afternoons I have a one-on-one lesson at the Calade with a volunteer called Valentina, an earnest, slender blonde.

During one lesson, I fumble my way through the excruciating small talk of 'conversation practice'.

I bought my daughter a new backpack, I tell Valentina: '*Le sac, c'est* "Hello Kitty" *en anglais*,' I say. '*En français, c'est ... bonjour, ma petite chatte?*' I am trying to be cute but Valentina laughs, horrified.

'*Non, non!*' she says. '*Er, chatte c'est un animal, oui, mais aussi ...* it is *le ... le sexe.*' – 'The cat is an animal, yes, but also ... the sex.'

'*Pardon?*' I say.

'*Le sexe* of the woman,' she says.

'The woman?'

'*Oui, les* woman, when they have the ... sex ... you know.'

It is very difficult to understand.

'Lesbians?' I squeak.

'*Pardon?*' says Valentina. The room is full of other students conjugating verbs and talking about snow holidays. I don't know how Valentina and I have travelled down this dicey path, and worse, I have no idea how to retrace my steps.

'Um ... Woman sex with woman, *en anglais* ... is ... er ... lesbian sex,' I say.

Valentina looks worried. '*La chatte* is the woman *sex*,' she says in a strained voice.

Le sexe, I remember with a flash, is the general French term for genitalia.

'Vagina?' I whisper.

'*Oui*,' Valentina says encouragingly.

'Oh!' I shout, the thrill of understanding overriding my need to keep my voice down. 'Pussy! *Oui!* Hello, Pussy!'

'*Oui*,' Valentina agrees. 'Hello, Pussy!'

We both smile, relieved.

I am developing a sort of 'Franglish Theatre' mode of communication, a combination of English, French and mime. I'm adding mouth sounds like a real Frenchy to give myself thinking time: tongue-clicking, tutting, raspberry-blowing. I use the French slang word *bref*, which is kind of like 'anyway' to imply that I would say more, if I had time. I also use *en fait* or 'in fact' a lot. And the phrase *C'est vrai?* or 'Is that right?' wins me a few seconds, even though I'm aware I must look like a hillbilly rube asking 'Is that true?' in response to every statement. My French is all about using hacks to buy microseconds during which my brain can try to extract something recognisable out of the word soup somebody has served me up.

It's hard work improving my French, but I learn more than just language in my Calade classroom. If the personal is political, it is kind, nurturing, patient places just like this that create an amazing connection to a country for a new arrival. It's a slow burn. A long con. Some students come for years to these weekly classes. They go on excursions on the Calade minibus, get help with their paperwork, fumble through conversation practice and learn, bit by bit, what it means to be the very best kind of French citizen.

There is nothing monied or fashionable about the Calade. A glamourous Sommières does exist, a society of oysters in the square and mansions on the hills. There is a bourgeoisie here. They send their children to the private school, St Augustine, and they dine by the river in large sunglasses. But that is not my Sommières. My Sommières is a badly heated classroom and black instant coffee and second-hand clothes and laughter and companionship. It is generosity of spirit and connection that is hard-won, without the ease of shared language and culture. I fall for the Calade, hard.

Keep the line on your left

A couple of weeks have passed, and Keith and I have started walking the kids to school alone, trading off turns, which frees up great chunks of time for both of us. But this system depends largely on the mindset of the children. Sometimes we're both required to be emotional support peacocks in order to get all three through those gates.

Walking to school alone increases my confidence and loosens the strings of my intense attachment to Keith for practical help with life, but the biggest severing of that dependence comes when I force myself to drive to the supermarket. The Intermarché is not far away, but the route winds through several narrow streets, across the Roman bridge to the other side of town, and takes five or ten minutes, depending on the traffic. The first time I do it, I nearly wet my pants.

Everything is arse-about in this little Peugeot, from the mirrors to the indicators. I feel utterly incapable, but I repeat to myself the mantra Keith has taught me: just keep the middle line on your left. I'm going to ride that line and hope I survive.

I start the car and edge my way out of the carpark onto the road. I haven't driven anywhere for weeks, let alone on the wrong side of the street, but although I feel rusty, my muscle memory kicks in, over-riding the strangeness of operating in mirror image. I make my way through the town without incident, although there's a lot of turning on windscreen-wipers instead of indicators, and a brief mounting of the footpath. Through the whole ten-minute trip, my palms sweat, my heart pounds and I pep talk to myself out loud like a mad Tom Cruise in full method-acting flow.

When I finally pull into an Intermarché parking space, I laugh with relief and joy. I made it! I hope nobody sees my victory fist pump, another embarrassing Tom Cruise moment. Once inside I enjoy a delightful supermarket session, with no children colonising my concentration. Finally I'm running my own show again. I wheel my trolley around the aisles, reading labels and acclimatising myself to my new space. I sketch my menu on a scrap of paper, modifying and editing as I translate packages and puzzle over novel ingredients.

I try to find fish fingers (our comfort-food requirements are high) but they aren't where I expect them, so I ask a man working in the frozen-food section.

'*Est-ce que vous avez le poisson de ... de ...*' – 'Do you have the fish ...' I waggle my fingers at him hopefully. Alas, he looks at me blankly.

'*Pardon?*' he says.

'*Poisson avec ... du ... pour ... les ...*' I'm scrambling. I wave my fingers more enthusiastically. Something clicks for him.

'*Ah,*' he says. '*Bâtonnets de poisson?*'

He points in the right direction, and I find them. Success! *Bâtonnets* means 'fingers'! I commit another word to my inner dictionary. (Later Keith says that *bâtonnets* just means 'sticks' of some kind, making my jazz hands pointless and bizarre. The man must really have wondered why I was adding such a flourish to my request. I fear my reputation is growing at the Intermarché. A warning picture in the tearoom may be the next step. 'That Australian might be a cunt,' I imagine him saying to his colleagues, 'but man, she's got pizzazz.')

I make it through the checkout without incident, produce my new Sommières tote bags to hold my groceries and load everything into the boot. But I'm not finished yet.

Those glorious baguettes from the *boulangerie* with the filthy-fingered genius baker are starting to repeat on us a little. I feel fine, but Keith has been slightly blocked from *bouche* to tush and he blames it on all the white flour. It's true that we have turned into absolute carb monsters. You get a baguette! You get a baguette! Everybody gets a baguette! We've switched our standard order to '*céréale*' or whole-wheat bread, but we're still left with a little constipation situation.

I decide a visit to the pharmacy is in order. These stores are always marked with a neon green cross outside, indicating the church-like importance that the French give to the apothecary arts. The French love their pharmacies, and with good reason: they are fantastic, a wonderland of hair- and skincare, vitamins and supplements. The packaging and typography are lovely, each little pot of hope feeling more seductive than the next.

It's no wonder the 'French Girl' beauty-industrial complex is a billion-dollar behemoth. This 'look' involves a thick head of insouciant wavy curls, sometimes pulled up into a casual knot – never frizzy, but never 'done'. The casually elegant hair is set off with a fresh-faced glow and a certain raffish way of teaming a Prada sandal with a hat found in the dog basket.

The French Girl face features a bold lip or a dark eye, but never both at once. It revolves around the 'natural' look, and markets innumerable serums, moisturisers, powders and primers, as well as hair oils, nail polishes and body lotions. The look values perfect skin over contouring makeup (although it will sell this to you, too). This is big business: while makeup can be a cheap treat, good skin comes at a price. That natural French Girl look might require a ten-step morning-and-evening routine of tending carefully to the face – which, in the casual-sexy way of the French, 'ends at the nipple'. Thus, French Girl beauty meets at the lucrative intersection of self-care and self-loathing: buy this beautiful, fragrant, pleasing product because you deserve it, you disgusting ogre!

It's all smoke and mirrors, of course. In truth, French Girl beauty requires just one thing: that you have the genetic heritage of a Danish supermodel. With this quality, you could throw up every meal you ingest, smoke a pack a day and wear an old man's flannel pyjama set belted with a curtain cord and you would still cause men to ride their bicycles into walls.

Nonetheless, minutes spent in a French pharmacy caressing bottles of Avène and La Roche-Posay are delightful. Sadly my visits so far have been less than glamorous: first head lice and now constipation. I approach the counter, take a breath and launch in. I've been practising this request after looking up a couple of key words on Google Translate: 'powder' and 'fibre'.

'*Est-ce que vous avez le* "Metamucil"*?*'

Blank stare.

'*Est-ce que vous avez le POUDRE de FIBRE pour le constipation?*'

I am intent on making it clear that I am not looking for a suppository. French medical care is notorious for applying medication up the bum for every eventuality from toe fungus to male pattern balding. I turn to theatre.

'*Le poudre,*' I say. I poke my rump out and waggle it a bit. '*Pour mon postérieur.*' With a flash of brilliance, I remember the word for 'drink'.

'*Le boisson pour aujourd'hui,*' I mime drinking, '*et demain, et demain, et demain ...*' I chug back several imaginary beverages and pat my bum. 'Drinking the bum-powder today, and tomorrow, tomorrow, tomorrow ...'

'*D'accord,*' says the pharmacist. '*Oui, oui ...*' He fiddles with his computer for a minute. '*Et ... voilà!*'

With a gallant gesture, he invites me behind the counter and points at the screen, where he has booted up Google Translate. My relief soars and then quickly sours as I encounter a French keyboard for the first time. None of the letters are in familiar places. I thought I looked like a moron prancing about in my one-woman show (*Constipation! The Musical!*)

but I top even these efforts with my slow, mistake-riddled performance hunt-and-pecking out my request on the pharmacist's keyboard.

We get there in the end, establishing haltingly that the pharmacist will get some medicine in. I am pleased with the outcome but must also face the possibility that the pharmacist believes that I have constipation due to alcoholism and he has ordered me a specialised suppository. It's just another data point against my entry for the Dignity Olympics. Ambassador of Australia mode, activate!

It's time to face the return drive. I roll my neck, shake out my hands, buckle my belt, check my mirrors and turn the key. The trip home is harder. The traffic has increased, both car and foot, and I must white-knuckle a tricky roundabout and a queue of cars over the bridge. I don't understand the rules of engagement around giving way, and I can feel my heart beating in my throat as I give myself the full Tom Cruise out loud.

'You're fine! You're doing it! You're doing it!'

By the time I pull into our carpark near the tower, I am trembling and cortisol-poisoned, but thrilled. I made it! Getting the groceries from the car to the kitchen is an epic marathon. I decide on the lesser of two evils: the single trip, donkey-laden with bags, rather than the two-journey option. I circle the tower and stagger down the steps past the convent. Once I'm in the house, Keith bounds out of his office to haul the bags up those winding flights of stairs to the kitchen (French buns! French buns!). I collapse at the dining table. I am spent and sweaty, flushed with a spicy adrenaline hangover. But I am victorious!

On being alone for the first time

I'm making a list:

Police: *La police nationale* or *gendarmerie*
Fire brigade: *Les sapeurs-pompiers*
Ambulance: *Service d'Aide Médicale Urgente* or *SAMU*
Poisoning emergency: *Urgence d'empoisonnement*
Emergency numbers: *Numéros d'urgence*
It's an emergency: *C'est un cas d'urgence.*
My name is ...: *Je m'appelle ...*
My telephone number is ...: *Mon numéro de téléphone est ...*
Please help – we have a medical emergency and I do not speak French. My phone number is zero-three-one-three-eight-three-four-four-three-nine: *Aidez-nous – nous avons une urgence médicale et je ne parle pas français. Mon numéro de téléphone est zéro-trois-un-trois-huit-trois-quatre-quatre-trois-neuf.*

For the first time since we arrived, Keith is away for a couple of days. He's gone to visit a university in Lyon where he'll be collaborating with researchers and writing academic papers. He'll probably spend a couple of days there every month, and he's really looking forward to the chance to practise his scientific French. Meanwhile I am super nervous that I will have to use my everyday version.

I already miss Keith. I miss his lovely face and his ready smile. I miss his capable companionship. I am shitting bricks. What if there is some medical emergency? I paw at my expanding list until it's slightly tattered and I try to practise the phrases: 'My child is bleeding.' 'Send an ambulance quickly, please.' It is very hard to get to sleep in my little dungeon.

In Australia I am used to managing family day to day with Keith away. The glories of modern work mean that his small tech company can operate in a global market from the converted-cowshed office at the bottom of our Coledale garden. It's the Cowshed at the End of the Universe, just as Keith likes it. But he must unavoidably go to Europe, China or the United States to mingle with his fellow eggheads a couple of times a year for a week or two at a time.

Sod's Law dictates that when Keith is away, appliances explode or children bloom all over with mysterious rashes. But at home I have my car, my support networks, a language I can speak and my mother to listen to my complaints. I am entirely capable of handling a crisis.

In France I can't drive further than the supermarket or communicate more than the basics. I am making some tentative friends, but we're not at the ugly-crying 'Help me, Sharon!' stage yet.

Everything will be fine, Keith and I reassure each other, as long as nothing goes wrong. I stick to my haunts. School, Calade, Rue Canard. School, Calade, Rue Canard. I try to Tom Cruise myself. You know what you're doing, lady! You've got this!

Managing all the school drop-offs and pick-ups alone is dangerous because my lack of understanding is usually made up for by Keith. If I've missed a trick in the morning he can figure it out in the afternoon. He is the one that can navigate conversations with teachers, and I am the one that smiles like a loon.

Today is especially tricky. Biggles had a run-in with the terrifying Madame Montagne yesterday. She is hardcore even for France, where strict, sarcastic and shouty teachers are trained at the Academy of Glaring and Throwing Chalk. Even I am scared of her, and I don't know how Tab copes with her as class teacher, although Tab says she is not always as stern as she seems. Biggles tells me that Madame yelled at him, but he can't explain why.

When I approach Montagne, she is very matter-of-fact. I start the conversation in English, forcing her to follow suit, which clearly annoys her.

'Yesterday? Yes, Beegles will not talk. Eventually I speak to him in English, and he answer me, so I say, "Oh ho ho, you can speak after all, can you? Listen, everybody, Beegles can talk!"' She re-enacts this part of the anecdote with sarcastic scorn. 'I must be very angry with him, very strong; otherwise he will not learn.'

I feel a clenching in the pit of my stomach. I know this sensitive child very well. When overwhelmed with stress, he shuts down, unable to express himself. He is introverted, my Biggles, brilliant and wonderfully made. He does not find social rules easy to follow, but he is never rude or unkind, and it is horrible to think of him in that classroom, just nine years old, copping Montagne's angry sarcasm.

This school operates on a different plane to anything I am used to. It's very hard to know what to do. I must advocate for my child, but I must also respect and accept the rules of this new culture we have chosen to live in, while considering the individual complexities of both Madame Montagne and Biggles himself. The whole situation gives me the Migraine of Stupidity.

School in France, I am coming to understand, is profoundly different from school at home, stemming from the way they frame the psychology of the child. I haven't been here long enough to understand how it works, let alone how to push back against it, so the kids, Keith and I are all feeling our way in the dark.

There is, I feel, some benefit to these very difficulties. It's good for the kids to come to terms with situations that feel unjust and unfair. Learning to rally, to deal with a complex person, to slap on a smile, to rise above your rage and keep your shit together: these are true life skills. Once we're home we can try to work through the fallout. The tricky part is riding the line between the character-building parts and the soul-destroying parts of the experience. Best-Guess Parenting.

Madame Montagne is formidable and unbending. She is also funny and deeply intelligent. Mabey's kindy teachers are warm and loving with the tiny children in their charge but unafraid to roar at them like dragons. And Biggles's teacher Madame St Clare is sweet and calm with Biggles, but she runs her fingernails down the blackboard to bring the class to order, and once, when the children do not respond to this, she blows on an actual foghorn.

My conversation with Montagne is fruitless and wrenching. Biggles storms into school angry. He will not kiss me goodbye, this boy who usually clings to me like a baby monkey. My heart hurts. Kat sees my face and comes over. She drags me off with her for coffee at Gigi's house. God help me, Kat and Gigi together. They are more rock'n'roll than a Kate Moss / Keith Richards sandwich.

After an hour with them I am at peak Migraine of Stupidity, because they both talk at once very fast and with great passion. I have no idea of the subject. Anal sex? Global warming? Béchamel sauce?

Gigi rolls a cigarette and asks me if I smoke. 'Only when I'm drinking,' I say. She cocks her head, nods and fetches me a bottle of passionfruit rum.

'I dreenk zis rum last night wiss my 'eadphones on and beeg angry music,' she shares.

I am impressed but decline – it isn't yet 9am and I'm just not French enough to pull that off. Plus, if anything does go wrong today, I can't imagine trying to cope with my Emergency List once I've got Gigi's passionfruit rum on board.

My friends are so sweet, but I am extremely relieved to make it up Rue Canard and inside the doors of the Wormhole, where I can have a big, releasing, restorative cry before the alarm goes off for the lunchtime school run. At lunchtime, though (thankfully, it is Wednesday, when French children only have a half-day), Kat approaches me at the gate.

'Now you 'appy? We have picnic. By river; we go today?'

I take a breath. I'd rather shoot myself in the labia than manage another social event today. We launch into a Franglish exchange.

'*Merci*,' I say. '*J'adore les pique-niques! Mais ... aujourd'hui, non. Mon fils, il est très timide.*' (I love picnics! But not today. My son is very shy.) '*Alors, le pique-nique ce n'est pas une bonne idée aujourd'hui. Peut-être* next *semaine?*' (So, the picnic isn't a good idea today. Maybe next week?)

'Next week, okay. Your son. She like cheese?' she asks.

'*Oui*,' I say, confused.

'The game, cheese! My son play cheese.'

'Oh, chess!' I say. '*Oui, il adore* chess.'

'My son will bring cheese to school for recreation? They play cheese for then?'

'*Oui!*' I say happily. '*C'est très, très bon!*'

'I make this thing to the *Directrice*,' Kat says, and marches to Montagne at the gate. She launches into her rapid-fire French, pointing at me, and at Biggles, and waving her hands around.

'Okay,' she says on her return. 'My son, she will bring the cheese tomorrow. They will play and your son will be the happy. Okay?'

'*Oui*,' I say, feeling the tears prickle. '*Merci beaucoup.*'

I make it inside the Wormhole with the kids and to the privacy of the toilet before I cry again, unravelled by Kat's kindness. We watch Harry Potter that afternoon, eat baguettes and play *Monopoly*. Nobody loses an eye or bleeds from an important vein. I have, thankfully, no need to refer to the Emergency List.

The next morning at the gate, Kat's son Laurent approaches with his chess set. Biggles goes in beside him, and I watch through the fence as they sit together on the ground setting up a game. I see my boy castle his king, his favourite move, and I see Laurent castle in response. I can see that the children will not need to speak in order to communicate through the game. The bell rings. Biggles looks up and sees me at the fence. He runs over to kiss me goodbye, and I exhale a breath that I had not known I was holding.

As I walk home I think about my big girl, who looked strangely red in the face at drop-off and mentioned a sore throat. Is she getting sick, I wonder? One thing at a time. Thank God that Keith will be home tonight to help me work out the French for 'tonsillitis'.

Sommières market

I feel like a fish out of water everywhere but one place: the Saturday street market, an institution of the town for centuries (the earliest proven date is 1183, a mind-bending fact). From Monday to Friday life is all about the kids, but on Saturday the market is for me. I trundle my nana trolley (a purchase that makes me feel like a true local) down the cobblestones of quiet Rue Canard to reach the buzzing town square. Music threads around the stalls that clutter every street of the *centre historique* as buskers play piano accordions and clarinets behind black hats on the ground seeded with glinting euros.

The knife-sharpening man is there, operating a formidable machine that looks as though it dates from the Industrial Revolution. The Lebanese olive seller offers '*un goût*' – a taste. Each tapenade and olive marinade proves more delicious than the one before (and more expensive, I learn, after my first market outing when I buy a towering pile of confit garlic and dips that costs me every euro in my wallet).

The cheese man offers '*un goût*' too. Wizened and elfin, he has a tracheostomy tube and cannot speak. Instead, he points and cuts, offering a piece from the tip of his knife. The paella lady stirs her huge aromatic platters with enormous spatulas, while several charcuterie stalls sell *sanglier*, the sausage made from giant wild Provençal boars. Marketgoers relax in the sunshine over wine and fresh-shucked oysters at the crowded picnic tables under the archway of Rue Mazelle, and lines snake out the door at Farine. At the soap store shoppers buy bags of powdered clay, *terre de Sommières*, renowned for its stain-removing properties.

I make my way to the small gourmet *boucherie* and wait in line patiently for my turn to discuss menus with the tall, barrel-chested butcher. I'm here to buy five *steaks haché*: a delicious take on the good old Aussie rissole. It's mince, but not as I know it; made solely of a piece of beef sent through the mincer and shaped into a disc, it's a favourite of French children. I also buy some pork rillettes, the pâté-like dish of shredded meat cooked in its own fat. We'll eat this with buttered baguette and a jar of gherkins.

Organic vegetables, herbs, baguettes and pastries are a feast for the eyes first, then tipped into the nana-trolley to be enjoyed a second time for lunch. The noises and smells of the market are unfamiliar and thrilling but I find their procedures refreshingly clear. This is part of why I love the place so much; unlike the rest of the week, where I am constantly met with my own ineptitude, I know how Saturday works. My terrible French is not the barrier to communication that it remains at the school gate.

There I run out of French two sentences in and must just smile like a gormless fool, when I am not actively humiliating myself. This week, a woman I know a little walks past me and I see that she has cut all her hair off. Instead of 'beautiful hair' ('*beaux cheveux*') I call '*Beau cheval!*' to her – 'Beautiful horse!' (In fact, I worry that I get the feminine/masculine wrong too, so I perhaps shout 'beautiful man horse' at her, which in my experience is exactly the fear women have when we cut all our hair off, which makes me feel even worse about it.)

At the Intermarché one afternoon I scream when a mouse jumps on my neck, before I realise it is just the furry hood of the shopper next to me. When I make these mistakes I don't have the language to fix them.

But at the market my French is up to the task. It's all transactional, and never veers off into unmanageable places past the limit of my sparse vocabulary. How much is the lettuce? Superb! Four slices of pancetta, please. Perfect! See you next week! I know how to ask for a *'panier'* or basket when choosing vegetables, and every week my vocabulary improves as I puzzle out the names of the items casually and beautifully lettered on little black chalk boards in the French cursive the children are learning at school.

At the end of every exchange, *'Bonne journée!'* says one person (Have a nice day!) and *'Bonne journée à vous'* or *'Et à vous'* replies the other (You too!). There is a lot of *'Je vous en pris'* and *'De rien'* (You're welcome). In general, the French indulge in a charming excess of *politesse*, like a sprinkling of fairy dust on the most mundane of encounters, and as I complete these social niceties and fill my trolley with soap and tomatoes and baguettes and *sanglier*, I feel less stupid and hopeless.

Surrounded by daytrippers, I'm starting to feel at home, greeting people I know, patting dogs and executing the gentle acrobatics of the triple-cheeked kiss. My Saturday experiences give me a quiet sense of mastery, allowing me to hope that, in some distant future, I might feel 'market confident' in my everyday life.

Down by the river lives the other market: the *brocante* of my dreams. To the south is the bar and restaurant L'Esplanade, where we drink rosé and eat hot chips in the sunshine, and to the north lies the small stone arena where the bullfighting happens in the summer. To the west runs the River Vidourle, and to the east École Albert Camus and my beloved Calade. In the large, dusty paddock between, the *brocante* is a wonder. Imagine the best op shop you can, and then multiply that by a factor of ten. The history of this area is rich and long, and this is reflected in the age of the objects collected and displayed on tables and sheets under the trees.

At the *brocante*, to my ongoing heartbreak, I can't really buy anything. We will be going home at the end of the year as we arrived, with only what we can carry; there's only so much I can fit in those space-sucking bags. But I can browse and dream picking through the ancient hand-embroidered linens, old coins, glassware, furniture, vintage tin toys, dusty magazines and unexpected objets d'art.

I trundle my trolley full of fruit and bread and cheese and vegetables back through the town, *chock-chock-chock* along the cobbles. Then I put the key in the door of the Wormhole, round up children to help haul the trolley up the stairs and collapse on a chair in the quiet, peaceful safe haven of my kitchen. I've got a pile of luscious tomatoes and olives ready to be marinated with chicken thighs on the bone in a slow-cooked Provençal dish, and to my knowledge, I didn't offend, upset or confuse anybody during their purchase. Happy days!

The Sisters' Bar

There's a poster on the school gate advertising a Halloween party for the P & C, to be held at the community hall near our house. Everybody is asked to bring a dish, and Tabby and I think it might be a great opportunity to show off some Australian cuisine. For some random reason, I even packed a little packet of Australian flags on toothpicks, so we're pretty jazzed about our plan to wow the town with our lamingtons.

Things start to go south from the beginning. Everything that could go wrong with this recipe does. We have the wrong flour, the wrong butter, the wrong chocolate, the wrong coconut and the wrong pan. Instead of light sponges bathed in chocolate and rolled in flaky coconut, we've made flat, dense rocks covered in seized-up chocolate and patchy coconut. Our lamingtons look like they are recovering from a heinous sunburn. Perhaps they are rather an appropriate national dish? I put the Australian flags in them and hope for the best.

Next: costumes and makeup. There's no way of pulling together anything particularly clever so we go for the classic 'vampire family' vibe with some plastic teeth from the Intermarché. I do a basic zombie makeup: a powdery pale base, lots of brown under the eyes, black eyeliner and some smudgy lipstick à la Robert Smith from the Cure. I ruffle my hair up and stick a few twigs in it so that I am serving up a 'crawled from the grave' look.

As soon as we enter the hall, I suspect we've read the vibe wrong. There are P & C crew in medieval costume behind some tables with games and food, but the parents sitting around at all the tables are in their normal clothes. They give us Resting Suspicious Face as I take the lamingtons of shame to the food buffet.

'*Bonjour!*' says Biggles's teacher, Madame St Clare, who is dressed in green velvet and a pointed hat. She looks amazing. Gorgeous. '*C'est quoi?*' – 'What's that?'

I look sadly at my plate. '*Euh, c'est ... un gâteau d'Australie,*' I say – 'It's ... an Australian cake.' Even the flags stuck into the small brown mounds are flaccid. My offering looks quite like a plate of droppings from a large, unwell marsupial.

'*Bon!*' says Madame St Clare, unperturbed.

Alex, behind a trestle table, kindly helps Mabel bob for apples and the children enter and pity-win a drawing competition, but every conversation Keith and I have with the school parents is pretty excruciating. After an hour and a half, it seems reasonable to escape. Once home, I am appalled to look in the mirror and see that my makeup has worn off just enough to leave me with a greyish, ill complexion and black, smeared panda eyes. I look like something the cat dragged in, as scrofulous as my platter of uneaten lamingtons. Ambassador Mode, activate!

~

Another day dawns. Juliette, my Celtic buddy from the Rue Canard *brocante*, invites me out for drinks and introduces me to what will become my favourite bar in town. It's called L'Estaminet but Keith and I always think of it as the Sisters' Bar as it's run by two long-haired sisters in their twenties. It has a tiny courtyard outside, and two rooms with low arched ceilings inside that extend back deep into the Sommières stone.

Tonight a Gaelic band is playing. They have impressively squeezed a flute and whistle, an accordion, drums and guitar into the corner of the tiny bar. Juliette and I smoke Marlboros (I feel a momentary pang of guilt about breaking my promise to Tab; it passes) and drink her favourite wine: a Languedoc red called Yin Yang.

'I drink only thees wine,' she tells me. 'Thees and wheeskey.'

Juliette introduces me to her friend, a stonemason whose name I immediately forget. He asks me to dance. He is small and round, my stonemason, like a gnome, with exuberant eyebrows and curly black hair, and even though his English and my French are both terrible, our spirits are immediately compatible and we polka around the tiny dance floor together with joy.

When the band takes a break, Juliette and I go for a smoke in the courtyard. A man approaches us. About sixty, he has shoulder-length, straggly, mouse-coloured hair streaked with grey, and he is cultivating a punky Captain Jack Sparrow look with tight jeans and a shirt opened low on his chest. Several necklaces of rope and metal adorn his neck.

'*Bonjour*,' I say.

'Ooh, bong-jour!' says the man, making fun of my accent immediately. My Spidey senses go on alert. He's clearly an arsehole.

'Zis is Terry,' says Juliette, making no attempt to hide her eye-roll.

'*Ça va?*' I say to him politely.

'Oh, speaky French, do we?' says Terry. 'Ooh, lovely! Bit of French from the *Anglaise*, eh?'

'Australian, actually,' I reply.

Terry hoots with laughter. 'Fuck me, even worse!' he says. 'What's a fucking kangaroo doing in fucking Sommières?'

'Well, we're here for a year,' I say, 'sending the kids to school.'

Terry's not listening. He's just scanning my sentences for something to mock. I've met his type before: the tiring rock'n'roll man-child who finds himself charming. Our conversation limps along: he's Scottish, he's been living outside Sommières for a dozen years – 'it's a fucking hole of a town but what are ya going to do' – until, thank God, Stonemason pops up at my elbow.

'*Terry, ça va?*' he says, and gives me a wink. He knows he's saving me.

'Toilet,' I mumble, and I sneak off to buy a new round of Yin Yang for Juliette, Stonemason and me. When the band starts up again, I return the favour and go and rescue my dance partner from Terry.

As the night wears on, the room heats up and the music and dancing get loose and wild. The stonemason and I career inexpertly around the cramped room. The musicians stomp on the floor as we barrel into other dancers and into the stone walls. The dance floor takes on a mad energy as we all swap partners, smiling and laughing, while the fiddles race to the end of their exuberant songs.

I pop off to the toilet and realise how drunk I am. The bathroom has botanical posters on the walls and a floral handtowel with crocheted borders hangs from an ancient nail. Storage boxes are piled in the corner. I try to straighten a small, gilt-framed painting but I am swaying slightly and my ears are buzzing. I think about the idiosyncratic decor of this odd little toilet tucked into the old wall. It feels more like being in an eccentric elderly aunt's house than in a bar. It is so different from home, where interior aesthetics favour neutrals, timbers and shades of beige.

Kat appears. She's been at the bar next-door to the Sisters' with some school mums and she drags me off to hang out with them for a while. They are merry, and very welcoming, but I can't handle the dynamics for long. There are some heinous French men flirting with Kat's crew and the machismo is unbearable. Kat and her friends are into it but I can hardly control my face when they start flattering and flirting with me, basing their seduction on innuendo about kangaroos and pouches.

I hear the Gaelic band starting up their final set next door. I excuse myself, return to the Sisters Bar, order another round of Yin Yang and hit the dance floor again with Stonemason.

It is late when Juliette walks me home up the empty cobblestoned streets. Like a Georgian gentleman, she insists on escorting me and, arm in arm, we chat and laugh all the way. She delivers me to my door where, after some fumbling, I manage to fit the key to the lock, make it downstairs and pass out, starfished next to Keith, Gaelic violin still ringing in my ears and that final glass of Yin Yang gently poisoning my hardworking liver.

After the party: the comedown. In a display of poise and glamour, I wrestle with the detachable toilet seat in order to vomit a few hours later, and I am resting my head on the cool tiles when I realise, to my horror, that I am due down the road for a haircut in less than an hour.

I can't cancel the booking. I don't have the number of the salon and my appointment is the first of the day. The hairdresser, right on Rue Canard, will be opening up for me and I cannot pull a no-show.

I clutch the godforsaken detachable toilet seat with difficulty as it slips and wobbles. Up comes the banana I ate at three in the morning as a pill cushion for the Nurofen I was taking for the stabbing headache that wouldn't let me sleep. Up comes the big glass of water I forced myself to drink.

I moan like a cow in early labour. I can't imagine how I'm going to walk to the salon, where I am due in just twenty minutes. It takes another ten before I feel strong enough to stand. I manage to wash my face, brush my teeth and tie back my hair. Using slow, careful movements, I get dressed. There is no time for a shower, so I spray myself with perfume in a futile attempt to mask the toxic stench of old alcohol that is seeping from my pores. I'm aware that my hair holds the charming fragrance of Eau de Stale Marlboro Lights. At least I'm in France, I console myself, where everybody smokes. The fag smell would score higher on the walk-of-shame scale at home in Australia, but here, it's not so bad.

The kids and Keith are still asleep. With just a couple of minutes to spare, I fetch my handbag and keys and leave the house. The morning air is bracing. It helps, a little, and I feel relatively confident that I am not going to spew. I will make it to my appointment, even if I look like the wreck of the Hesperus.

It's Saturday – market day. I pass the stalls, every cigarette that wafts past churning my guts and activating my wine flu, until I make it to the salon.

'*Bonjour!*' chirps the hairdresser.

'*Bonjour,*' I manage.

'*Bloopy-bloopy blah?*' she says. '*Bloopy-woopy bloopy blah blah?*'

I grimace. '*Je – parle – français – juste – un petit – peu,*' I say weakly. '*Je – suis – australienne.*'

'*Ah, oui,*' she replies, her smile fading.

'*Pour mes cheveux,*' I soldier on grimly, '*juste – le gris, non! Pas de gris. Et le couleur, juste naturel. Très, très naturel, mais pas gris. Et la … la …*'

I've managed, badly, to communicate 'Just cover the grey with a natural colour', but I cannot remember the French for 'cut'.

'*Le* scissor,' I manage. '*Pas de* scissor. *Juste—*' I swallow. '*Pas de gris.*'

'*Voilà,*' she says, and to my eternal gratitude she does not speak again for the next hour as she paints on the dye, washes it out again and blow-dries my new look – *pas gris*. Without grey.

Throughout the excruciating process, the radio plays. Clearly my hairdresser needs the company: the pale, shaky mute Australian in her salon is not bringing much to the party in that regard. The terrible French pop music gets worse as the hour wears on, culminating in an electronica Chipmunks mix that the hairdresser turns right up and bops along to. Every beat slams along with the pulse in my throbbing head.

Finally, the ordeal is finished. I pay and make my way home past the market stalls, which have kicked into full swing by now. I pass the char-cuterie booth, the knife seller, the cheap summer gear and the expensive linens. I keep my head down and give the minimal salutations I can get away with.

Despite myself, I am starting to feel quite elated. I have made it, and now I am headed home for a bath and a coffee sporting fresh new hair. I did not flunk my appointment and let down my hairdresser, even though the whole experience was humiliating, and clearly I must now peer with interest in the opposite direction every time I pass the salon on Rue

Canard, like I do when I pass Scary Cool Guy's vegetable shop. (If I keep making friends like this, I will give myself a neck injury.)

But the fact remains that the night before was a slamming good time. And the day can only improve. Granted, I'm not achieving French Girl Poise. But if I just tweak the goalposts to celebrate the accomplishment of not puking on the doorstep of a hair salon, then I am bloody winning!

As for the hair, I am pleased enough with the result, considering the whole exchange was enacted through mime and nausea, and the hairdresser herself was sporting an intense head full of blonde tips and varying other shades, like an exuberant cockatoo. My very subtle, boring brown nothing-burger of a hairdo feels like a safe escape.

The mums at the school gates on Monday morning do not agree. They feel my hair looks exactly the same, and that I've been ripped off. They are indignant. Perhaps they are expressing their affection for me and our growing friendship by protecting me from being taken advantage of? In general, my French friends give a *lot* of advice. It is given with great kindness, and it is often very helpful, but it is usually unsolicited, and it comes at me with force. Always, there is the same subtext: You need my help, because you are not French, and therefore don't know the French way, which is the best way. So, this advice is my duty as a Frenchwoman. Look at me. Are you listening?

'What ees zees?' Kat asks as she lifts a strand and lets it drop disdainfully. '*Le coupe? Le couleur?*'

'*C'est naturelle?*' I say hopefully. '*C'est okay, oui?*'

'*Non!*' they all agree, with great energy.

'What is word ...' Kat ponders. 'Ugly!'

Yes, my mums conclude with great kindness: the new hair is really ugly. Gigi punches me companionably in the shoulder. Back in Wollongong, my new hair would have been met with a supportive wave of words, no matter how hideous the chop. That's how my Australian women roll. They are publicly supportive and then later they quietly buy you a hat. But French women are not backwards in coming forwards, and it all comes from a place of love. I have to laugh. I find it all pretty hilarious.

'You must complain,' says Gigi.

'Oh, it's not that bad,' I say.

'No! Is terrible,' Kat insists, shaking her head. 'It look very, very bad. I will help get you money back.'

House of quiche
and horrors

'**Z**is is no good, ze way you are managing zis,' says Vanessa. 'Zis is very bad, actually. It's really rotten.'

Vanessa the fixer is lecturing me from the lounge room. She's here for her Thursday-evening language lessons with the kids. It's always a bit of a tough night, Thursday. It's the end of a long day, almost the end of the week, and the last thing the children want to do is grapple with more French. I struggle too. I love Vanessa. She is a force of nature, exactly the person you want on your side as you navigate a new culture. She's like a dog with a bone, and nobody is better at solving problems. She's a born fixer. But Vanessa never turns off the Fixatron, even when you are not asking for help.

The combination of new bacteria, stress and the sudden change of season has hit us like a ton of bricks. In the last fortnight of October, we're beset with a nasty virus. As soon as one child stops vomiting, another seems to start. Asthma attacks, ear infections and fevers make their appearance, and a hacking, spluttering cough becomes a nightly soundtrack. Infections migrate from sinus to throat to chest. The medieval-dungeon bedroom is probably not helping our respiratory health. I suspect we have galloping consumption. France! You glamorous bitch mistress!

In this pre-Covid era, none of us have the kind of deep-rooted reaction to cold and flu symptoms that will come to seem so normal in just a couple of years. At this time, a runny nose or a bit of a virus is standard-issue stuff with three children at school, and there's a certain virtue-signalling around 'soldiering on'. Soon, the pandemic will turn us all into panicky hypochondriacs, alert to every sniff and snuffle, and the shift of thinking around illness will seem profound and permanent.

But not yet. Now, my approach is still a little bit toughing-it-out, a little bit chicken-soup-and-cuddle-therapy and a lot of letting the virus run its course. I'm very loath to introduce antibiotics and I view homeopathy as hocus pocus. This, to Vanessa, is close to child abuse.

Vanessa is very into homeopathy, obsessed with the pharmacy (French church) and a fan of medications of all kinds, including antibiotics. I only bring medicine in when fever is involved. Google Translate is, as usual, unhelpful: liquid Nurofen should be administered into 'three or four outlets' of the child, I'm informed. I know the French are into suppositories, but this seems excessive.

'Zey are steel not to ze doctor?' Vanessa asks me with horror.

'It's fine, Vanessa,' I say through slightly gritted teeth. 'I'll take them if they are still sick next week.'

'But zey were sick last week!' she says incredulously.

'It's just a cold, Vanessa,' I say. 'It's a virus. I know how to manage a virus.'

'But what are you geeving zem?' she asks me. 'What medicines?'

'Just some Vitamin C,' I say. 'Everything's okay, Vanessa. They're a bit run down but I've got it under control. Okay, we'll start with Mabel today? I'll bring you a cup of tea.'

I shut the door to the lounge behind me. As I start climbing the stairs, I hear Vanessa grilling Mabel.

'Now, what is your mother giving you? Are you 'aving any medicines? 'Ow often is zis cough you 'ave?'

I know it all seems a bit Black Death-y, but I think Vanessa might

112

have forgotten that living with a clutch of small children is like living inside a petri dish. They pass germs back and forth like some devilish game of captain ball. While all three are starting to recover from their respiratory virus, Mabel picks up a gastro bug at kindy and heads it back into the field. The spew-flu then enters for a day or two, wreaking havoc on the kids' subpar immune systems.

I've had to develop specific criteria for missing school. My rules are as follows: for a day at home, you must have a temperature, green snot, recent diarrhoea, unsightly rash or croup. If you 'feel sick' generally but do not fall into my categories then off to school you go. If a sickness falls outside the categories but I think they'd better stay home, I have to be very quick to make the decision myself – 'Don't get up! Don't speak! You're staying home with Mum today!' – so as not to allow any acting that could make a child feel as though they have won the toss. Here in France the line has to be held hard. If the children can get out of going to school, they will pull any trick. Who wouldn't?

The girls are heavily invested in who has had what days off and for what specific reasons (they are both talented actresses in the soap-opera genre) and I'm sure they file away any bits of theatrical business that work for the other. Oh, I see what she did with the sitting on the footpath wailing, one sister will think. That's good – embarrassing Mum gets results ... The other will watch and learn too: My God, are those real tears? I bet she put a bit of shampoo in her eye. *Genius* move.

As we limp to the end of the school term, our energy wanes while our social life picks up. The school gates are exhausting right now because, as I make friends with the school mums, I'm required to talk more and more, and my French is at least fifty per cent faking comprehension. Every week, my vocabulary grows, but I still only understand a fraction of anything said to me. It's very hard to communicate on a deeper level – and especially to crack jokes. Keith's French is good and it gets better by the week, although he insists it's only average.

We have a few school mums over for lunch this week, with all their kids, which is wonderful. The house fills with babies and children, I make quiche (when in Rome) and we sit around the wooden kitchen table laughing and sharing stories. I serve food, bring drinks and cuddle babies, using all the language that isn't words to express my gratitude for the friendship of these beautiful women.

I thought Tab had managed to elude Mabel's gastro bug, but the evening of the mums lunch, Tabitha appears at my bedside at midnight, sick and miserable. I search out a spew-bowl and sit with her on the couch under Big Bertha through the early hours of the morning. Cuddle therapy: the last and best tool in my box.

I feel terrible that I have invited my new friends into our house of horrors and have to explain it to them in French the next day.

'I am so sorry – my big girl, she is big sick. The vomit. Big, big, big, the vomit. After lunch I eat you, in tonight, the not tonight, but tonight of Wednesday. Big, big, big the vomit my daughter. I am so sorry! Lunch my house, the house of vomit. My God, it is bad.'

Oh, the shame.

'Come in!' I might as well have said to our new friends. 'Welcome to our *maison* of disgrace. We've been culturing some delicious bacteria for you. Can I offer you a cheeky upper-respiratory chest infection? Perhaps a tasty strain of gastroenteritis for the adventurous among you? Please, eat the food. Use the toilet! We are delighted to have you.' Ambassador Mode, activate!

The school mums are all very kind.

'*Pas grave*,' they all say. '*C'est normal.*' It's okay. School kids vomit.

The end of term is in sight. All the children's clothes are falling apart. The cobblestones have wrecked our shoes, all the socks are lost and somehow every one of Biggles's T-shirts has turned into a rag with holes.

My back is sore and my brain is exhausted. Keith and I are both working really hard, much harder than we had expected, to keep this show on the road. Still, there is no point where we question or regret our decision. Even with all the vomit, and the phlegm, and the incomprehensible homework, and the bitchy vegan shopkeepers, life is wonderful. I can only think that it will become better and better as I get my systems in order and improve my French. The children are tired and depleted, but holidays loom like a beautiful mirage in the desert.

Hopefully this bacterial hazing ceremony has inducted us into the life and germs of our new town, and from this point we will start to thrive. I may just add some cod-liver probiotic olive leaf to the quiches in the meantime and pray that the children are well again by next Thursday. I could not take Vanessa's outrage if they are otherwise.

Barcelona cooking school

Finally: *les vacances*. It could not have come sooner. Time to relax, to restore, to enjoy lots of *grasse matinée* (sleeping in), to *flâner* (wander with no purpose in mind) and to *lèche-vitrine* (to window-shop or, literally, to lick the windows, a task almost possible at Catherine's pastry shop).

But we're not in Sommières today. We've blown town! I'm at the thirteenth-century La Boqueria market in Barcelona taking a cooking class with Tabitha. Tab is perfectly capable of holding a conversation with the other attendees of the class, managing a sharp knife and even piping up with a savvy question or two. Still, I keep a tight hold of her hand as we wind our way past gleaming fish, towering cakes and enormous hanging pig carcasses on our tour with a Spanish chef.

La Boqueria on Las Ramblas is an undercover market, where close-packed aisles and stalls overflow with fresh food under a low roof speckled with old stained-glass windows. There is beautiful art deco tiling and typography everywhere, and Tabitha and I scramble to keep up with our guide as he threads expertly through the jostling crowd. Exuberant Spanish shouting fills the air and I jump as an old woman in gumboots sloshes a bucket of water onto the floor of the fish section. A man with a flamboyantly waxed moustache and a tight T-shirt flashes beautiful teeth as he gives us green olives to taste. I squeeze Tabitha's hand and she grins at me. We're delighted to be on this shared adventure.

Tab is eleven now: old enough to have a private mind and life – unlike her smaller siblings, who are still largely open books to me – but young enough to need lots of hands-on management and nurturing. It is a beautiful age. And as adolescence approaches, I feel the need to shift gears. I love the silliness and magic of young children, but I am ready for the teen madness that Tabitha, with all her comedy and theatrics, is sure to bring in spades. Our relationship deepens and changes with every year that passes, and I look forward to this next stage.

Over a few hours, and a glass or two of red wine for me, we learn how to make *pan con tomate*, the classic Spanish tomato bread (grate the tomato, use just a quick pass of fresh garlic over the toast), and vegetable soup (no cream, no stock, just a little butter at the end). We make paella, using as the secret ingredient a frankly terrifying squeeze of 'liver juice' from a squid's innards, and Catalan custard, pillowy light and sharp with lemon. Our flirtatious chef, Lolo, scolds us for mismanaging the garlic ('Never crush with the flat of your knife, lady!') and teaches us tricks for chopping the 'hat' and the 'knot' of the onion.

After our class Tabitha and I stop in a little city supermarket to pick up some bread before meeting the others. The narrow little store is crammed and bulging with colourful groceries.

'*Hola*,' I say to the cashier. '*Cómo estás?*'

'*Estoy muy bien!*' says the zippy cashier in his flat cap. '*Cómo estás?*'

'*Buena!*' I reply. I am, indeed, *buena*. I'm in Barcelona, hanging with my best gal, and speaking the Spanish! I mean, I've used it all up now, but what a twenty seconds it was!

'Er – bread?' I say. (Sadly, I've already forgotten the Spanish for '*pan con tomate*'.) The cashier looks at me quizzically. 'Do you speak English?' I ask.

'*No inglés*,' says the man sadly.

Bread, bread. I think hard. What is bread in Spanish? What is sandwich?

Tabitha pipes up.

'*Parlez-vous français?*' she asks.

'*Ah, oui!*' says the cashier.

'*Avez-vous le pain?*' asks Tabitha.

'*Ah, oui!*' he answers, pointing us to the far end of an aisle. '*Juste au bout!*'

We are all happy to have made ourselves understood. Together, Tab and I count out the euros and make our goodbyes.

'*Gracias! Adiós! Merci!*'

I could not be more delighted.

Keith and the kids pick us up in the Peugeot and we wind our way through Barcelona's tangle of one-way streets to the port, where we are staying in a rickety old sailboat, the cheapest accommodation I could find on Airbnb. It is charming in many ways, with little beds tucked in odd places and the gentle sway of water beneath our feet. The romance of our maritime adventure fades a little when we are banned from pooing in the toilet, a small detail the grouchy old sea-dog of an owner stresses as he checks us in.

'You can piss here, yes,' he says, pointing to the tiny head, or toilet, 'but you must shit at the marina!'

It's a detail I feel he could have included in his listing. Over at the marina, a few hundred metres away, where we trot for number twos and showers, there is no hot water. The nights are punctuated by the steady rhythm of children hitting their heads on the roof and wailing, and the lapping of the swell is interrupted by the high-pitched whine of mosquitoes. We are too busy slapping, scratching and soothing small heads to get much sleep. In the morning the pattern of the bites suggests that there are also bed bugs or fleas. Poor fresh juicy young Mabel, in particular, looks like the 'after' illustration in a medical pamphlet.

In a cheap little bistro in Las Ramblas where plants clamber up the walls, we have lunch with Keith's old student Marc. The children eat *patatas bravas* and listen as Marc passionately explains the fight for Catalan independence. This long-simmering battle has burst into revolutionary flame while we've been here. Windows everywhere are decorated with the yellow-and-red stripes of the Catalan flag, and when we are caught up in a street protest, Mabel clutches me tightly with one hand and scratches with the other.

It's only a few hours' drive home via Salvador Dalí's incredible house-museum in the fishing town of Cadaqués. Poor carsick Mabey, still covered in bites, throws up in a popcorn box in the back of the little hatchback as we round curve after curve of the Spanish coastline.

We arrive home to Sommières a little bedraggled, stinky and consti-pated (a toilet ban combined with a diet of *patatas bravas* will do that to a gal) but I am exhilarated; the idea that we can pop down the road to Spain for a few bucket-list days in Barcelona is mind-blowing.

I'm keen to get my systems in gear so that Term 2 doesn't kick my arse as roundly as Term 1, and I am delighted to be home to my loo. Yes, that detachable seat is dangerous and requires me to hang on for dear life. But at least I'm allowed to poo in it. Hooray! One for the gratitude journal.

The Bar du Nord

It's November and once again, time for '*la rentrée*'. But this time, a smoother entrance. Tabitha and Biggles sail down the cobbles on the second-hand scooters we bought in Barcelona, and sweet Franc doubles Mabel on the foot pegs of his bicycle. I'm relieved to see them enter the gates smiling. I start to make my way back home when I hear a familiar voice.

'*Rachelle!*' Chloé is shouting. '*Attends! Attends!*' ('Wait! Wait!')

I turn to see my glamorous friend running up the road. Her hair has changed again – it's still in a fall of tight plaits but they are now blonde.

'*Mon amie, elle est là,*' she pants, and even though she is out of breath her mellifluous voice is still beautiful. My friend is here, I translate to myself. What friend?

'*Elle est australienne!*' Chloé manages to say.

Behind Chloé is a dark-haired, thirty-something woman in a bright puffy coat.

'Hi,' she says shyly. 'Chloé said that you're Australian?' Unmistakably an Aussie accent.

'Oh my God!' I say. 'Are you the other Australian I've heard about in Sommières?'

'Yeppers,' she says. 'I'm Nell.'

Chloé is beaming with pride. She rattles off a farewell string of French that Nell answers fluently. I don't catch a word. Chloé trots back down the street.

'*Merci Chloé!*' I call. '*A bientôt!*'

Nell and I trade information. She is married to a Frenchman called Jo, they have been living in Canada for years and recently returned to Sommières, his home town, with their two little girls. She grew up on the New South Wales mid-north coast. Nell and I are both delighted to relax into loose, slangy Australian. Even when speaking English I've had to become used to enunciating carefully and speaking slowly, and the relief I feel in not editing myself at all is like sinking into a bath.

I have a coffee with Nell and her friend Frances in the square, and we make plans to meet up again. Heart full, I head off towards the river with my laptop in my backpack. A little dive on the river called the Bar du Nord has caught my eye. I still haven't found a good place to sit and work and I'm always on the lookout. I'm trying hard not to let my own writing disappear in all the busywork of looking after the family.

Here in France I've been writing a little for a website called *Living in Languedoc* and I've sold a couple of pieces to Australian magazines, but mostly I am working on my book. The battle to finish *Mothering Heights* has taken on an epic quality. I'm wrestling with my own demons. Laziness? Lack of grit? ADHD? Incompetence? Choose your fatal flaw! I am determined to finish this book, but to do that I have to first teach myself *how* to write a book. This requires wrestling with my devil self that wants only to watch *Architectural Digest* house tours and montages of unexpected animal friends, and dive headfirst down subreddit rabbit holes exploring topics like 'inventors killed by their own inventions'. I want to read the internet like a book that never ends.

I find personal growth in the difficult discipline of writing. I push myself to fight the monster of procrastination and put a flat hand to the face of my own self-critic. Over time it dawns on me that I might actually yank, wrench, pull, urge and cajole this massive, unwieldy beast of a manuscript into some sort of a book-shaped object, just as I am, day by day, shaping our France life into something recognisably 'home'.

I write in pockets of time, in sporadic bursts, in funny little places. In the Calade, after class and before the lunchtime pick-up, I work in a plant-filled corridor on a barely used floor of the building. Perched on an uncomfortable wooden chair, I can usually get a decent half-hour in before my back revolts.

I quite like grabbing half an hour to write before I do the shopping at the cafe attached to the Intermarché. The ladies behind the counter are initially rude to me but grow kinder over time. The coffee doesn't get better, but I get a lot done, perched on a stool at a plastic table, listening to young tradies argue about cassoulet above the tinny muzak. The Intermarché holds good writing magic for me.

When I open the heavy door of the Bar du Nord, a smoky, yeasty smell slaps me in the face. It's a narrow room with a long, zinc-countered bar top and six or so small round tables along the opposite side. Black-and-white stills from old movies are tacked above the bar, and the mid-morning clientele is faintly seedy. I order coffee from the friendly grizzled bartender and settle back in the corner. Hiding behind my laptop, I check out the scene.

There is a bunch of old men playing cards and drinking pastis. Another man is reading the paper and a middle-aged woman is talking to the barman at the counter. After the obligatory Resting Suspicious Face, the patrons of the Bar du Nord leave the Australian lady in the corner alone.

It's early in the day for a sesh but the woman at the counter has had a few. She starts reeling about, setting her sights on different men at the bar. Her techniques are fascinating. She pats one gentleman vigorously on his bald head, Benny Hill style. Then she gives another an intense shoulder massage until her belt falls off. It takes a very wobbly five minutes for her to manoeuvre the belt back in place, but she takes it as the opportunity for a sort of 'get dressed, but make it sexy' routine, bending down and drawing the belt back up her legs to her hips, slowly and with much gyrating, all the while maintaining eye contact with her discomfited mark.

A man appears at the door. He's walking with some difficulty, using a cane. The woman whips around, sets her lady-radar on him and races over. She helps him inside, gets him to a table and then triple-kisses him lingeringly. He is initially grateful and a little chuffed, but soon his face falls as he realises that he has fallen into the path of a sex pest. I am finding it very difficult to get any work done at this point, especially when the woman sets her gaze on me. She holds her jacket open and nods downwards proudly, like 'What do you think of these?'

'*Oui, très, très bon,*' I say politely. As breasts go, they look bouncy and exuberant – good traits for show-boobs, I think. I love the nutty disin-hibition of the Bar du Nord. But it's too interesting for me to keep as a primary worksite.

My alarm beeps. Time to get to the school pick-up. I pack up my laptop.

'*Au revoir!*' I call to the louts and scoundrels of my new favourite joint. '*Bonne journée!*'

They give a cheer in return and I shut the door on their smoky world, turn right and head up the alley to school.

Toujours le clown

At the Calade the French is almost all above my head, but I adore my classmates, especially Josephine, my Brazilian sausage. I fumble through. One day, we discuss the different words *'seule'* ('alone'), *'sel'* ('salt'), *'saler'* ('to salt') and *'salle de bain'* ('bathroom'). I put them together in my sexiest tones: 'Alone in the bathroom, I salt my chicken.' The class laughs.

'*Non, non,*' Nanette says.

'*Oui!*' I insist. '*C'est mon secret!*'

It brings the house down, and I am thrilled. I made people laugh in French! Peak happiness! This erotic chicken-based gag is as good as my comedy can get, however. Mostly, my contributions are limited to moronic points about the weather.

'The sun today – yes! But no wind. Yesterday is big wind,' I say.

'*Oui,*' my companions nod kindly to their stupid Australian friend. 'That's right! Yesterday was big wind!'

I cringe. There is little as awkward and anxiety-inducing as standing in pained silence with another person, unable to temper the air with any talk, whether small or large.

I always thought that this aspect of France life would be character-building for the children, but I hadn't realised that it would be the same for me. It's painful, but I feel myself expanding, and this brings me joy.

Life contains some technical issues, too. The dishwasher covers all the crockery and glassware with a white film, the electricity keeps shorting out and now the washing machine has thrown in the towel. One morning, in a sophisticated display of dignity and grace, I hurt my back by finally falling off the detachable toilet seat. I tumble three steps down the mobius staircase another day, which hurts more, but at least I am wearing pants for that episode.

Autumn has well and truly kicked in. One day, it seems we are in T-shirts, and the next I am digging the puffy jackets out of my space-sucking bags. The mistral, a fierce wind known for driving people crazy, blows like the dickens. I nearly fly off my feet over the waist-high barrier on the bridge one day as I cross it towing my nana trolley. Portrait of a dickhead in France.

I'm trying, too, to give our bedroom a makeover. I can't do much about the lumpy double bed or the icy walls, but I buy a fluffy mattress topper and a huge new doona with a soft mustard-coloured cover from Amazon France. I pin some posters from Paris museums on the wall and hunt high and low for decent pillows.

One happy afternoon I discover the Croix-Rouge, the Red Cross charity shop, where I stock the family up on beanies and mittens and coats. Fashion designer Maurice even comes along one day and gives me sartorial advice on cut and fabric. As the temperature drops we nestle into the damp earth of the town, sending our trailing roots out further and further. Our friendships deepen every day. Sometimes I even try to take us outside of our usual routine of school, Calade and Rue Canard.

I go to the gym one night (French buns! French buns!) with Nell the Australian. The woman behind me in the aerobics class is kitted out in belted white jeans, pantyhose and a button-down linen shirt. Even at the *actual gym*, I marvel, the French disdain activewear. The trainer asks me to wear socks next time, and I decide not to tell her that I can't: I put all the family socks in one bag at the laundrette and then accidentally threw that bag away with the garbage. Why? Because I am a genius.

Our aerobics session concludes with a wonderful episode where we dance-prance around the room in a circle. At the end the trainer asks us to vote for her cousin in the finals of Eurovision. It's fun, but I don't go back. The school run and the mobius staircase are quite enough of a gym contract for me.

One weekend I spy, among the latest screed on chemtrails at the noticeboard in town, a poster for a 'horse-dancing' event at a local pony club. The boys aren't interested. They'd rather go on a hike, so they drop us at the riding school on the edge of town before they head to the mountain, promising to pick us up in a few hours. We wave them off happily, but I feel slightly anxious. I much prefer Keith around to buffer my French for any new socialising.

The gals and I venture in to find fifty or so people milling about a dusty circular horse-training manège. The crowd is fancier than the Sommièrois we're used to. Today I'm surrounded by shiny boots and gleaming bobs, and lots of women in heavy makeup. Here, it seems, are the bourgeoisie from the hill, the ones that shop at the market on Saturdays and send their children to the private school, St Augustine. I don't recognise anybody.

We find ourselves a spot at the edge of the ring, and soon rousing classical music begins playing tinnily from the speakers. The show begins and I am ... confused. I've never seen a horse-dancing show before, so it's hard for me to ascertain exactly how weird they are supposed to be, but this one is absurd in the extreme. A rider enters the ring with his horse. He is dressed as Spiderman, his leggings diagnostically, religion-revealingly tight.

Spiderman does a few mediocre tricks on his horse and rides out to scattered applause. He's followed by Supergirl leading a trio of miniature ponies. This act is a lot of fun as the ponies escape immediately from her grasp and run wildly around the manège before stopping in front of us to drop a pile of lazy turds. It takes Supergirl five or six minutes to corral her charges and she leaves the ring despondently.

An artistic interpretation of *Aladdin* follows. A woman in a synthetic black wig twirls in the centre of the ring like Kate Bush, while a man dressed in a snug unitard rides his horse in a circle around her. A French version of 'A Whole New World' blasts from the crackling speaker as her harem pants drag in the mud.

Darth Vader comes on next standing atop two horses at once. He holds the reins in one hand and flourishes a sword with the other. It is difficult to judge Darth's horsemanship, so distracting is the lycra that bisects his testes as he straddles the horses and rides around the ring, his groin at eye level with the audience.

The show is short and strange. I love every minute of it. When it is over the girls and I go to get a snack from the small hall behind the manège, where cookies, cakes, cordial and urns of coffee are set out along a lino countertop. We sit around a small table with our terrible coffee and crumbly cake for a while, but we have brought no cards or books and we have no friends to talk to. It seems as though we have gatecrashed a small event for the pony club (and possibly swinger) community, and it is at least an hour until we can expect Keith and Biggles to return.

Suddenly a lady sitting next to us thrusts a large baby at me. She points at the carpark, gibbers a string of French and runs out the door.

'*Non*, wait—' I call. Tab and Mabel look at me, wide-eyed. The baby does, too, and then it opens its mouth and begins to scream.

'*Ooh* ...' I say to the baby. '*C'est bon, bébé ... C'est bon* ...' I pat its bottom and bounce it up and down.

'Did you catch what she said?' I ask Tabitha.

'Something about her car?' Tabitha says. 'Maybe she had to move it?'

The baby takes a breath and recommences screaming at a higher pitch. '*Maman!*' it bellows, and then it wriggles so hard I nearly drop it. The baby is desperate to get down. I set it on the floor and let go for a moment to change my grip on its little T-shirt. Suddenly free, the baby toddles off at speed. I chase it around the small tables. People watch me as they eat their little cakes.

'*C'est bon, bébé!*' I reassure desperately.

'*Maman!*' the baby screams.

Once I capture it I must pick the baby up again. It doubles its efforts to escape, and I cannot explain myself to the disapproving people around us. To make things worse, the baby smells like it has done the poo of five babies. The girls try to help, but the baby is having none of us. We all pat and mutter soothing nothings, but it seems an age until the woman comes back, takes the baby from me and commences an enthusiastic explanation. I hear only a string of Bloopy Blahs.

'*Je parle français juste un petit peux,*' I say miserably, grabbing my girls and leaving to wait for Keith and Biggles out the front.

I realise on this outing how much of a comfort zone we have built in our small community. Being surrounded by the local pony-club bourgeoisie makes me realise that we understand only a tiny part of the culture here. The Sommières of dancing horses and aerobics bunnies is a mystery. I realise again that we are *marginaux* and misfits, and that perhaps we should stay in our lane.

Soon the little Peugeot appears. Keith and Biggles are tired, dirty and happy, and a little while later we are all home behind the lovely safe doors of the Wormhole. There is mushroom pasta for dinner, not a baby or a bifurcated scrotum to be seen and wonderful, simple English to communicate in. Novelty and excitement are all very well, I decide, but there is quite enough of that for me in everyday life where I am on the verge of an international incident just buying the milk.

I am Penis

Even when we are not chasing drama, it finds us. The social intricacies of the children's gang play out like a season of *The Bold and the Beautiful* (and I am the one gazing, confused, into the middle distance). Amélie suddenly refuses to speak to Tabitha at school and won't explain why. Sabine is reliable and kind, but she is very quiet, communicating only with a shy, sad smile. Franc cries at the front door when he asks one morning if the children can play and I say that they are still asleep. They don't love me enough, he wails. When Alain is upset, he angrily slaps himself and cries, 'Bad! Bad! Bad!'

One day we organise for Franc, Amélie and Alain to come over to play. I know these youngsters pretty well by now. Their naughtiness is inventive, and they cycle through tears, laughter and anger like they are attending an intensive personal-growth retreat, so I am ready for some shenanigans. But not ready enough, as it turns out.

These kids speak only French so there is a lot of guesswork involved, and mostly the six of them play *cache-cache* or hide-and-seek. I am happy that they have found a common game, accepting the trade-off that involves a wild child-tribe crawling through every inch of my house. I make food to ward off the hangries, and I use Google Translate when I cannot make sense of the questions or the problems. It is high-maintenance mumming. Midway through the hectic afternoon, the doorbell rings.

It is Albert, an elderly man who owned the château in town where Keith and his sister worked for a period twenty-five years ago. Although he looks like an Italian gangster dressed for a favourite niece's birthday in his linen suit and cravat, and leaning on his cane, it seems he is just here for a casual visit. I take a breath and recalibrate the social complexities of my afternoon: Albert is lovely, and possesses the most delightful giggle my ears have ever experienced, but he speaks only French, of course.

I leave Keith to make conversation and go to check on the children. Amélie is crying and Franc is looking sheepish. They both rant at me indignantly. I cannot puzzle out what has happened, but Amélie is eventually mollified with a hug. In the kitchen I make coffee and biscuits and carry them downstairs on a tray. Then Keith and I talk with Albert, politely, and in French – 'And how are your daughters? Are they living in the town?' – while the six children barrel in and out of the room and we all shout *Ferme la porte!*' – 'Shut the door!' Albert giggles, enjoying the chaos, but my laugh becomes a little hysterical. The pressure of trying to host a polite afternoon tea in the grounds of a monkey-house is getting to me, and I am relieved when Albert takes his leave after an hour or so.

Returning to the kitchen, I find shards of glass all over the floor. Amélie confesses to smashing a jar. My sweeping is interrupted by loud pops and bangs from the bedroom and I run downstairs to find that Franc has found the little bungers we bought at the Intermarché for an upcoming festival and is setting them off with delight. Fireworks in the bedroom? The afternoon has officially devolved into the Playdate from Hell.

I decide it's time to channel the angry nuns of my own school life. I go full penguin.

'Non! Non! Non!' I repeat. Luckily, this word is the same shouted by a mother in both languages. Angry Mother energy transcends language, as does its twin, Soothing Mother. Today I need to pull out both. Franc and Alain have complicated home lives, and their behaviour

can be unpredictable and difficult, but their sweetness is pervasive and they usually calm down quickly with some nurturing attention. Amélie's soap-opera drama is harder to manage. She can be very loving but she's big on throwing 'This relationship is over!' tantrums, which are confusing and exhausting for Tabitha. ('*Pas amie! Amie! Pas amie! Amie!*' she shouts. 'Friend! Not friend! Friend! Not friend!')

It's tricky to help the children manage their friendships. All my cultural cues are missing, and even when factoring out the individual differences of kids (all of whom are nuts in their own way, whether here or at home), there are larger forces at play.

At any gathering of adults in France, children are well behaved. I never see them whingeing and whimpering, pulling at their parents' sleeves and moaning, 'I'm *bored*,' as is commonplace at home. I never see parents loaded with handbags full of snacks or toys to help the children get through the event. Kids are expected to manage boredom on their own.

This is impressive, and I take mental notes, but I see a dark side too. There is a certain emotional sensitivity baked into kids in my Australian home town, where talk of bullying and emotional wellness is frequent. I don't see this here in any obvious way, even taking into account that my liberal beachside bubble is not representative of larger Australia any more than Sommières typifies France.

The classic understanding of French parenting holds that children are raised within a strict *cadre* or framework but left to figure out the details within that *cadre*. The idea is that they grow by having autonomy. There's a strong antipathy to the '*relation fusionnelle*', I read, or a bond in which the child's and the mother's needs are too connected. (I wonder if this is why I cop a few raised eyebrows at the gate over Biggles's prolonged cuddles.) Expectations are high for how children will behave in a public setting and how they will relate to other adults, and the rules of *politesse* are drummed in, but child drama is left for the children to manage themselves. This results, at times, in kids who are both strikingly sophisticated and brutally cruel.

We relate to each other across the gap between Australian and French culture, a gap made wider by the very specific culture of our own house, where there is a significant amount of emotional micromanaging. Keith is very kind and will sit with the children talking through their problems for hours. When they fight, I tend to go a bit Dr Phil.

'What part did you have in that escalating, do you think?' I ask the children, and, 'Talk me through how you could have handled that differently,' and even, 'Can you see that you are triangulating here?' I've even employed the Dr Phil classic: 'Do you want to be right, or do you want to be happy?'

I don't channel Dr Phil for all my parenting tips. I'd rather withhold croissants when the children are naughty than send them to wilderness re-education camp, for instance. But like Phil, my parenting does have the earnest stink of psychobabble about it.

I want my kids to have emotional intelligence, and I am driven by my own ghosts: a childhood in which my brother and I fought like Demogorgons. I don't want that culture to exist within our family, and I'll employ some over-the-top relationship managing to avoid it, for better or for worse. And these days, my little French bonus sons get a dose of it too.

At a street fair one day, Alain pulls my sleeve and points at a boy with Down syndrome dancing nearby.

'*Regarde*,' he says, pulling at his eyes to make them into slits, '*un psychopathe!*' Alain laughs with delight but I am aghast. I take him aside and sit down with him and, in my poor French, talk to him about why such a word is unkind. He is confused but he wants to please me. He agrees to modify his language. 'Am I in trouble?' he worries, in his sweet way. 'I don't want you to hate me.'

'*Non, Alain*,' I assure him. '*C'est juste une bêtise.*'

Bêtise is the word for a 'small mistake' in France. A *bêtise* requires a correction as opposed to a *punition* or a stronger punishment. I learn the importance of pronunciation the hard way on the Playdate from Hell when Franc starts violently hitting Mabel with a pillow.

'*Je suis punis, Franc!*' I tell him, grabbing the pillow out of his hand when he won't stop and Mabel is crying. '*Je suis punis!*'

Franc laughs so hard that actual tears roll from his eyes and Alain gasps for breath on the floor. I am trying to say, 'I will punish!' but my grammar is always awful – 'I am', I say, instead of 'I will' – and *punis*, most unfortunately, sounds rather like 'penis' when spoken with an Australian accent.

Socialising like a Frenchy

To have friends opening their hearts and lives and homes to us: for this I am grateful beyond words. Mabey's kindergarten class seems to have an endless stream of birthday parties, which gives us a wonderful stickybeak into a series of interiors, always one of my favourite things. And every lunch, dinner or drinks invitation gives us a different insight into France. One day we get an invite to lunch from Biggles's friend Ajax.

Ajax and his brother Martin live with their mother, Riri, in a small apartment next to the old clock tower. The apartment is very basic, with beautiful huge old flagstone floors and walls. So close to the river, it will be freezing in winter.

We make a quick stop at the Lidl, the supermarket within walking distance, to collect a hostess gift of cake and chips. When we arrive, Ajax greets us at the door with a formal triple-cheek *bise* and takes our coats before ushering us into the lounge. His gallantry is easy and unpretentious. Riri has no English at all, and her French is fast and accented. It's hard for me to catch much. Keith carries the conversation. The meal is served in courses: a *pâté* to start, followed by a plate of fries and *steak haché*, and then a cheese course. The boys serve each dish and clear the plates with no fuss, and then they present a chocolate cake paired with an enormous can of whipped cream. Riri smiles indulgently as the boys lean back in their chairs and squirt huge mounds of it straight into their mouths.

After lunch, Riri sits by the open window, smoking and smiling at her boys, cat on her lap, as a heater bellows air pointlessly below her feet.

Outside a parade passes by. It's a beautiful day. The children play *Fortnite* on a giant screen, and sweet Ajax gives Mabel a Winnie the Pooh stuffed animal that immediately joins the Friendy family. Keith's cat allergy is playing up. I see him scratching surreptitiously as he gamely holds up the conversation while I sneak glances at the clock. It's clear that Riri's family is struggling. Dad is out of the picture and Riri has only her work as a nail artist, her table set up in a corner of the lounge room. I am torn – I wish I could give Riri a little business, and it would be a wonderful social circuit-breaker, but Riri's nails are terrifying: two inches long, they are bright-red talons filed to a sharp point. My French is just not up to the task of requesting a short, square black manicure and the alternative is unbearable. I would, within seconds, poke myself in the eye.

After we return from Riri's house we have a couple of hours at home to regroup before we must leave for *apéro* at Kat's. We all scatter to our various corners to read quietly. What is *apéro* actually, I wonder. Is it dinner? Will there be food? I give the children some scrambled eggs and cucumber, just to be safe. Like Ajax and Martin, Kat's children give us the *bise*. But where Ajax and Martin were goofy and loud, Kat's kids are a mix of sullen adolescence and sophistication.

Kat's small apartment off Rue Flamande explodes with the debris of three children: toys, electronics and clothes. We cluster on two over-stuffed couches while Kat serves wine and a plate of savoury hot cheese puffs. Jacques, her husband, is a tall bald man with a single large hoop earring. He speaks no English at all, but a couple of wines in he becomes loquacious and babbles intensely at me, giggling. I nod and say, 'Oui, oui,' hoping that I'm not agreeing to a wife swap, or a far-right immigration policy, or to babysit the children while he and Kat go to a wealth-building seminar in Portugal.

The children gather around a giant screen in the corner to play more *Fortnite*. Again, the noise and graphics of the game dominate the small room, and then fifteen-year-old Étienne starts streaming French hip hop at high volume through his phone. Pre-teen Céline smells the cork of the wine bottle and nods. Kat and Jacques just raise their voices over the din.

Jacques and I are discussing the upcoming Christmas holiday (I think).

'*Je suis excitée!*' I tell him. He nearly spits out his cheese stick and Kat explains, through her guffaws, that I am telling him, 'I'm so horny!' My heart sinks – not only have I complicated my already incomprehensible relationship with my friend's husband, 'I'm excited!' is one of my stock phrases. I dread to think how often, and to whom, I've said it.

Home from this party, I have a terrible headache. The French, the *Fortnite*, the confusion of it all. I sleep badly. These experiences are why we are here: to expand beyond our narrow sphere, to see how others live and to grow as humans. We are so very lucky to be invited to the homes of our friends and to be shown such generosity and kindness. But bloody hell, it's tiring, and sometimes the effort to fit in makes me feel very, very foreign.

The art of friendship also involves ditching bad decisions. I still see Australian Nell often, but I no longer go for coffee with her friend Frances after a disconcerting experience at the Bar du Nord. Frances is not taken by the seedy charm of the joint. I get it. She may have been bewitched by an outback bar full of Aussie Mick Dundee types where I would have had to make a quick exit. But the Bar du Nord itself doesn't mark the death knell of my friendship with Frances. Rather, that moment comes over a discussion the three of us have around the Australian referendum on gay marriage.

'It's a great day!' I tell them. 'Australia just legalised gay marriage!'

'Oh, I don't theenk so,' says Frances.

'Oh, yes,' I reply. 'It was still against the law in Australia. It's been an ugly campaign, but it's over now, thank God.'

'Zis is a mistake,' says Frances. 'First, zey will allow sex like zis, and next it will all be about sex with the animals. Who I choose first, my dog or my cat?'

My jaw drops. Frances sniffs as she inspects her cup for cleanliness. These moments happen in France. I make a leap of assuming a certain set of values in another person and realise at some point that I have got them all wrong – for good, or for bad.

I miss, desperately at times, the ease of my Australian friendships, where we talk endlessly about parenting, about politics, art and books and cooking. We cackle like witches over coffee, walk dogs, drink cocktails and dance at parties. We're all adept at the gentle art of 'sledging' or 'taking the piss': the comedy of mild psychological abuse that is something of a national pastime. We go for walks, drop off sympathy lasagnes and cheerlead each other through difficult times.

There is a friendship gap caused by a lack of shared language that is often overcome by deeper, truer mechanisms: instinct, touch and something indescribable – hormonal, perhaps – that bonds us to those we are attracted to. But as a lover of words and jokes and flights of shared conversational fancy, it is deeply painful for me that all I can offer to every conversation with my French-speaking friends is a beating over the head with the Obvious Stick.

This is part of the reason I bond so intensely with Alex, my trilingual anthropologist. We have a shared sensibility that transcends all our differing reference points, and I find it easy to slip into vulnerability with her. I can, I feel, be authentically myself with Alex.

I love spending time at the farmhouse, where we hang out with the family, including Alex's dad, who is gentle, English and charming. Alex grew up here, just outside Sommières. She even went to École Albert Camus. The children roam the farmhouse as we sit around a huge open fire, eat cheese and discuss the world. One night, Alex invites her friends Andre and Momo from the village. They have small children too, speak English and will become good friends. Momo, a classic French *Bobo* or bourgeois bohemian, with a pixie face under a cap of brunette hair, reminds me very much of many of my friends at home. She's a trained geologist, home with babies right now, and her child Claude is in the class below Mabel, the preschool cohort called the *grande section*. (Mabel and I call them the 'Big Sexies'.)

I really like this crew, but there are a lot of moving parts to keep on top of, emotionally, at a gathering like this. I keep one eye on the children as my brain works hard to incorporate reams of new cultural information. Social anxiety kicks in. I drink three glasses of wine quite fast, in my sophisticated way, and then smoke one of Alex's rollies. Feeling queasy, it takes me a minute to extract myself from the deep, soft couch. I go to the toilet to get my bearings. I sit in the gentle dizziness for a while and inspect *Viz* annuals and children's novellas from the 80s on a little shelf on the wall.

Back in the lounge, wood smoke curls about the room. We laugh and chat and get to know each other. It's a great night. After dinner, Alex's dad asks about the early colonial history of Australia.

'Well, there was this one night after the arrival of the Second Fleet,' I tell the room. 'The boat was full of female convicts, and it was months late, and the colony was starving. They'd run out of food. The night the ship arrived, there was a storm, a really intense biblical storm, wild stuff, and this crazy scene unfolded, which is sometimes called the Foundation Orgy.'

My audience is interested.

'The sources are messy and it's disputed, but the story is that the convicts and the women just had a massive outdoor sex festival – the whole economy was fuelled by rum at that time, so everybody was pissed. One version sets it all up as a huge party, but the other reading of it is a bit darker – that it was a mass sexual assault.'

Alex shakes her head and her father tuts sadly.

'So, the women have been on the ships for six months. The clever ones have been shagging the sailors to get better conditions, but they're all sick, exhausted and filthy. They've got malnutrition, probably lice ...'

I pause to hiccup once or twice as I reach for my wine. Where is it? Has Keith moved it? Never mind, I'll get another one in a minute.

'The convict colony is almost out of food at this point. They are wretched. There have been almost no women living there at all, and the soldiers are drunk on power as well as rum. Sydney is basically on the edge of mutiny all the time.'

Mabel appears beside me asking for a drink of water and I gently put my hand over her mouth to stop her interrupting the flow of my story.

'Finally, the supplies and the women arrive, and everybody just loses their minds. They are shagging in the dirt, on the rocks, in the rain, like some kind of eighteenth-century Glastonbury, or Woodstock. But really, it's brutal. Terrifying! Like Dion-siss-siss! Do – no nysis? Dine-Isis? Di-oh-nissisuss!'

I realise I am shouting. Keith is looking at me, with the pained expression I know sadly well. Momo and Alex are gaping.

'Well,' I say weakly. 'Isn't history fascinating?'

Becoming Sommièrois

One December morning, we hear a commotion on leaving our place. When we get to Juliette's *brocante* we find her red-faced and screaming at the man I've come to think of as Bad Fonzie. He lives with his family in a flat above her shop, and this fight has been coming for weeks.

Bad Fonzie, in his sparkling-white oversized T-shirts, looks mean and shifty. He likes to drive fast up Rue Canard even though there are only inches to spare on either side of the narrow laneway. When Bad Fonzie's dusty Fiat Panda appears, pedestrians press themselves into doorways. His wife, stringy-haired and dishevelled, is always screaming at the kids. They don't seem to go to school, unlike the kids of Bad Fonzie's best mate, whom we call Rico, a tall, rangy man with a mane of black hair and a lovely smile who is always walking his kids to École Albert Camus, hand in hand. The story goes that Rico's brother was stabbed and killed by another brother a few years ago outside the Sommières post office. I generally smile at Rico but try not to make eye contact with Bad Fonzie and his wife.

Bad Fonzie and Juliette, fingers in each other's faces, are arguing at top volume. Faced with this conflict I would dissolve into a puddle, but Juliette is made of tough stuff. I grimace at her and mouth '*Ça va?*' She nods and I usher the children past all the neighbours, who are out enjoying the diversion. Later I'll find out that Bad Fonzie threw a chair out of his window, narrowly missing elderly Lucie and her tiny dog beneath. This was the final straw for fiery, loyal Juliette, and the bad air between the neighbours exploded into a raging argument. At least, I think that's what happened. I always have to factor in the possibility that I have everything totally arse-about.

Layer by layer, we are growing to understand Sommières, a town full of the energy of the old and the new. It's a home to migrants and old-timers, transients and travellers – a place soaked in the past but always in motion towards the future. It's an intoxicating combination of brash youth and crumbling ruin. The wildness is all part of the package, like a deliciously bad boyfriend you can't help but forgive.

Sommières is not a rich place. It's like a poor cousin of some Provençal village, a town of hustlers, and the metrics of value are not money and possessions. We fit in here strangely smoothly. While it's an enormous privilege (Spank! Spank!) to be able to travel halfway across the world and set up a temporary existence, we are not here because we're rich, but because we're portable, so we don't live an extravagant life.

Like our friends, we pick up clothes at the Croix-Rouge and the *vide-greniers* (garage sales), trade information about two-star travel deals and spend our euros on luxuries like nights out at the Sisters' Bar and dinner parties around the expandable kitchen table. Friends bring us hand-me-down toys. We bake cakes in thanks. We budget our pennies, like the inhabitants of this village have done for thousands of years.

'A medieval town asleep on its feet,' Lawrence Durrell called Sommières in a letter to Henry Miller in 1957, and it hasn't changed greatly since then, the population still hovering just under 4000. Larry also said that he had seen 'nothing prettier' in all his travels. Both sentiments still ring true, especially on these wintry mornings.

Like a fractious baby, Sommières is particularly lovely when it is asleep. In the early mornings, and on Mondays when the shops are closed, the streets are deserted, and as we walk we are embraced on both sides by solid stone. The comforting walls surround us, letting only the briefest slices of sky splinter past encrusted archways and windows with pale-blue shutters. They are my favourite times, these putty-grey moments, when we are alone in the streets and feel like we might belong, just a bit.

We veer left today, picking up speed so we can take a detour and still make it to school before the gates close. We want to see the river, and we now know the short cuts through the alleys, as the streets become increasingly imprinted on our mental maps. Up the Rue Marx Dormoy we go, past the butcher and the toyshop, and under the clock tower. I glance down the tight passageway that contains hidden steps down to the Place du Marché.

We stop briefly to marvel at the bridge. It's the second-longest viaduct built in Europe by the Romans, with piers that are three metres thick. There are only seven arches visible. Ten others have been swallowed by houses at both ends, and they now make up cellars and archways underground. The central feature of the town, the bridge is both a Roman relic and a functional piece of everyday engineering. For us, it exemplifies the constant sense of living inside a place suspended in time.

At the school gate, Kat is subdued, and I notice a ring of bruises around her upper arm. I can't help but think they look like somebody has had an angry grip on her, and I rail at the pain of being hamstrung by my lack of French. There is just no possible way to bring any tact or sensitivity to the questions I want to ask her. I feel rage that anybody would hurt Kat. She is so special, with her sharply-drawn dreams, her maximalist apartment, her roaring laugh, her generosity, her filthy jokes, her fierce love, her earthiness. I settle for giving her a long hug goodbye.

The nuances of the school-gate culture are finally becoming clearer. There are different cliques that hang under different trees, including a trio of cool dads in threadbare cardigans and caps who repair bicycles, ride souped-up steam-punky contraptions to the gate and generously give us repaired machines for the kids from their underground workshop. A motorbike dad roars to the gate with high-decibel theatricality on his mechanical penis. His face tatts and vest look menacing until his small, beautifully dressed daughter runs and leaps into his arms.

This gate life is becoming so familiar to me that the memories of school at home feel like the odd dream. In Coledale, parents are often barefoot and occasionally in wetsuits. They suck at water bottles, unselfconscious as babies, or clutch handmade lidded ceramic mugs containing coffee spiked with unlikely substances like butter and turmeric and mushroom dust. Here in Sommières, people smoke at the gates rather than drink coffee, and there is occasionally the unmistakable tang of jazz tobacco in the air. In Coledale a parent would never light a fag, let alone a joint. At a pinch they might vape some sort of bone broth–infused cannabis oil purchased via the Byron Bay Online Wellness Co.

At the cafe in the square, where in that first week I tried and failed to write, the men of Sommières gather to drink coffee or red wine and chat in the sun. We often wave to Cédric there, and the waiter, Ponytail. Sometimes Kat sits with them, but it's mostly men. I ask one day why. Their wives kick them out of the house for the day, she tells me, and there's no work. There is a sense of gentle boredom to this group, as they smoke and chat and greet each other with kisses.

Past the *tabac* on the corner, the teenagers mill about in their immaculate tracksuits, calves zipped tight and sharp fades cut into their dark hair. They shout and giggle and do tricks on their bikes. There is a pair of identical-twin teenage boys in this crew, with gorgeous faces and flowing hairstyles, and they like to ride their bikes slowly on one wheel while blasting French pop from a ghetto blaster on their shoulder. They seem to think they look menacing, but in truth they give off more of a Cliff Richard vibe. I feel for the teenagers. There's not much to do in Sommières, and very little green space. We've started making use of the skate park, which is situated next to the soccer oval, a verdant and lush field behind a locked gate only open to the soccer team on the weekend. We skate around the dusty bowl on our second-hand scooters, looking enviously at the forbidden green oasis next door.

Opposite the *boulangerie*, on the stoop of an apartment building, there is usually a little group gathered around the young pregnant woman with the messy neck tattoo I noticed on our first day. Eventually, there is a newborn baby on the scene. Throughout the growing and shrinking of the belly and the appearance of the baby, she sits on the stoop and smokes. People buy baguettes, cats prowl and her elderly neighbour, kyphosis-humped below her jet-black hair, tuts crossly as she hauls her shopping trolley past the group up the steps and into the building. Nobody offers to help. It takes weeks of passing the stoop and watching the micro-interactions before we realise that it's a dealer's house. The Romanies run the drug trade on this side of the river, we're told, and the Arabs the other. Like an old showgirl lifting her petticoats, Sommières reveals herself to us in layers: the fine linens, the workaday cottons, the delicate lace and the stained rags.

Back at the Wormhole, I close the door and slump onto the couch. I have made some sort of minor fool of myself in the street and shame is stinging. Thoughts of home overcome me. The sound of surf and frogs and birds; the bitter tang of a good strong flat white.

That night, Keith and I watch the drama *Marseille*, starring sexist old cretin Gérard Depardieu, and the sleaziness is almost unbearable. Every female character is a sex object except the middle-aged judge who is pushed off a mountain in the first episode. In the news, an outspoken Black feminist and anti-racism campaigner is ousted from a government body. I think about Juliette and Bad Fonzie. I think about Kat's arm. I feel sad.

The next afternoon, I wait at the gates beside Élise, a school mum I don't know well. She's very kind but has no English at all. I do my best to keep up my end of the polite exchange but it goes tits-up for both of us very quickly.

147

'What are you doing this weekend?' I ask: a safe, classic hairdresser opener.

She glances at me sideways. 'I'm sorry, I am busy. I have family visiting from the north.'

'Oh, that's great!' I say. 'No, I just ask because ... I wonder ... what you like to do.'

'I like the markets,' she offers.

'Me too!' I say with relief. 'I love the markets. Especially the *brocante*.'

'But I have family here so I cannot go on Saturday,' she says firmly.

'Yes, of course, it's fine,' I answer. I can barely cope with this small talk at the gate. The prospect of a full day's market date is horrifying. I don't know how our conversation has entered this treacherous territory.

Élise and I look at each other with barely disguised dismay as together we stumble, victims of misguided *politesse*, further into a social engagement that neither of us wants. Élise clearly feels that I have asked her out twice and she is being terribly rude.

'Tomorrow, I could have a coffee,' she offers.

'*Oui*, tomorrow, perhaps,' I stutter.

There is a pause.

'Oh no, I remember that tomorrow I am busy!' I say. I barely stop myself from a compulsive 'Next week, perhaps', replacing it with a safe 'Life – it's busy, right?'

'Yes,' she agrees. We are both relieved. Life is busy. Too busy to be trapped into accidental coffee dates. Another lesson learned. I mentally add the Australian small-talk staple 'What are you up to later?' to the 'dangerous' column of my cultural cheat sheet. Australian conversation underplays everything. What are you up to? Not much. How are things? Not bad. We've even invented the phrase 'yeah nah' to underplay the word 'no' itself. When this understated obfuscation meets French Directness, chaos ensues.

Biggles scrubs up

This week I face the task of dragging young Biggles into the land of respectability. This is a full-service job; he is a disgrace from nose to tail. Biggles is a pants-optional sort of person, and clothes are becoming an issue for us here, especially as December gets colder.

At home, where the kids wear a school uniform, it's much easier. I have to sew up a rip every once in a while, the hats are constantly lost and the uniforms have often been handed down through a series of ragamuffins before they get to mine, but it's low-maintenance drama. Our little beach school is full of kids dressed in the same style. Uniforms cover the weekdays and on the weekend, the kids pair some questionable combination of garments from the dress-ups box, stay in what they wore to bed or grab the closest thing to hand. Sometimes they don't bother with clothes at all. I try to keep everything clean, but shirts get holes, shorts fray and if an item appeals to the kids, they will squeeze into it or tie it on, disregarding the fact that it is eight sizes too big or too small.

When we have an event or party to go to that requires all three to be in a decent outfit, it usually involves a shopping trip. But here in France, other children never look like they got dressed from the rag bag: every day is 'proper outfit' day. It's killing me. As the temperature drops, the kids require more layers of clothing, as well as numerous accessories like thermals and beanies and gloves.

The shops here in town are really just boutiques for the Saturday-trippers, way out of my budget. I've had a terrible hit rate shopping online here – I can't seem to get the sizing right and the complex return policies are a nightmare to translate. I can't drive as far as Montpellier and Nîmes, the nearest cities, because that would mean certain death. My driving safety zone extends as far as the Intermarché or the expensive Urban Sport next door, but those give me a choice between supermarket style and sports luxe, and the cobblestones eat expensive shoes as quickly as cheap ones. I've tried both.

The Croix-Rouge is my saviour. Tucked down a side alley, it has confusing and mysterious opening hours, but there are racks and racks of second-hand clothes and the ladies behind the counter (one very large and one very small) are kind and patient with my awkward French. I load up with layers of sweaters and jeans, and on the coat rack I find the most beautiful woollen Little Red Riding Hood coat for Mabel. She is thrilled. Kat and Gigi deliver hand-me-down beanies and we pick up winter gloves and socks from the rack at the Intermarché. All in all, the girls are not hard to pull together, but Biggles doesn't make things easy.

He has decided, as part of his grouchy anti-France stance, that he will only wear black. I think his theory is that if his clothes are drab, people won't pay attention to him and interrupt his interior monologue about *Monopoly* strategy. Also, he hates to get his hair cut, so I usually let his thick blonde mop grow out as long as possible before getting it cut short. This week I said that if he let me cut his fringe, he could probably get away with avoiding the barber a bit longer.

He agreed, but the theatrical wriggling in the bathroom as the scissors approached meant that my first cut made the fringe a bit short on one side and it required balancing out. Then I had to balance a bit more on the other side and before I knew it I'd given poor Bigsy an intense mullet. I knew I needed to call in the professionals, but it was a few days until the salon in town opened. Biggles had to front up to school with a short fringe and long mop, business at the front, party at the back, wearing his emo blacks and looking like Sharon from Payroll in 1987.

Biggles complains that his hands are freezing, but he misplaces his gloves constantly. I work hard to keep him warm because his asthma is triggered by the cold, but he is so naturally disorganised that this is an ongoing losing battle. After school one day Bigs realises he has lost his whole bag. This is the third time that one of the kids has lost their school bag. How? I don't know. I don't think we ever lost a full bag and contents before, but in France, apparently, we are just that bright.

Madame Montagne is not impressed.

'Je suis désolée,' I say. 'Biggles ... er ... *perdu son sac.* His bag is lost.'

She rolls her eyes.

'Je ne sais pas pourquoi!' I say.

'I don't know why, either,' she replies.

I look to Biggles but see only his mane bouncing halfway across the yard, like a spooked golden retriever. He is also terrified of the Directrice and escapes at the first opportunity.

'Also, 'e needs new shoes,' she says. Biggles is in his boots because his runners have completely disintegrated. ''E cannot run in zese shoes.'

'Oui,' I say. *'Oui, bien sûr.'*

I back away, bowing from the waist like a lackey in a royal court, and set off on a mission to sort out my little ratbag. I buy a new school bag, a new *agenda* (diary), new trousers, gloves and a beanie. After class I drag him kicking and screaming to the salon to be sheared, and then to Urban Sport for a new pair of runners. These must be black, Biggles insists, with no writing or logo and no 'funny feeling'. Mission completed. I cross my fingers that he doesn't lose everything immediately.

Despite appearances the children are, in fact, doing well at the moment. It's often only one child downhearted on the way to school these days. France remains tiring for them socially, but this has the unexpected benefit of bringing the three siblings very close. The Friendys remain their best companions. Laughter and falsetto squeaks ring out from the big bedroom as they spend hours immersed in their imaginary games.

I keep finding garlic in their beds. The Friendys use it to ward off vampires, I'm told. Mabel turns the top bunk into her office, from where she runs a business called ILoveYou.com, which sells lollies and medical supplies. She loves to put on her 'work jacket', my little faux-fur cape, climb the ladder and settle in to type busily at a computer she has made from cardboard. She constructs and refines the rules for an imaginary place called Tu-Tu Land, where children are pushed around all day in beds on wheels and thrown into jail for cleaning their rooms. She writes songs up there too, among them the heart-rending 'A Lady Called Lin':

> Please be with me and not with him
> That makes me feel like you put me in a bin
> And don't drink gin with him
> I don't want to be with a lady called Lin

'I farted. It tickled. My butt cheeks wiggled. It smelled like a pickle and I did it again,' the children chant, when they are not singing 'Harry Potter in 99 Seconds', a song they learned from YouTube. They thunder up and down the stairs and cuddle up together under Big Bertha to read. They seem to recognise, as only the trio of them can, how wonderful it is to play games that you understand with safe and predictable playmates.

Tabitha enjoys her clutch of nutty friends at school and she becomes, every day, less afraid to speak up. Biggles is handling the stress of it all. Mabel also has the benefit of classmates who are all barely out of babyhood and have not learned to judge each other yet. So Mabel can't speak French? Well, Pierre wets his pants and Mignon cries every morning at the drop-off! Everybody is weird! Even just a few months in, Mabel is communicating well enough to have turned into *le chef* or the boss of the kindy class. She's invented a club, *La Licorne*: the unicorn. Unicorns, it seems, are a universal language of six-year-olds. Overall, the kids may look like they fell out of a laundry basket and landed hair-first on the kitchen shears, but they are steady enough on the inside, and that's what matters.

French food

Living here is a cook's dream, even if the coffee is a crime against humanity. The supermarkets have self-service orange-juicing machines, endless wine aisles and outstanding cheese and charcuterie. I'm hip to the ins and outs of the Intermarché now. My faux pas of the early days are behind me, and the Intermarché has become my happy place.

All five of us eat every meal at home, barring occasional trips to the pizzeria or the *crêperie*. The children eat four meals, once I factor in that crucial after-school *le goûter*, so my kitchen here turns out eighteen covers a day. Luckily I love to cook. The kitchen is in a constant state of flux – cleaning up after the last meal and rolling out the next – and the whole process hinges on the shopping.

There is a small blackboard in my kitchen, which I use to write the menus that help me stay on top of my busy little restaurant. This week, the menu looks like this:

Monday: herb-crusted Provençal lamb, salad
Tuesday: eggplant parm with roasted potatoes, salad
Wednesday: Toulouse sausage with broccolini and corn on the cob
Thursday: pesto penne
Friday: quiche and salad

Saturday: schnitzel with market vegetables
Sunday: roast chicken, roast veg and gravy

With my bags hanging from the cart, I start my shopping at the left-most aisle, where books, electronics, stationery and kitchenware live. This is where I pick up gloves, undies and socks, and random paraphernalia. I know that the washing-up gloves are kept separate from the washing-up liquid, in a cleaning section where I find the surprisingly effective sponge called a 'Scrub Daddy'. I step carefully over the wet tiles in the fish section.

Past the orange juice machine: I love this fresh juice but hate the single-use plastic bottles, which leak onto the moving counter so that the cashiers glare at me. Early on I decide that if I am buying juice every week, I'll bring the bottle back to re-use. But the day I do, I forget to fill it. When I've finished sending my groceries through the till, the teller and I both spy the bottle lying forlornly, used but empty, in the bottom of the trolley. The teller raises an eyebrow at me. I look as though I have done a naughty but I cannot explain myself. It is the green, I say weakly. I am the earth, you see. In a rush of success, I manage, 'It is not bad me! I am ecology!' Over time I learn to smack down the lids of the orange juice bottles and twist them on hard.

I head down through the dry goods next – washing powder, toilet paper, pasta, snacks, rice, shampoo. I love the health and beauty aisles. Even the everyday supermarket brands are so pleasing here, despite their traumatically tiny fonts. Even the head-lice treatment has a mellifluous name: Marie Rose. It's enough to make one imagine the tiny insects wearing berets and debating existentialism.

I mostly ignore the bread aisle – we buy our daily baguettes at the *boulangerie* – but I always pick up a half-loaf of 'Harry's American Sandwich', the sweet white bread that Mabel loves. This, with peanut butter, is her comfort food. (It's also Keith's and my most effective disciplinary tool. When Mabel is naughty, she is given three warnings before losing peanut-butter sandwiches for a day, and the peanut-butter log is kept on the wall of the kitchen. Her record is three days without her comfort sandwich, a devastating experience that Mabey takes care not to repeat.)

Muesli and cornflakes; coffee and tea. Through the chocolate aisle I roll – hazelnut and almond, I decide today. I pick up some of the little sacks of fruit puree that the children sometimes have for *récréation* or recess. Biscuits, crackers for cheese, and canned goods: tomatoes, tuna, tinned artichokes, lentils and beans. At the far corner are long shelves of alcohol. I pick up some beers for Keith, some red and white wine for dinner, sparkling rosé to have on hand for guests and a little bottle of limoncello to serve as an after-dinner *digestif.* Into the trolley goes a bottle of the lemon *sirop* that we love, along with a few bottles of Perrier.

I buy one or two of the mozzarellas we like in the blue bag from the cream aisle. In the meat section I always like the chicken Marylands for cooking on the bone, and I pick up mince and sometimes a fat spiral Toulouse sausage or two. The pastry lives in a fridge here, and I collect some puff for a pie top, as well as some shortcrust for quiche, because I have now learned the difference between the words *feuilletée* and *brisée* – sadly, through trial and error.

Milk, litres of it, and lots of butter, and then I pile in the fruit and vegetables, delighting in the fresh, plump tomatoes and eggplants and potatoes and zucchinis and grapes and apples.

At the cheese counter I buy cheddar, some creamy cheese and a little blue. '*Une tranche,*' I say to the woman at the deli counter after we nod to each other in recognition. 'A slice.' A little more ... a little more ... *parfait!* I'm no longer afraid of the cheese section. I can approach and have a full conversation contained to the safe limits of cheese and the weather, polite and warm and utterly devoid of faux pas. It leaves me exhilarated. I no longer start every interaction with, 'I'm sorry, I don't speak French but ...' or even 'I only speak a little French.' If I stumble, I pull out the phrase, 'My French is poor, but I am practising.' By now I can frequently complete an entire shopping trip without the hot pink blush of shame. This pleases me enormously.

I've always cooked a lot. I love to write menus and think about food, making that 6pm gathering at the kitchen table the anchor of our day. Here in France the food is lovely, and it's a joy to cook with it. But there is a learning curve. Sommières has a different food culture to beachside Wollongong.

At home my friends and I can talk at length about poo. It's greeted as hilarious and reasonable conversation in Coledale, a town populated with lovable cosmopolitan wankers who believe that 'food is medicine' and can hold forth at length about the 'gut brain'. In Sommières if I introduced my stool as a conversational topic to a group of school mums, I would likely be run out of town with pitchforks. At best my reputation would decline from 'harmless buffoon' to 'terrifying deviant'.

At home, too, a dinner party invitation requires factoring in the myriad vegan, gluten-free, dairy-free, low-fructose, GAPS and paleo diets of my friends. This is not an issue here in Sommières, where baguettes form the sturdy, constipating base of the food pyramid for everyone I know.

Lunch, the main meal of the day, is a serious business. Everything stops between twelve and two, when you head home to eat or partake in a bistro's *menu du jour*, which includes an entrée, a main and a dessert, followed by a cheese tray from which you pluck a few slices of whatever takes your fancy. You pair the meal with a glass of wine and, later, a small coffee, and you may finish with a digestif, often a fiery *eau de vie* that helps to settle your food and perhaps even tear the very lining from your lungs. An average Thursday lunchtime is an occasion to be savoured.

Part of my Australian school morning routine was packing lunch, as well as Crunch&Sip: the vegetable snack Australian kids have in the classroom mid-morning. In France, kids either stay at school for *cantine* or go home for lunch, and there is a very relaxed approach to *récréation*.

There is strong discipline around eating times at school – kids don't tend to snack between meals – while at home, children graze all the time, like goats.

'There's something I miss about packing school lunches,' I muse to Keith one day as we lounge around the flaky chaos of the kitchen table. The children have scattered to the four winds to relax before they return to school, and the two of us are about to clean up the carnage.

'Here's what I'd do,' says Keith, dressed in his raggedy track pants with his woolly socks propped up on the table. 'Every day: Vegemite sandwich, muesli bar, apple.'

'Every day?' I ask.

'I could do that for ten years,' he says.

'I believe you,' I reply, 'but making lunches can actually be really lovely. Bit of this, bit of that … Little surprise here, little treat there …'

We both start getting into our arguments.

'I would refine the system, you see, so that it was absolutely efficient in terms of time and motion,' he says.

'Those cute bento boxes with little bits of fruit and vegetables in compartments,' I muse.

'One! Two! Three!' Keith exclaims. He nearly drops a piece of cheese as he waves his arms about. 'I'd get the process down to about forty seconds. Once they're teenagers, double the sandwiches and chuck in a banana as well,' he says.

'You can get these ones that are fully leak-proof, so that you can even put yoghurt in one of the compartments and it won't spill onto the olives,' I say.

We gaze at each other for a few moments.

'Yours sound nicer,' Keith says.

'Well,' I reply, 'they come with a price. Every twenty-eight days I will explode in a Level 5 meltdown over the pressure of packing fancy lunchboxes every day for thirteen bloody years.'

'Yes,' says Keith. 'Mine come without danger.'

In France, children who stay at school for *cantine* are fed three courses, with the impressive menus posted at the school gates each week. (This Friday, for instance, the children are eating tomato salad, Boeuf à la Provençal, courgettes, yoghurt and grilled apples.)

After school, children have their third meal of the day, *le goûter* or afternoon tea, which is typically fruit, pastry or bread, with a favourite snack being chocolate tucked inside a baguette. But life is not all gooey Brillat-Savarin cheese and heirloom Provençal peaches: Sommières is quite economically depressed, the dentistry is patchy and sugar intake is high.

The devotion to children here is expressed through their impeccable clothes and haircuts rather than their 'wellness' reflected through the prism of their diet, as is the culture in my hometown. Food is a signifier for pleasure here, not health. In Coledale it might be virtuous to deny sugar and wheat, but here in Sommières a complex, 'nutrient-dense' and time-consuming diet would show merely that you don't know how to live, or how to express love to children.

At the end of my trip, my trolley is groaning.

'*Bonjour*,' I say to the cashier, refraining from adding my automatic '*Ça va?*' She has her job to do, and I have mine, and this is no time for chitchat. (In some months, however, I will start saying '*Ça va?*' to the servers again, because that's how we roll in Australia, and I like watching them weird out a bit.)

I have mastered the art of unloading enough groceries at a time to fill the small conveyor belt while at the same time preparing my bags in a row to start packing at the other end – heavy things at the base, breakables on top. I dart back and forth, emptying my trolley as the cashier rings the groceries through, and soon the job is complete. It's hard to see the totals on the register, and I must rely on my French to manage the euros. I do this with varying degrees of competence.

'*Merci*,' I say to the teller. '*Bonne journée!*'

I manoeuvre my heavy trolley out past the Intermarché Christmas tree, lit and dressed for the upcoming season, and pack the bags into the boot of the little Peugeot before driving back over the bridge and up through the streets to the carpark behind the tower.

I have laid down enough muscle memory for the drive home that I no longer have to Tom Cruise myself. I can easily swerve around hapless tourists stepping out onto the narrow road while I plan my *barigoule* of spring vegetables with asparagus and snow peas.

Often I park at the edge of Rue Canard where there's a sneaky shortcut close to the door, run home and grab Keith. (We stopped actually leaving the car there when we finally realised that the spot was illegal in daytime hours, but not before parking fines began to arrive, one after the other.) Now the sneaky-park is used only for quick drop-offs on shopping day. Keith will unload the trunk, whiz the car up the hill and then return to cart the shopping up the endless stairs. If he's on a call or otherwise engaged I carry the bags myself, a gruelling final step in the long process. In the kitchen, my mountains of food cover the wooden table. I unload them into the kitchen shelves and the fridge, writing my weekly menu on the little blackboard as I go.

I set some beef, mushrooms and pearl onions aside, ready to go into the oven for a slow-cooked *boeuf bourguignon* for dinner, and then I make myself a cup of tea and sit down. There are just a few minutes before my alarm will go off for school pick-up, after which the afternoon shift with my three little buddies will begin.

I myself am fattening up like a prize pig. My not-*not*-sexual almond-croissant relationship is to blame for the extra pastry-weight on my belly. But I choose to embrace the extra padding (more to love?) with the knowledge that I am actually fitter and stronger than when we left Australia. It's all the stairs. (French buns!) Those stairs, and all that tasty, tasty gluten.

Wintering over

The season of ear infections and cold-induced asthma has begun. It's icy enough now to freeze a small dog's balls, and the windscreen of the car is often frosted over in a thick sheet, so that we must pour bottles of water over it in order to melt the frost off a patch large enough to let us drive. It's a constant battle to find gloves and coats and get them on the children, who seem to have some innate, genetic rejection of outerwear, no matter how cold they are.

The house is very difficult to heat. We've hung a big quilt to block off the sunroom from the kitchen, put heavy blankets on windows everywhere and heat only the essential rooms, but our electricity bills are still outrageous. It hit minus six degrees the other night, and my most used phrase currently is '*Ça pique!*' ('It's bloody freezing!') At the Calade I restrain myself from teaching the class the Aussie phrase 'Colder than a witch's tit'. I feel I might be growing as a person.

Morning routines reflect the challenges of the season. In the kitchen, I pour my coffee from the little French press, angling it so that hot liquid doesn't spill from the broken tip. Replacing this pot is on my to-do list for the next time I am at the 'everything shop' near the Intermarché. Keith walks in, carrying Biggles in his arms. He deposits him on a kitchen chair next to Tabitha, who has made it down the ladder and has her head pillowed on her arms on the table. Keith leaves to fetch Mabel.

'Good morning, little friends,' I say brightly. 'How'd you sleep? Hot chocolate coming up.'

Keith deposits Mabel and then he too flops heavily onto a chair. I'm at the stove making porridge. We've somehow developed a new system where Keith carries the kids from bed up the spiral stairs every morning, and once in the kitchen I post hot food into them and crack jokes until they are awake, with their bellies full and a smile on their faces. We seem to have arrived, without intending it, to a place where we run this house at full Little Emperor level.

As the winter bites, Sommières starts to contract like a hedgehog curling away from danger. Only the locals are left, apart from on market Saturdays, which means the streets no longer sport tourists and walking groups swinging their giant cameras and hiking sticks.

Life inside the Wormhole is shrinking too, as we battle our heating issues. The wiring set-up in this ancient, newly renovated house is not designed for the load required. It shorts out when we run too many appliances, and a cord gives Biggles a terrifying shock one day. Ever the scientist, Keith starts a spreadsheet trying to track how much power we can run without overloading the circuit. We curl up together in the downstairs lounge most nights, eating there and turning off the heating in the kitchen, or we stay up in the kitchen to get our exercise through after-dinner table tennis, using a portable net that we set up on the dining table.

In the night we heat only the two bedrooms we use, and so by morning every other part of the house is freezing. After breakfast is done, it's the chilly bathroom for clothes and teeth and hair, and then the bottom room to fossick through the bag we keep on the back of the door with gloves, hats, neck warmers and scarves.

Walking to school along deserted streets, Tabitha and I chat about the latest drama with Amélie. At school yesterday, Tab had found a smooth rock and decorated it carefully with her new metallic pen, a prized purchase from the fancy stationery shop in town. 'For Amélie', she wrote on it, and gave it to her friend. Amélie scribbled on it and gave it back. 'For Tabitha', it said. 'No, it's for you,' Tab tried to say. 'And back for you!' Amélie said. When Tabitha wouldn't accept the gift back, Amélie grew angry. *'Pas amie!'* she shouted, and burst into tears.

Tabitha says she tried to explain but just could not find the words. She says that the kids laugh at her every time she opens her mouth, and it makes her scared to speak. I know the feeling – Amélie's mother, Gigi, never stops finding my accent and phrasing hilarious, and even though she is good natured and jovial about it, it's exhausting to have somebody crack up every time I speak. I have accepted that I sound like a fool much of the time, and I must push through that in order to communicate, but this is much harder for Tabitha to do. She's still so little. She's learning fast though and clutches in her hand this morning the letter to Amélie she wrote last night using Google Translate: a sentimental, flowery missive of apology and anguish that is very, very French.

I feel like crap, and I look like crap too. Every day I wear the same puffy coat on the school run. Underneath I am braless and wearing the outfit I went to bed in. The coat hides all. Pale as a moth, I want to buy some light fake tan to give my face a little lift but can't find any in the pharmacy. I look on Amazon France and activate Google Translate to understand the product description:

The skin melts of pleasure, the tan rises in beauty. An irresistible caramel colour to guide the application. First glance, first pleasure: hot and deep, subtly sprinkled with golden shards, the colour of the delicious tanning cream does not dye, but allows to direct the application without being wrong. An exquisite ganache texture to coat the body with softness. Creamy and melting, enriched with moisturizing aloe, it is a real treat of skin that slides under the fingers to evenly coat the body with softness and wrap with freshness of a peach.

Best think carefully about this purchase, I decide. I don't want to start a riot.

Everybody in town is getting sick. During the day I make a pot of chicken soup, a tray of brownies and a big lasagne. After school the children and I make a little round of the streets, delivering soup and brownies to Ajax, who has chickenpox, and lasagne to Esmé, who is pregnant and exhausted. This is something we do in Australia when our people are sick, and it feels wonderful to make these offerings to friends here who have been so generous to us. It's like my Sommières spiritual guide Larry Durrell said: 'a city becomes a world when one loves one of its inhabitants'. I feel this deeply.

One day, Chloé hosts a beautiful lunch for us. A table laden with food fills the small lounge room as she and her sister Liesl tell us stories of life in Rwanda before they fled as refugees, their antics as a large, loving group of siblings cut suddenly short by the death of their father in war, after which the whole family, bereft, was scattered across Europe. Mabel gapes with wonder at Clémentine's bedroom. Across a double bed, a Frozen bedspread is pulled tight and topped with a tower of frilly cushions. Dolls and toys line up along the wall. Liesl sleeps on the couch. Both she and Chloé are studying hard for professional qualifications. It's clear that much-beloved Clémentine is the focus of the family, holding all the hope of their new lives.

Around the table we share tearful toasts to absent friends, and then we delight in watching Mabel and Clémentine play *Dance Dance Revolution*, their wild hip-shaking fuelled by handfuls of jelly babies.

~

Another afternoon Kat, Momo and I help Alex clean out the capacious barn attached to her farmhouse. She's planning a party. We make barely a dent in the mess, but we have a good laugh. I try to pretend my back isn't seizing up more with every passing minute.

We chat about the upcoming Christmas holiday. Kat is a great one for travel and always has a plan on the boil. She likes to drive places with the kids and sleep in the back of the car, and she and I trade tips on budget Airbnbs and savvy travel deals. We are heading to Poland, I tell her, and planning a visit to Auschwitz.

Momo blinks at me, concerned.

'This is okay for you?' she asks.

'Well, I think it's important,' I say. 'You know that saying: "If we do not understand the mistakes of the past, we are doomed to repeat them."' Alex translates for me.

Momo bites her bottom lip.

'It's too ... sad, no?' she says. 'Too much trauma.'

'Yes, I imagine it will be very sad,' I say. 'But Keith and I can handle it.'

'But the children!' she finally bursts out.

'Oh!' I realise Momo's concern. 'The children won't be going. They are too small.'

Momo is relieved. She has imagined, I realise, that Keith and I are taking the children to a concentration-camp museum as one of our 'resilience building' exercises. Momo, an 'attachment' parent, is very engaged with the emotional life and development of her two children. She and I have long discussions about pedagogy and child psychology (at least, I think that's what we talk about) and out of our friends, Momo is the most concerned about the difficulties the children are having. She doesn't agree that the children should keep attending school even when they don't want to and is horrified when I try to explain the hard line that we hold against the children chucking a sickie.

Kat shows us her latest modelling snaps. She has taken to working as an amateur model for aspiring photographers and thrills in the cheesy fashion shoots she's been doing on the local riverbank. Kat is giving Blue Steel in every frame, and the photos are utterly hilarious.

Socially it is excruciating. How do I convey my complex emotions at the sweet, naive comedy of it all? How do I share the side eye of delight that Alex is shooting me without hurting Kat's feelings? The Australian in me immediately comes up with a dozen gags about the whole thing, none of which seem translatable.

As the muscles in my back start to bite in spasm, I feel an invisible window start to slide shut, my pain and me on one side, the world on the other, the cold glass between. Momo and Auschwitz, Kat and the modelling, my limiting French and the dust of the crowded old barn: it all becomes a little much. I drive home in the cold, my back a dull bruise, to find another parking fine in the letterbox with a cheerful note attached from Vanessa: 'Naughty naughty!'

The next morning, my back is still sore as I walk the children to school.

'I hope I don't feel sick in class again,' Tabitha tells me. 'They'll send me to the office.' I can hear the thoughtful note in her voice and I know that my small actress is contemplating a plan that will end in a delightful early mark.

I stop on the street just past the fountain and turn to Tabitha.

'Listen, Tabs,' I tell her, 'I know you don't want to go to school today, and I know you still feel tired, and that sucks. But if the school calls me and I am sent to pick you up, you will be in trouble from me. Don't try it.'

Tabitha yanks her hand from mine and storms off. At the gate, she walks through without looking back or saying goodbye. I cry all the way home, tucking my hood tight around my head and taking a circuitous route through the alleyways so as to avoid running into anybody I know. I feel ugly, and I have a headache, and my back throbs, but my heart aches most of all. I'm being both an over-protective, overindulgent mother and a hard-arsed bitch. The middle ground seems, somehow, beyond my grasp.

The Migraine of Stupidity

'*Tu es excitée?*' Kat shouts across the square at me.

'Wokka wokka!' I shout back, and do a sexy little dance.

She honks an imaginary horn.

'*J'suis en retard!*' – 'I'm late!' I call. '*Bisous bisous!*'

My French is still terrible, but it gets better all the time, as I practise constantly in my travels about the town. The girls get ever more fluent, Biggles will activate his *Boulangerie* French if there's a chocolate muffin in the offing and Keith is delighted to get out of the house and practise speaking whenever he can. I listen to my *Coffee Break French* podcast and I try to watch the occasional YouTube clip and a spot of French news, but it's hard to get the motivation to study – it's so exhausting managing life in another language that once I'm back in the Wormhole, I just crave lovely relaxing English.

I teach my Calade classmates a few of our classiest Australianisms: 'I've had a gutful', 'Fair suck of the sauce bottle' and 'That looks like a dog's breakfast'. I consider other homeland classics: to 'go arse over tit', to 'piss-fart around', 'from arsehole to breakfast-time' and to 'bang like a dunny door' but in the end I decide they are beyond even my powers of mime. I decide, sadly, that one of my favourite Australianisms, the insult 'Get a dog up ya', is utterly untranslatable.

I love my Tuesday and Thursday mornings at the Calade, but these language-school days are tiring, and they often end with the Migraine of Stupidity. I've handed off my Tuesday afternoons with Valentina to Keith. My schedule has become too busy to fit it in, and our relationship never totally recovered from the Hello Pussy incident.

One Thursday at conversation practice we speak of national foods. I try to explain the obsession my liberal-bubble Australian beachside community has with the digestive system. I speak of people fermenting vegetables and sprouting nuts and regarding gluten as the devil's cocktail. These ideas are novel and ridiculous to my classmates, and not just because of my poor French. We laugh. A lot.

One day, Nanette tries to teach us the expression '*Qui vole un oeuf vole un boeuf.*' (One who steals an egg will steal an ox.) It devolves, as Calade conversations often do, from a translation of 'beef' to a parsing of the phrase '*gros testicules*' or 'big balls'. Nanette finally draws a set of balls on the whiteboard to illustrate the difference between a bull and a cow. Out of respect to the conservative Arabic women and the young shy African man in the class we try hard not to laugh, but the effort makes more than a few of us cry, especially when Nanette adds a jaunty hat.

Grammar is tough. Even mime can't help me with the '*passé composée*', the '*vérité générale*' and the '*impératif*'. The Migraine of Stupidity kicks in early on grammar days. Sometimes, to hide my ignorance, I put on the 'fake listening face' I learned from Keith (he uses it on me when I make him discuss doomsday prepper forums), but occasionally the class will try to help me. At some point I usually just pretend to understand so that the helping will stop: the awful, terrible helping that never ends in any satisfactory conclusion. Twenty people earnestly saying 'Bloopy Bloopy Blah' over and over in rising tones never magically makes 'Bloopy Bloopy Blah' comprehensible. '*Ah, oui!*' I must say eventually, praying desperately that the class will move on. Pretending comprehension to a group this large is emotionally disconcerting, like faking an orgasm at an orgy. (I imagine.)

Each week, *petit à petit*, I feel the groaning machinery of my old brain move puzzle pieces closer into place, Babel-fishing the gibberish around me into comprehensible language, but it is the hardest work I have done for a long time. My brain feels slow, creaky, the hard-drive too full of *Survivor* alliances and school-lunch hacks to take on new information. My compassion grows for what the children are handling at French school every day, and I gain a fresh understanding of the relentless experience of migrants and refugees.

Thursday afternoons are French-lesson days for the children. I'm in the bedroom, hiding from Vanessa, when Mabel comes down and starts rummaging through my bedside table.

'What are you doing?' I ask.

'Vanessa sent me to find the ear drops you bought me. She thinks you bought the wrong medicine and she wants to read the label. Also, she dropped off another parking fine.'

I groan. Bloody Vanessa. She can't help herself. I shoo Mabel back to the lounge. Keith is exhausted at the moment. He is working so hard, and when he clocks off from the Australian workday, it's to engage Dad-mode, immersing himself in helping the children with their schoolwork and emotional adjustment. The house, with all its strange quirks and mechanical foibles, takes significant work to manage, and at night lately he's been trying to save years of content from my old blog, which has been eaten by Russian bots. Twice a week he takes Tabitha to the hand clinic in Montpellier for physiotherapy on her little finger, repairing surgery she had last year. One of his final tasks of the day often includes climbing the mezzanine ladder to lie and chat with Tabitha while he massages the knotted scar tissue in her small hand.

I visit the fishmonger to make Keith a special dinner: *coquilles Saint-Jacques*, or scallops in cream sauce. The fishmongers at Le Corail in their high rubber boots are chatty and helpful, carefully wrapping me a package of fresh pink scallops. At home I poach the scallops in white wine, shallots and mushrooms until they are barely firm, and then I put the scallops and mushrooms aside and reduce the sauce, whisking in cream, tarragon, lemon zest and egg yolk.

Mabel lays five scallop shells out on a foil-covered tray and helps me divide the mushroom mix between them. On each we carefully place three scallops, spooning the creamy sauce on top. We season them lightly with cheese, salt and pepper, and slide the tray under the grill.

I prepare five small service plates, and when the sauce and cheese are bubbling and melted, I plate up the dish, garnishing each with a few tiny tarragon leaves.

'*À table!*'

Keith is delighted when he sees the special entrée and even more pleased when each of the children taste and push aside the dish. Keith, whose nickname as a child was Seagull, consumes everybody's *coquilles Saint-Jacques* one after the other.

'Thank you, my darling wife,' he says, pushing away the final plate. 'Could life be any better?'

Seagull's stomach-ache later that evening is worth it, he says.

Most excitingly, Christmas is on the way. Decorations are appearing about the town and the Intermarché is covered in tinsel. One day Mabel gets upset, worrying that Santa won't be able to find where she lives. Tabitha writes a letter from Mrs Claus and secretly pops it in our letterbox:

Dear Mabey,

It has come to our attentshun that you are a very good child indeed and so we are pleased to tell you that you are in the running for the Child of the Year Contest.

A winner will be chosen and you will be told of the winner as well as the prize you will get.

Yours sinserely,
Mrs Claus

Mabel is beyond excited. She cannot stop discussing it. Tabitha tires of the prank quickly but Mabel locks on, Australia's Highest Husky with a Christmas bone, unable to let it go.

Plus Belle Laverie

When the washing machine breaks down, managing our laundry becomes a complex task. It takes a few weeks but Keith, the Engineer of Everything, manages to fix it. In the interim I spend a large amount of time at Plus Belle Laverie, the laundrette in a seedy bit of town on the other side of the river. The lengthy instructions on the wall of the Plus Belle are totally beyond me at first, but eventually I become an old hand.

When I have unloaded my laundry into a few machines and inserted the proper coins so that the locomotive chugging begins, I settle back on the metal bench, open my laptop and try to get some writing done. The chairs are terribly uncomfortable but the warm, musty fug is a lovely contrast to the chill outside. One day a pre-teen boy appears at the door in a ratty T-shirt. He flicks dark hair out of his eyes, rests a fist on one scrawny hip and asks me for money.

'*Non, désolée,*' I reply. The boy narrows his eyes and waves his friend over. He's clocked my accent.

'Where are you from?' they ask me in French. I answer.

The two of them, blocking the doorway, practise their English on me for a while then ask me for money again. They are hungry, they say. Their mum doesn't feed them. They can see I am a nice lady. Just give them some money. I get up and start unloading my still-wet washing

175

from the dryers. The boys are making me nervous. It's afternoon, but the laundrette is in a very quiet corner of town at the far end of a carpark.

'*Désolée, non,*' I repeat to the boys. They get angry at me.

'Stupid bitch,' they say as I gather my belongings. '*Putain!*' They are laughing. As I push past them to get through the door, one of them flips me the bird with his left arm up and extended, slapping his bicep with the other hand. '*Va te faire foutre!*' he shouts. ('Fuck you!')

I get in the car and lock the doors with shaking hands. Ridiculous. Naughty boys. And now I have to dry all this laundry at home, which will take forever. When I get back I realise we're out of milk. *Va te faire foutre*, universe.

A few days later I try again. I'm back at the Plus Belle working away in the damp warmth when Bad Fonzie enters with three rough-looking birds (none of them his wife). My heart sinks.

'*Bonjour,*' I say politely, and turn back to my laptop. They ignore me. Bad Fonzie and his bad bitches confer between themselves for a couple of minutes, then two of the women go and stand outside the door and the last, a short blonde with a pneumatic bum, jumps up to sit on top of my table.

I type a sentence of nonsense in an effort to appear nonchalant. In one practised move Fonzie spreads the blonde's thighs and leans in for a deep and tender kiss. It escalates from here. Things get handsy. Moaning begins. The Lord's name is invoked.

Her generous rump is just inches from my laptop and I am paralysed. So often in France I'm stumped for the correct thing to do, and here I am, faced with yet another example. What's the polite behaviour when a pair of strangers attempts coitus on your laundrette table? Is there a phrase to suit the occasion? Perhaps it's well known in the town that you go to the Plus Belle Laverie when you like to watch. Am I expected to take off my glasses, shake my hair from its bun and join in, like a sexy librarian? Should I look up 'I prefer not to witness the intercourse of strangers' on Google Translate and announce it upon my entry?

'*Oh, mon dieu,*' Blondie moans. Bad Fonzie slaps her thigh. I close the lip of my laptop decisively.

'*Voilà,*' I say conversationally, as though my task is finished. I squeeze past the amorous pair, stop the machines and begin loading my soaked and heavy laundry back into its bags. This takes me a few minutes, during which Bad Fonzie's date progresses to an alarming place of near-congress. Finally, I have everything. I grab my backpack and, polite to the end, give the standard farewell.

'*Bonne journée!*' I call as I head out the door. They both laugh. Looks like they are having a *très bonne journée* indeed. I pass Bad Fonzie's two henchwomen, load my wet washing into the car and head home to drape it all over the kitchen. Again.

The party

I find Keith asleep at his desk on Thursday, hands on keyboard, chin on chest and snoring lightly. He wakes in a panic. 'What! Where am I supposed to be? Am I late for school?!' It's not the first time I've found the poor man frozen like a Pompeian businessman. He's absolutely buggered.

We are coming to the end of the school term, the busywork of the festive season is kicking in and I am starting to lose my mind a little. I know when my stress levels are rising because Keith starts to treat me like a package that might explode. He speaks slowly and gently, in the manner of an emergency clinician in the Community Outreach Team dealing with an unpredictable client. 'Incoming patient,' I imagine he might radio into the hospital. 'Possible psychotic break, meth psychosis or lady who can't work out how she's going to get the presents to Australia for Christmas Day and why everybody is INCAPABLE of PICKING UP their WET TOWELS for the LOVE OF CHRIST. Prepare all the Valium you have!'

The children are tired too. Tabitha is scratching her head with '*les poux*' – I am pretending I can't see it – and Biggles is complaining of tummy-aches. Anxiety? Cheese-greed? Looming appendicitis? Who knows? (Vanessa. Vanessa knows. DO NOT ask Vanessa.)

Mabel talks about the Child of the Year contest constantly.

'Mum, I'm so bored of that,' Tabitha complains to me.

'You started it, Tabs,' I tell her. 'You finish it!'

Some minutes later, Mabel runs screaming up the stairs. She's checked the mailbox for the seventh time that day and found a new letter.

Dear Mabey,

We are happy to tell you that the competishun is down to three people now and you are one of the three. Please keep being good and maybe you will be the Child of the Year!

Yours sinserely,
Mrs Claus

'Why didn't you say it was over?' I ask Tabitha. 'You've given the contest a whole new energy!'

Tabitha shakes her head and goes to hide from her sister in the mezzanine.

Mabel talks about the shortlist for days. How should she be good? Where was Mrs Claus hiding the cameras? Who might the other two children be?

Keith and I decide that the only way to return all the social largesse we have received over these last months is to throw a party. A proper Australian house party, including our friends from school, the Calade and Rue Canard.

Juliette invites us to Christmas lunch with her family and friends. The flat upstairs is too small to accommodate us all so our host turns her medieval cellar into a party den. She covers all the stored crap with furs and cloth and squeezes in tables, chairs and couches to accommodate us all. Upstairs, Lucie turns food out of her kitchen (a fantastical space full of plants and birds in cages) at a cracking pace. At one point I have a glass of whiskey, a glass of champagne and a glass of rosé flanking a plate of *sanglier* (wild boar), duck and pigeon.

Under the low ceilings of Juliette's *cave*, I look over at Keith, his face misted in cigarette smoke as his winemaker seatmate Bastien waves his slender fingers in the air, enthusiastically describing his grapes.

'We are going to have to lift our game on Saturday!' I call to him down the table, past the throng. He nods, mouth full, and lifts his glass to me in a toast.

Then the desserts arrive. *'Juste un goût!'* – 'Just a taste!' I beg to no avail as an enormous plate is passed down to me with a wink. Dessert is followed by herbal *digestif* cigars, and then coffee, and after the lengthy goodbyes (three kisses each) we are presented at the door with a parting shot of a delicious liqueur with a kick like a *sanglier*. We waddle home and collapse on the couch. No chance I am going to manage the 'Sunday prep' routines of preparing bags and clothes for school in the morning. We'll pay for today's shenanigans with a chaotic Monday tomorrow. It's worth it.

Over the next week I cook for our party. I construct tray after tray of sausage rolls and mini quiches and vol-au-vents and cram them into my little freezer. I do a huge shop for ingredients that I will use to make dishes on the day: mini toasts loaded with smoked salmon and dill and cream cheese; charcuterie platters and bowls of spiced nuts. Mabel will make her specialty Caprese sticks, with bocconcini and tomato and basil on toothpicks. I make a big casserole dish of chicken Provençal with olives and tomato and refrigerate it, in case people stay for a proper meal. Best to be prepared.

I pick up a few dozen wine glasses at the Croix-Rouge, buy plastic cups and napkins from the Intermarché and set up a bar in the sunroom. We stock up on red and white wine, rosé, sparkling wine and beer. We buy soft drinks for the kids.

On Saturday, the kids, Keith and I clean the house. We try to calculate how many guests we might be hosting but can't get any clear numbers. We've invited all the friends we have, but nobody seems to have made a firm commitment. Or perhaps they did and I thought they were commenting on the political crisis in Turkmenistan.

'Come to an Australian Xmas Party!' our invitation says. '5pm till late!' It is so hard to gauge times and expectations. It has to be early enough that people can bring their children and have a vaguely 'cocktail hour' vibe, because I can throw around a lot of finger food but not cater a full dinner for such an open-ended affair.

We put ice and beers in the bath, light candles around the place, cue up some Bing Crosby bangers on the stereo and get dressed up. At ten past five Keith and I look at each other, aghast. Nobody has arrived. I survey the piles of food. Keith pours us a drink.

'It'll be funny tomorrow,' he says.

I knock back my champagne, and then the doorbell starts ringing and doesn't stop.

I dash downstairs at six or so and put a sign on the door: 'Welcome! We are upstairs!' There is no way we can keep answering the door because Keith and I are running about like chooks with our heads cut off.

As the night wears on, many of our friends are astonished at the number of people cramming into the Wormhole, but watching the French interact at the party, it makes sense to me. The default position of the French is suspicion and the default Australian position is instant intimacy. Australians are famously easy-mannered. Some (how dare you!) might say ill-bred. But we are egalitarian to our bones, and this means we will talk to anybody, so Keith and I have collected friends all over town.

Not so the French. People will not talk to each other until they are introduced, and they will not introduce themselves. Until we say, 'Trevor, this is Brenda. She makes armpit-hair art. Brenda, this is Trevor, a part-time erotic taxidermist and rhythmic gymnastics commentator,' they will stand next to each other, silent, as though musing on the blood feud that has existed between their families for generations. But once introduced they will chat with pleasure.

Also, nobody will serve themselves a drink. Keith and I put bottles, glasses and ice buckets about the place, but it becomes clear to us early on that it is apparently rude to pour your own drink. Keith races about the kitchen filling empty glasses as fast as he can.

'Drink?' he says to Gigi and Cédric as they stand silently shoulder to shoulder, empty glasses in hand. Their faces break into relieved smiles.

'*Oui! Oui!*' they say. He quickly introduces them to each other.

'Please, help yourself!' Keith tells people hopelessly. Nobody does. Glasses empty far quicker than he can keep up, as the kitchen becomes hotter and louder and people spill into other rooms.

Nell's chef husband, Jo, hangs out by the stove and helps me sling canapes. We plate them up and get the children to carry them around. It is sweaty, noisy madness. Keith and I catch each other's eye on occasion above the throng, but mostly we work. We work hard.

People keep arriving, entering the kitchen with armloads of flowers and chocolates and bottles of wine. Albert limps slowly up the stairs with his stick, armed with a bouquet that takes up half the kitchen table. I settle him into a chair with a glass of red wine and introduce him, to his great delight, to the boisterous and sexy Kat.

In the bottom room Alex and Momo let the babies roam. The children, in a gang, thunder up and down the stairs playing *Cache-Cache* and *Loup Touche-Touche*. At peak-party, there are more than sixty people navigating the staircase of our tall narrow house – shrieking children, school parents, friends from the Calade and from the village – all the community we have collected in our months here in Sommières. Each of them, I think, was worried that nobody would show up to the party that the new residents were throwing.

Our friends are mingling. Juliette is deep in conversation with Josephine, Nell with Chloé and Kat with Cédric, while Bing Crosby is barely audible. The children and I roar with laughter over a Vegemite-tasting game, and Keith teaches our friends the Aussie phrase 'budgie smugglers', which brings the house down.

It occurs to me that this Australian house party has in fact worked some sort of Antipodean magic on the people gathered in it. The energy of this party is high, wild and festive. Perhaps we are more than just interlopers being indulged so kindly by the town. Perhaps we really do bring something to this diverse, idiosyncratic place. I find myself welling with emotion.

The party gets ever louder and then slowly ebbs away again until, sometime before midnight, Jo helps me dish out the chicken Provençal to the dozen or so stayers. I blurrily put the children to bed, Mabel clutching Pandora the Friendy, who is somehow covered in glitter, and go up to have a cigarette with Juliette on the terrace. 'I 'ave never been invited to a party like zis in zis town. I am so 'appy you have come here,' she tells me.

Downstairs, we sit, plates on laps, to eat our late supper. Juliette asks about the history of Australia. Somehow I find myself telling the story of the Foundation Orgy again.

'The storm is wild! The convicts are all pissed on rum. Completely pissed. Conshenshual? I don't think so!' I shout. Ambassador Mode, activate!

I realise Keith is wearing that toothache expression, and he's moved my wine again. It's time for bed. With triple kisses, we say goodbye to Albert, Jo and Nell, the final stayers, and tumble down the stairs into the dungeon bedroom, which the cartload of naughty child-monkeys has turned upside down playing *cache-cache*. We starfish onto the mustard bedspread, drunk, exhausted, exhilarated and feeling as though the ears of the house are ringing. A wild success? Wild, anyway.

Day one in Sommières: a new address and a year of adventure await on wonderful Rue Canard.

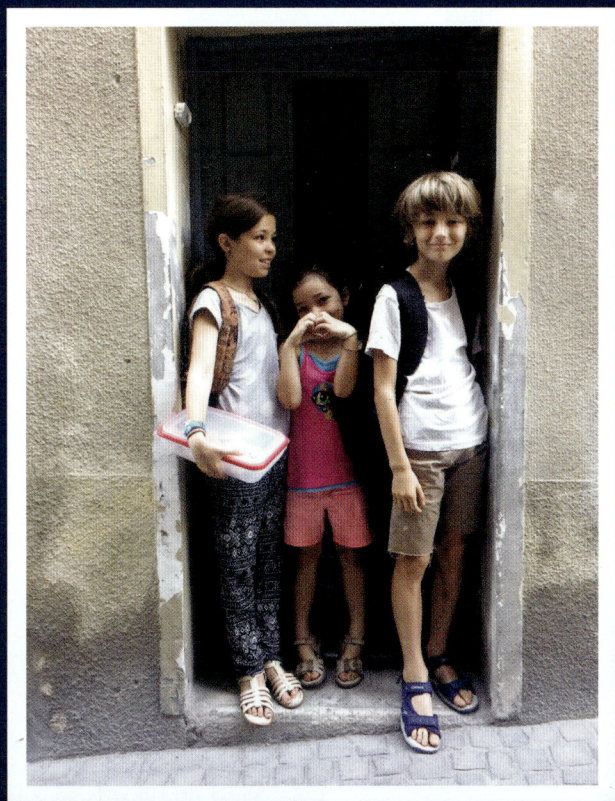

Three darling little kangaroos off to navigate life at École Albert Camus.

French coffee is a crime against humanity, so a decent flat white on holiday in Barcelona is enough to send me into a semi coma.

Sweet Mabel sometimes forgets her trousers, and at other times dresses like a tiny glamourpuss.

On the walls of my Calade classroom: the grammatical rules I never, ever master. *Putain de merde!*

Pale blue shutters provide a gentle splash of colour to the muted stone palette of the *centre historique*.

The Saturday market: the only place I don't feel like a massively incompetent donkey.

So much life is lived around this dining table, particularly in winter when the house (which we call the 'Wormhole') is so hard to heat.

Keith and I throw 80s shapes in our borrowed ski gear on the slopes of the Tatra Mountains outside Kraków on one of our many mini sojourns out of France.

Life on wheels. Keith is always repairing and replacing second-hand bikes, scooters and rollerblades as they are lost, stolen and chewed up by the cobblestones.

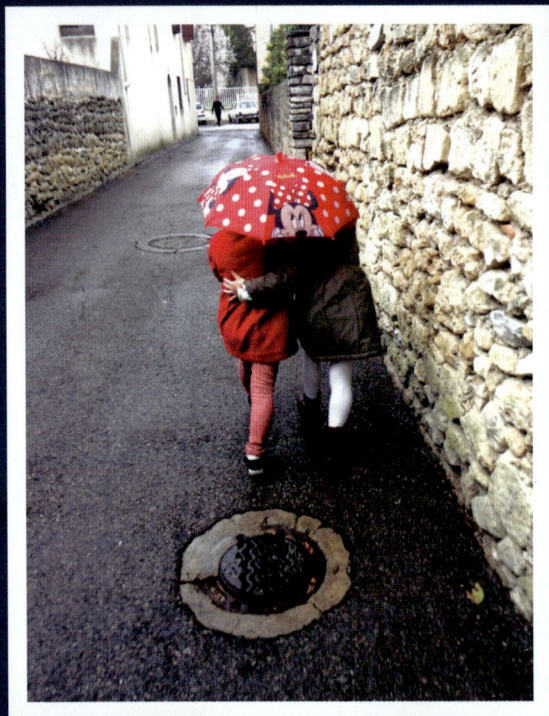

In big ways and small, our French friends always look after us.

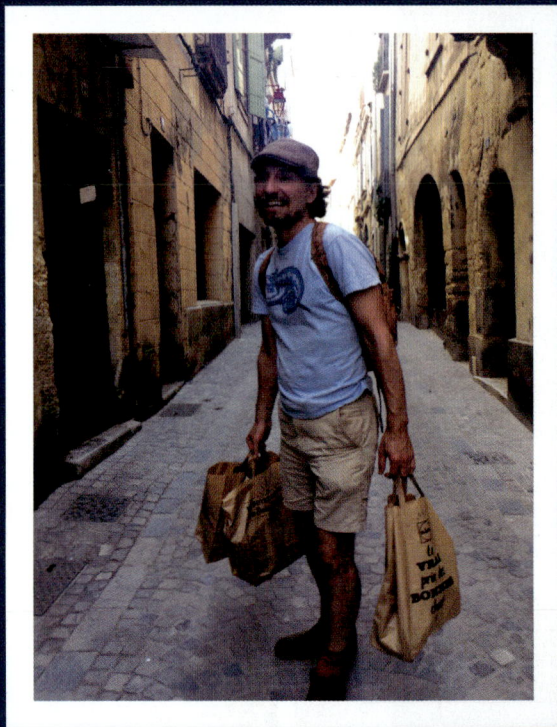

Keith in his natural habitat: loaded up with bags of food and readying himself to cart them up the endless spiral staircases at the Wormhole.

Sommière's Roman bridge is an everyday wonder of history and engineering. It looks pretty, but it's not for the weak: I nearly tumble over the edge one day battling the wild wind known as the Mistral.

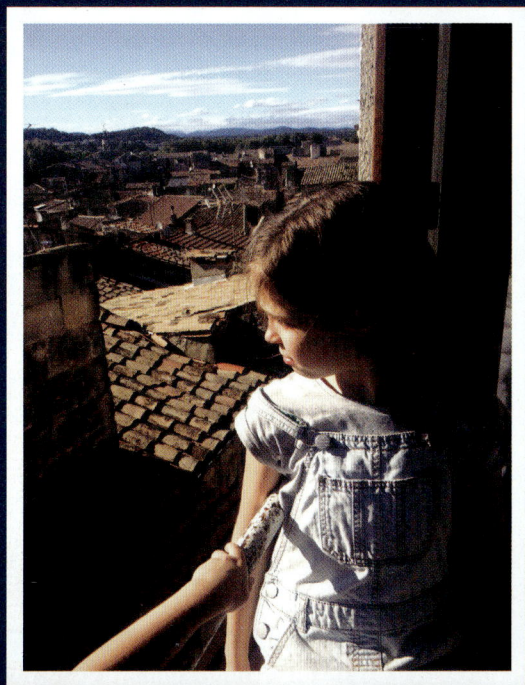

Darling Tab, gazing across the terracotta rooftops and probably thinking about The Hunger Games.

A sea of rooftops sheltering so many neighbours we come to know and love.

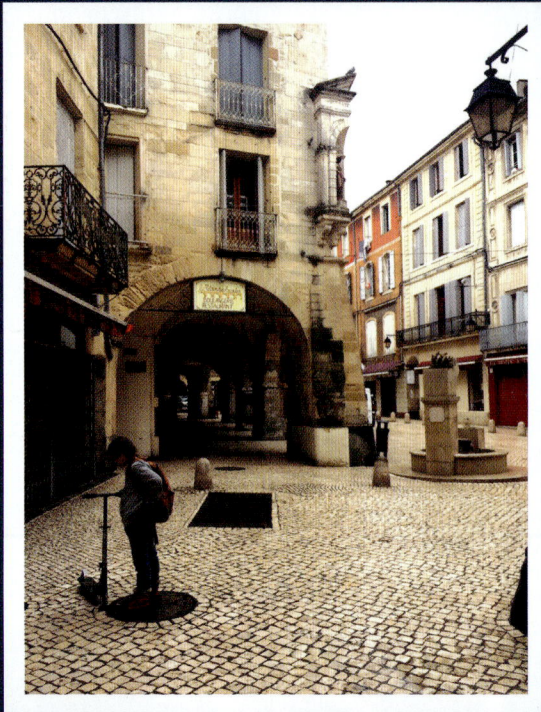

The square we travel through daily on our school run. We grow to know all its changing moods, seasons and cast of characters, and we are so sad to say goodbye.

White Christmas

The staircase leaks glitter for days. It's time for an introvert's holiday. We need to get away and restore ourselves, immersed only in our gang of five, and we're more than ready for our Christmas road trip.

We're starting with a few days in a remote cottage in the Auvergne – the 'green heart' of central France. The children are excited for a snowy Christmas and I long to spend my break lazing in front of the fire like a cat. Then a journey up to Normandy and back before returning relaxed and primed for a new term. We clean up the house, pack our little hatchback to the gills with books and Friendys and Christmas presents, and hit the road. I am deliciously aware that everyday mum-life is suspended: the parade of meals slung out from my hardworking kitchen, the constant tweaking of the schedule that scrolls like ticker tape through my head, the endless shrink-and-grow cycle of Mount Washmore on the couch.

Our tiny cottage in the Auvergne is perfect: isolated and basic. We find it with difficulty via winding, snow-clogged and deserted mountain roads. There is no internet or phone service. Mabel frets about Santa. Then Tabitha 'finds' a letter at the front door.

Dear Mabey,

Congratulations! You have won the Child of the Year! Please write in this box below what present you would like and we will get you whatever you want. No eckspense spared!

Yours sinserely
Mrs Claus

'What did I do *now*?' Tabitha wails when I pull her aside.

We settle in for Christmas Eve where I tell the children about the wonderful Icelandic tradition *Jólabókaflóðið* (Anglicised as *Jolabokaflod*), or 'book flood', where on the night before Christmas everybody receives a new book and a bar of chocolate. The children think it sounds amazing, and they cheer when I present my wrapped gifts. We're bathed in bliss as we sprawl around the wood stove eating chocolate and reading in this funny little house. The decor is a mix of the homey and the bizarre: lumpy knits and cuckoo clocks vie for space with a promotional chair from McDonald's emblazoned with the slogan 'I'm Lovin' It!' Is there anything better, I think to myself, than being warm and safe indoors as the cold wind gently rattles the windows, reminding you that you are protected with the ones you love? Tabitha even manages to wrap a tiny gift that finally puts her Child of the Year prank to bed. We make up some tale to explain why gifts on request are banned, and good-natured Mabel accepts it.

The next day the children make snow angels and I realise there is no oven in which to bake my Christmas roast. I rally and fry chicken on the stovetop. Then the gas runs out. I am stumped. What to do with all these carrots and potatoes?

'What about the wood stove?' Keith says in a flash of inspiration. Chicken soup it is, bubbled slowly into deliciousness on top of the small wood stove and eaten while we watch a VHS tape of *Jurassic Park* in

French on a tiny television. It is as unexpected as it is memorable. (And Santa still finds us.) My heart is full, my mental load light and Christmas in France most beautifully white.

After the Auvergne we roam the châteaux in the Loire Valley, explore dolmens in Brittany, visit the ancient island commune of Mont-Saint-Michel and wander the D-day beaches and war museums of Normandy. We play Murder Winks, eat pasta in cheap Airbnbs and roll in snow wherever we find it. We see an incredible amount of history, play cards in restaurants, read books and eat car picnics of baguettes and jam and apples. The children invent a disturbing back-seat game called Bad Husband (which involves pushing, shoving and chanting) and we all sing, in rounds, the classic nursery rhyme they have learned in school: 'Vent Frais, Vent du Matin'.

By the end all the road food has us farting like puppies. I imagine our little hatchback tootling along the highway with comic strip–type wavy stink lines rising from it. It's been a fantastic trip but after two weeks we are ready to drive an epic final full day to get back to the Wormhole. I miss my bath, and a nasty sinus infection has left me with a constant vice-like headache. On the plus side, the blocked sinuses mean I have lost my sense of smell, a blessing in disguise. I am desperate for my own bed, a proper diet and a *little* personal space.

Back with a thump

We get back just in time for *la rentrée*. The weather is bitterly cold, and the flood warnings for the Vidourle are on high alert. The swans, Charles and Camilla, are nowhere to be seen – hiding, I hope, in a sheltered part of the river. We're told to listen for the bell that rings for *l'inondation*: the town is well prepared from its many previous floods.

A storm is raging on the first morning of school, the wind blowing at 70 kilometres per hour. We run through rain, thunder and lightning, the spokes of our umbrellas inverting, and I slip over twice on the precarious cobblestones, wrenching my spine. When a child whinges that their trousers are wet I demand, 'Where's your backbone?' Pain and frustration are draining my empathy tanks. It's all a little gothic.

The week continues in that vein. Every task is just a little harder than it should be, and the house is in a state of accusatory chaos, with post-holiday unpacking combining with back-to-school debris. It's impossible to warm the old stone, and we're out of routine. The children drag their heels and complain. A cocktail of oestrogen and resentment percolates lightly in my veins, and my ongoing sinus headache doesn't help my mood.

~

On Wednesday morning we race against time to make it to school before the bell. Halfway there I stop to button Mabey's coat and realise she isn't wearing any pants. I look at her woolly stockings, gusset halfway to her knees.

'Where are your trousers, Mabel?' I ask.

'I took them off,' she says. 'They were itching me.'

'But you can't just wear stockings, Mabel!' I say.

'Is that wight ...?' she muses thoughtfully, mentally adding 'stockings are not pants' to the arbitrary list of world rules in her six-year-old head.

I imagine the faces of the teachers and the tidily put-together kids when Mabel unburdens herself of her overcoat and strides in, trouserless, to take her seat in class. We're already weird, the Feral Cheryls of the schoolyard. I can't let Mabel become No-Knickers McIntosh.

'Back! Back!' I shout. We race home and hurry Mabel into a pair of jeans before setting off for school at top speed. When we round the corner we see that the gates are closed. This is new. We've often scraped in by the skin of our teeth, but we've never arrived after the gates have been locked. Through the bars we can see the last of the children in their lines entering the school. We are just minutes late.

'We missed it!' we all gasp. 'We'll have to ring the bell!'

Ring it we do. Nothing happens. We ring it again. And wait. I make a few jokes about how the children might score a day off. The secretary must be away from her desk, I think. So we ring it again. A face comes into view at a classroom window overlooking the gate and then disappears again.

'That's Madame Montagne,' Tabitha says. She's as terrifying from the street below as she is face to face.

'So she saw us?' I ask.

'Oh yeah,' says Tabitha.

'Curiouser and curiouser,' I say.

We ring the bell again. It has been about ten minutes and I am getting a sick feeling in my belly.

A child's face appears briefly at the window this time.

'It's because it's buzzing in my classroom,' Tabitha says.

'What?'

'When the gate rings Madame Montagne goes to the window and calls "What is it?" and then the gate monitor gets to press the buzzer,' Tabitha says.

I'm slow, but it is starting to filter in.

'So Madame Montagne knows we're here, but she's not going to open the gate?' I say to Tabitha.

'Doesn't look like it,' Tabitha says.

'But she's not going to tell us that she's not going to open the gate?'

'I don't think so.'

'Rachelle!' calls Gigi, passing by, and I flag her down. She doesn't try to kick out my knees today. Perhaps she can see that I'm a little frazzled.

'*Non, ce n'est pas possible,*' she says. 'No school.'

In Franglish we establish, haltingly, that the rule is that when children are late they are not allowed to enter. No reason is possible, no excuse allowed. Gigi shrugs.

I look at the silent intercom. No message has come through it. There is a window above us but the teacher has not chosen to use it. Instead she's left us on the street for fifteen minutes, buzzing the bell like fools. I'm dumbfounded and I'm pissed off, but mostly I am prickling with humiliation as we all slink away. The children are quiet. They can see that I am upset, and it's always confusing when something has tilted the equilibrium of your parent.

Home we trudge. The Australian idiots. Stern-Mother France has let me know my place and, yes, it worked – I will make sure I am never late again, but also I am sorely tempted to let the teacher know that in the vernacular of my old country she should eat a large salty bag of dicks.

It is annoying but not problematic for me to take the kids home again. But what if I had to go to a workplace? A trip away? A medical appointment? What if we were late due to an asthma attack, a nosebleed, a car breakdown, rather than just a small child's wardrobe malfunction? It's the fact that nobody opened that window and spoke to us that hurts the most. I feel very, very far from home.

I am cold. I am sick. I miss the sting of the raging southern sun, the Australian sense of humour, the Wollongong school gate. I miss the food, my friends, my mum. I miss easy interactions with strangers. I miss joking. I miss being understood. I miss the bush. I miss the ABC. I miss colourful, abundant Australian salads, raw-food menus and sharp Asian flavours.

I miss coffee. Oh, how I miss good coffee. This week, the women at the Intermarché cafe laugh at me when I order. They are annoyed. I don't know why. My face? My accent? Did I stand in the wrong spot and break some unspoken rule of supermarket-bakery etiquette?

'*Les Anglais*,' one of them mutters, and the other shakes her head.

I have no snappy comeback to these rude cows because this week every French word I know has left my head, probably because of our holiday. For a fortnight we relaxed into the wonderful pleasure of speaking English to each other all day. I feel every deficiency in my skill set this week as I say '*bonjour*' when I mean '*merci*' and '*enchantée*' when I mean '*au revoir*'. Every sentence melts into word salad: '*Nos, vos, votre, tes, mes, ses, son, sa, leur, mon, ma, mes.*'

In a small town it's impossible to avoid encounters with people you know, and it gets deflating when every one occurs in a language in which at best you are a fool and at worst a wanker. I read one morning a quote that says, 'If you encounter an asshole in the morning, you've encountered an asshole. If you encounter them all day, you are the asshole.' This gives me pause as I have already encountered two assholes, and it isn't yet lunchtime.

But all the children actually cope with *la rentrée* amazingly well. Much, much better than me. To reward them for doing a great job with their first week back at school, on Friday afternoon I make them the meal they have all been asking for: Doctor Who's favourite snack, fish fingers and custard. They deserve it, even though I can't look, and they watch *Doctor Who* while cuddling under Big Bertha.

Eventually I get it together. My sinus infection finally improves. Thanks to some expert advice from Vanessa and a visit to the rich cornucopia of the pharmacy, I no longer feel constantly as though my face is on fire. My back recovers from its undignified sprawl on the cat-shit cobbles and I can handle the emotional baggage of being the local chump again. I find a new coat at the Croix-Rouge with Josephine and Maurice, and a man nearly as tall as he is wide winks at me in the street. He is wearing a T-shirt that reads, 'Man I Feel Like a Woman'. The storm has passed, the sun has come out; I am not an asshole, and neither is *la belle* France.

The hot desk of a hot mess

The mistral bites outside, but the Bar du Nord is as cosy as an old jumper. I'm working on *Mothering Heights* in the frowzy fug, powered by the grizzled bartender's bitter coffee, and I am immersed in stories of nappies and sleeplessness when an argument erupts over a card game and pulls me into the present.

'Non, non!' shouts a small, wiry man at his friend. He grips him playfully around the neck and rubs his head. *'C'est pas possible!'*

The bartender winks at me as the half-dozen card players argue good-naturedly over their spread, all talking at once. An old woman at the bar rests her hip on her shopping cart as she kickstarts her day with a glass of *vin rouge*. They all ignore the smoking ban.

I am finding new momentum with my manuscript as I slowly and painfully winkle out the patterns of the messy past. In the Intermarché coffee shop, in Fonzie's laundrette o' passion, in the corridors of the Calade and in the bizarre, delicious soap opera of the Bar du Nord, the book is taking shape.

I signal to the bartender for another cup of coffee. He lifts his chin cheerfully. The men laugh and deal out another round. Among the gentle clatter I write stories of a life long ago and half a world away, concocting images of a visiting kookaburra and a taut pregnant belly bared to sharp sun on a hardwood deck among the gum trees. It is sometimes strange and destabilising to be living this mental life out of time while also living a real life out of place, but the more I dig into my memories, trying to order and understand my own chaos, the more I understand myself.

I approach life with a certain enthusiasm and spirit, an energy for life something akin to that of an under-trained labrador, which propels me gleefully into glorious projects and conversations and relationships. But operating on chutzpah and cortisol is unsustainable: I soar and crash, soar and crash. I make lists and concoct plans and research ideas, working twice as hard as I should to harness the essential disorganisation of my brain.

I sit on my glasses and crack their lenses. I lose the paperwork. I say the wrong thing. Then I lie awake in remorse, make the apology, repair the damage, re-read the instructions. The price for my vivaciousness is exhaustion and irritation: the dredging of an empty well. Before I learn to protect my energy I throw it to the winds – take every drink, crack every gag, engage fully with every person I encounter – after which I must retreat to my blessed solitude, wrung out like a damp rag.

It is at times an unbearable energy, both to exist in and to live with, and it takes me time to understand how to operate my own machinery with more care. Keith is the steady anchor that grounds this current, and so are the children, and my writing too. The antidote to the exhaustion of my flighty monkey mind is the slow, private steadiness of work, and the attendant calm of discipline.

The softly-softly process of threading fragments into a coherent narrative sharpens my perspective. I see tiny unexpected increments of improvement in my own chaos as I teach myself the craft of writing a book. Focusing on the process rather than the outcome, I breathe through my own inadequacy as I wrestle my rusty thoughts and clumsy sentences into something approaching clarity. My hot desk is a hot mess, but perhaps I'll fake it till I make it. And if not I can live with the stain of being a failed artist. I may be bleeding my vulnerability all over the page and presenting my insides, soaked in cliché and unlovely metaphor, for public ridicule, but oh well! What's a little shame between friends? Humility is good for the soul, they say.

Time horizon

'*Arrête! Arrête!*' I shout as I chase a little boy up Rue Canard. 'Stop! Stop!'

Shopkeepers lingering and smoking on their stoops laugh as I pass. They are enjoying the spectacle of the hopeless teacher being bested by the cheeky villain child. My foreign accent makes the schadenfreude a touch more delicious.

I'm an 'excursion mum' today and I'm failing utterly at keeping Léon in check. This child, with a will as sturdy as his little legs in shiny track pants, is the naughtiest boy at École Albert Camus. His wickedness has dynamite, and he has immediately sniffed out my utter lack of authority. I'm trying to keep the boisterous boys at the back of the line from disappearing down tempting alleyways as we walk to the library for a talk by a children's illustrator, and Léon keeps escaping.

There is a beautiful anthropological notion of the 'time horizon'. It refers to the way we frame our lives based on what we know might come next. Our time horizon alters our thinking in many profound ways, including our sense of safety in the world.

For Keith and me, the minute we arrived in Sommières a countdown began. We are aware that this pocket in time is limited, that this version of 'home' is suspended in an alternative reality, and it will soon be over. But for the children time has an altogether different meaning.

The horizon is invisible to them. Every present situation has the potential to last forever when you are forced, by the indignity of smallness, to go where you are told. Get in! Turn left! No more questions!

As parents Keith and I have the right to direct these children down any route we choose. Our whims dictate their destinies, and we have thrust this France experience upon them, trading off the disruption in their time horizons with the gifts of experience and novelty. There are times when this trade feels powerfully inadequate, and the ethics of it make me uneasy. Have we opened up possibilities for them? Or have we in fact destabilised them in some quiet, important way? Best-Guess Parenting strikes again.

I pause, resting my hands on my knees. Excursion-mum duties kill me but (the recent locked-gate incident notwithstanding) École Albert Camus has been so wonderful to us that I want to do my part to help. Some outings are tougher physically, some emotionally.

One day I help Tabitha's sixth-grade class on a visit to the *collège*, the local middle school that her class will graduate to next year. I walk at the back of the line with Tabitha, and I notice that none of the children talk to her. This group, on the giddy verge of adolescence, is excited for *collège*. They have no interest in engaging with a transient who has no place in this next part of their time horizon.

At the *collège*, Tabitha sits alone at a table. The library smells of disinfectant with a faint top note of body odour. The boys and girls joke and giggle with each other, but Tabitha is quiet, listening to the teacher. I can barely grasp a word she is saying, and I wonder how much Tab comprehends. A sick wrench of sadness fills me as I think about her days. How much of my sweet girl's time is spent like this: an outsider, quietly waiting to be told what to do, and always sure she is about to humiliate herself?

Tabitha does not usually hang out with these kids. Her class is a composite with the next level down – Year 5, the *deuxième* – and she interacts at lunchtimes with Franc, Amélie and Alain from this group, as well as Biggles. They don't share many of Tabitha and Biggles's spheres of reference, but they are at least within their time horizon: the next day, the summer.

Tabitha is a diminutive child, commonly wearing clothes two sizes smaller than her age, and she's a foot shorter than many of her friends at home in Australia. Here in France, the population is generally more petite, and the size differential is not so obvious. Tabitha's demeanour is jovial and expressive, and she doesn't look small to me, usually. But this afternoon Tabitha looks more than tiny. She looks diminished, sitting quietly alone at her round table as the teacher drones on incomprehensibly and the other children whisper to each other in their puppy-close cliques.

Guilt plucks at me as I shift my sore back in the uncomfortable plastic bucket chair. Parenting is such power. Am I abusing mine? On the way back to École Albert Camus I pull Tab close and make plans with her for a special sleepover up in the mezzanine. She is delighted, but I blink back tears on the walk home thinking about her small hands folded tightly on top of that lonely, scuffed expanse of library-table laminate.

Another day I have agreed to be excursion mum on a kindy-kid trip to the aquarium at La Grande-Motte, a kitschy resort town near the sea full of astonishing 1960s architecture based on the Egyptian pyramids. (Keith and I call it The Big Moot.) I get to school with Mabey on time, but when the teacher asks me where Mabey's lunch is I realise I've missed a memo. My heart sinks.

'*Cinq minutes!*' says Momo, who is also helping out today. The Big Sexies are part of the group, and her son Claude is coming. She runs out the gate and across the dusty square, her slender legs pumping fast in their black stovepipe jeans. The teachers start herding children onto the coach. Mabel is nervous, but a few minutes later children are still boarding when Momo, panting, screeches to my side and hands me a paper bag.

'I 'ope is okay,' she says. Inside there is a ham sandwich, a banana and a piece of cake quickly wrapped in greaseproof paper. Momo has raced to her kitchen and speed-packed a lunch for Mabel. I feel tender gratitude for the epic kindness of my French friends.

On the bus, while Momo and I chat, I hear Mabey. She's upset. Two of the boys have grabbed her precious Emirates airline sick bag (she is much attached to her objects, and this is a favourite) and they are pretending to throw up in it theatrically. Mabel's voice is rising in pitch. I have to intervene.

'*Attendez! Non!*' I say. '*Pas malade jouer!*' (No sick play? Dear God. The humanity.)

The boys take no notice of me at all. I try to grab the bag as it flies past and miss it, rendering myself even more of a buffoon.

'*Arrêtez! Arrêtez!*' I squeak, but my pathetic yelpings are drowned out by the teacher who has appeared beside me. She roars a stream of French at the boys. Her voice is so loud that I physically rear back.

'Listen to this woman,' the *maîtresse* bellows, 'or I will throw you back to school!'

The lecture has an immediate impact on the boys, who hand Mabel back her sick bag and hang their heads. The teacher closes her mouth and transforms once again from a monster to a sweet-faced, kindly woman with a headband holding back her swinging ponytail.

'Okay?' She smiles, hand on my shoulder.

'*Oui*, okay,' I manage. She trots back up the line.

I try to channel French teachers on these excursions, but I am never able to manage the shape shift. French teachers speak to adults in calm and gentle tones, laughing and chatting, then whip around and roar like dragons at the children. They do not raise a sweat. They do not lose their tempers. They just give the children both barrels, shut the nonsense down and return to their conversations.

My most difficult excursion by far is to a Roman museum in Provence. Keith is along for the ride this time as an excursion dad. There is an everyday connection to ancient Rome in Sommières that never gets old for us: the children, learning about Roman history, are surrounded by relics of it, not least their walk to school every day past the beautiful bridge.

Today the children have made their own Roman coins with a pressing machine and filled in work sheets after examining the architectural dioramas lining the walls. Biggles has already embarrassed his parents and delighted his teacher: when the children are asked to draw a portrait of the *maîtresse*, Biggles draws Madame St Clare with angry eyebrows and a wide-open, screaming mouth. He is not trying to cause trouble. It really is how he sees her.

She loves it. '*Oui!*' she says, a twinkle in her eye. '*C'est moi, exactement!*' I adore this teacher.

After lunch, I half-understand the instructions we are given to disperse in small groups for a walk in the surrounding forest. I go where I am sent, along with a shy young student teacher who speaks no English. Keith is sent in the opposite direction. The student teacher strides ahead, and I take up the rear, following the group down a series of forest paths that take us ever deeper into the countryside. The sounds of the museum slip away behind us as I walk with the group through the scrubby, dry bush, chatting to the kids and mentally calculating how long until I can go home to my bath.

It's around twenty minutes later that we stop at a fork. The student teacher smiles at me expectantly. I smile back.

'*Où maintenant?*' I ask brightly. 'Where to now?'

'*Pardon?*' she says, confused.

Her stream of French takes some time for me to comprehend but both our smiles fade as we realise that we have both assumed that the other is in charge. I discover that her confidence was merely teenage enthusiasm. She steps back into the messy clutch of children, making it clear that I am the leader of this troupe.

It's hot. One of the children asks for water. I hand them my bottle and they quickly drain it. I am, at the best of times, directionally illiterate.

Today I have zero idea where we are, and no idea at all of the direction of the museum, but all the children, as well as the student teacher, are looking at me to lead us home.

Mon fucking *dieu*.

'Allons-y!' I say with cheery bonhomie – 'Let's go!' I retrace our steps up the path, trying desperately to note any familiar trees or landmarks. The children are no help.

'We are lost?' one asks. *'Perdu?'*

'Pas perdu!' I scoff – fake it till you make it! – but there are some forty minutes of increasing panic before I finally navigate us back to the museum, where nobody seems bothered by our tardiness. I am hot, exhausted and adrenaline-poisoned, and my back is stabbing me with sharp needles. I would feel elated at the fact that I have delivered us safely home, but I have no space in my body for any more feelings. It is full.

The meaning this year will have for the children and the lessons it will hold are a mystery. I have to pick my way through and try to lead, one excursion at a time, even though I so often have no idea where I am going. Sometimes the task is heartbreaking, like helping Tabitha process her visit to *collège*, and sometimes it is just ridiculous, like my inability to assert authority over Léon, the nine-year-old scoundrel.

Back to that excursion. I shoot a sad sideways glance at the Wormhole doorway as I pass it, panting. The rest of the class is climbing the stairs past the convent, but Léon is taking off in the wrong direction, throwing me a quick triumphant look over his shoulder. How I wish I was behind that door, lying on my sheet-draped couch with a cup of tea at my elbow, reading a memoir about somebody else's French adventure.

Shoulders back, I channel Madame Montagne.

'Léon!' I roar. *'Arrête. MAINTENANT!'* – 'Stop. NOW!' I snap my fingers and beckon him back to the group with a glare that says, 'Do *not* mess with the Ambassador.'

The midnight thread

The south of France conjures up certain images: a crisp white shirt and a flat leather sandal; a slash of red lipstick on a bare, clear skin; a brunette throwing her boyfriend's possessions out of the window in a fit of sexy rage; poetic toasts given at long tables set with heavy silverware under pergolas foaming with bougainvillea.

This south of France might exist, but not in my part of town. And not in the winter.

I'm yawning as I shepherd the children through the square. The town stretches like a scruffy dog starting to wake up. Ponytail is setting out his chairs, and the man from the *tabac* is standing in the doorway inhaling his first cigarette of the day.

A clickety-clack sounds from around the corner, and then a group of beautiful women swoops into view like a flock of exotic birds. They are wearing high-heeled boots and flowing coats in a tonal wash of rich, lovely colours: charcoal, olive, camel, scarlet. Their hair streams behind them in highlights of gold and chocolate. Ponytail, Tabac and I stop and watch as they cross the square and sashay through the alleyway beyond us. We look at each other and exchange appreciative, querying glances. Who were those exotic Parisians? What are they doing here? Then we return to the previous moment: Ponytail teases a pile of dirt from a cobbled corner, Tabac takes a deep drag and I hurry the children on their scooters before we are late for school.

'Quick, kids! Before the gate closes!'

Life here is made up of different threads woven together into a dense, complex tapestry. The occasional glamorous thread, like the visiting Parisians, throws sparks into the patterns of grey and brown surrounding it.

I too am made up of different threads. I live mostly in the threads of mum life and supermarket life, and the colourful threads of my rich inner world, but every once in a while I engage in the sparkling thread of night-life.

One evening I go out with Juliette to the jazz bar across the bridge. In the bathroom Mabel sits on the toilet lid and watches as I put makeup on: a bit of foundation, a bit of mascara. It's all familiar so far. Her eyes narrow as I add some blush and a line of gold to my eyelids. Mabel does not like me going out. By the time I draw on a strong lip she starts asking questions.

'Why do you have to go, Mummy?'

I try to add a loose curl to my shoulder-length mass of hair. I'm wearing a semi-sheer camel-coloured shirt I found at the Croix-Rouge over my jeans, and I've pulled out the pointy-toed calf-tight cowboy boots.

'Sometimes people just need to go out at night, Mabey,' I say eventually. 'To have a few drinks and talk to each other.'

'But what for?' she says. 'It's cold outside! Talk in the day!'

I'm finding it hard to rebut her arguments. Honestly, I don't want to go out either. *Ça pique*, it's freezing, and I'm feeling pre-emptive anxiety about the pained look on people's faces as they experience my nitwitted conversation. I used to be a queen of shenanigans. I loved the night-life. But the older I get, the more I yearn for time alone with a nice hot cup of tea and a grisly true-crime documentary. I try to channel my inner party animal.

'Because night-time is the right time to party?' I offer. Mabel is sceptical.

I snap shut my powder compact. 'Good as it gets, Maybs,' I shrug.

'You're as beautiful as a kitten, Mummy,' she says loyally.

After kisses and farewells I shut the door on Mabel's disgruntled face, leave the Wormhole behind me and set off down the cobbles. I cut down Rue Flamande and cross the bridge. It's exhilarating to smell the damp night and smoke a cigarette as I strut, just because I can. I disengage my mum brain and drop down a notch, into an older identity.

Before I turn the corner to the Place de la Libération I hear a discordant four-piece stepping up and down a squalling jazz ladder. Not many punters are inside. Behind the bar a smiling man in a flat cap talks me through a long list of wines lettered onto the black chalkboard. The bar is comfortably shabby, with fittings that look as though they've been built out of offcuts and discards. Rows of polaroids are strung around the walls. Wine in hand, I go looking for Juliette. I find her smoking outside in a small clutch of people.

'*Rachelle!*' she cries in her raspy voice, and pulls me into a hug. Juliette is wearing a red velvet dress, calf-length and slinky, with black boots and a bejewelled bolero jacket. Her blood-orange fringe slices a fresh line across her forehead, and the makeup on her almond-shaped eyes is flawless. She introduces me to the group around her. I take a breath and ready myself for the work of communication.

Three wines in it's both harder and easier. My tongue is looser, and my brain parses the body language to contextualise what's happening, balancing out my limited vocabulary, but everybody talks faster the more they drink too, and often I lose the plot of the conversation completely and cannot get it back. Are we still talking about the Barrier Reef? Pesto versus marinara? Psychoanalysis?

As usual, once I have used up The Spiel on each new person the conversation trails off quickly. I've only got ten minutes of material.

If I was up for action, the men would perhaps push through, but I'm not there for any kissing, French or otherwise, and everybody tires fairly quickly of indulging the conversational charity case.

I linger on the outside of group conversations, escaping to the toilet more often than necessary just to have a moment in the quiet, breathing in and out and inspecting the posters on the wall. I look perhaps like I am bulimic, or suffering a touch of diarrhoea, but I always leave the bathroom feeling restored for another half-hour.

I'm operating, four months in, at what I've come to think of as Politician French. I can speak much better than I can understand, and once I've said '*C'est quoi?*' twice and my brain is still registering only '*Bloopy bloopy blah*', I have no other options but to take control of the reins. Like a shifty politician, my conversation unfolds thus: Thanks for your interesting thoughts! Let me reply with a statement that has absolutely nothing to do with the subject you have introduced. Beige stockings! Cross-eyed babies! I'm sure I look both dumb *and* odd, a seductive combination.

I spend much of my time skating along on the sniff of an idea, the gist of a conversation, reaching for the ring always just out of my reach, relying so heavily on theatre and comedy that I barely know what I am saying.

Deep into the evening I feel my social battery wearing down. The men, alcohol-fuelled, are getting more flirtatious and I can't easily shut the encounters down. I rely on the tedium of my conversation to turn them off.

I find myself in conversation with a woman in her sixties seated in a wheelchair. Dressed in layers of lace, she is talking to me earnestly through a curtain of waist-length black hair. I am utterly lost. Is she really saying that she can't walk because her son-in-law threw a fridge at her? Clearly I can't ask this question. I am reduced to operating on pure empathy. I tut-tut gently and offer those minimal encouragers of 'active listening': *mmmm, mon dieu, c'est vrai?* ...

Juliette comes and pulls me away by the arm. 'Don't talk to Éloïse! She's crazy! And she gets mean.'

'The story about the fridge?' I ask.

'Oh, that's true,' Juliette says. 'Bastard broke her leg that time.'

This fucking town, I think. Suddenly I feel like I'm wearing a hat a size too small. Here comes the Migraine of Stupidity. I'll cut my losses, I decide, and leave before the night gets too late. Juliette is settling in for the next quartet. Her eyeliner is melting a little and she is pointing her cigarette to punctuate her words. I realise I will be walking home alone. I have to get the kids up for school tomorrow and I have reached my limit of French and experimental jazz.

I say my goodbyes and I head for the bridge, the wail of the saxophone fading into the dark behind me as I cross over into the sleeping old town.

I try to Tom Cruise myself as I walk briskly across the cobbles – This is fine! You are fine! – but it is not long before my imagination conjures rapists. The streets are deserted, but as I head deeper into the old town, the squirrelly alleyways and the squat bulk of the silent apartments overhead feel menacing. The air is shot through with sudden laughter, and I pass a small clutch of men who pause and regard me silently. Inserting my keys through my fingers, I turn a corner past the group into a dark street, and before I think about it, I start to run.

The running unlooses my grip on myself. Bad Sommières, somewhat theoretical and darkly romantic in the daytime, feels horribly real in this moment. From every new alleyway I expect an attack. I imagine being unable to speak, to plead for mercy. What is French for 'help' again?

The wine in my blood mixes with cortisol and adrenaline, poisoning me with terrifying imagery of Sommières stories so casually shared. Fridges thrown. Brothers stabbed. Children slapped. Wives beaten.

Every window above is shut and silent, and I am alone and vulnerable, ready to be just another moment of historic violence in this Gothic town. These dark streets feel ready to absorb my blood like all the rest.

When I finally arrive at the Wormhole, I scramble to get the key in the lock, stumble inside and collapse against the door. I am too elevated to cry, but I feel sick, my mouth coppery with chemicals.

Downstairs I crawl into the hard, lumpy bed beside Keith's comforting warmth. It takes a long time to get to sleep. I used to be a creature of the midnight streets, energised and inspired by the exciting possibilities of the darkness, but not anymore. Daily life is adventure enough. The Ambassador, it seems, has reached her limit.

Snow and pierogis

School terms are intense here, but they are wonderfully short. Every few weeks, a break. Not long after my late-night imaginary encounter with Bad Sommières, we take off for Poland, where we take the dirtiest bus in the world to a downmarket Polish ski resort in Zakopane, at the foot of the Tatra Mountains.

I hang out in a musty pine-panelled restaurant, wearing the baby-blue 1980s op-shop ski suit that I have borrowed from the Calade. The kids are on the slopes with Keith, but I can't ski and I can't learn because of my pesky bad back. It is prone to strange behaviours and is unlikely to respond well to those learning-to-ski falls that involve one leg pointing to Norway and the other to Albania. I'm happy though. I have a hot coffee and a good book, there's a crackling fire at my back and I'm surrounded by dramatic Poles. The people-watching is next-level.

Keith and the kids get back from their session, roses in their cheeks (the temperature outside is minus fifteen), and Keith orders the specialty 'hot beer with cloves' of the Tatras, which tastes comedically bad – even worse than it sounds. The kids are delighted to drink hot chocolate and warm up their cold noses. I help Mabel pull off her boots. Keith has been employing the childhood snow-boot insulation system of his mum on this trip – one sock, plastic bag, second sock – and we are all dressed in a motley collection of gear gathered from the community cupboard at the Calade, friends, the Croix-Rouge and the winterwear shelves at the Intermarché.

At the thermal baths of Termy Bukovina I die of happiness in the circular hydrotherapy pool of my dreams. All around the edges is a series of jets at different levels, and a bell rings every couple of minutes to let you know that it's time to move along a stage so that over the course of a complete circuit you receive a full-body hydrotherapy massage. There is one strong jet at glute-level. Ooh la la, I think, as I raise an internal eyebrow and muse on the possibilities, but the lady beside me is not discreet. When the bell rings, she moves to the jet, turns around and straddles it like a boss. Get it, girl!

Poland is a blast. It snows for our whole visit, and we have an amazing time in Kraków, a city soaked in history, with grand and beautiful Gothic, Baroque and Renaissance architecture. Mabel sleeps in my lap through unforgettable front-row seats at the Kraków Philharmonic, and we wander the old town, Kazimierz – the Jewish quarter – and Nowa Huta, the brutalist 80s Soviet 'display city', built as propaganda to represent a socialist utopia during the early years of the Poland People's Republic.

We explore a nuclear fallout shelter in the basement of the Museum of Poland under the Communist Regime and refuel at Ariel restaurant on Szeroka Street, a delightful warren of Jewish history where the food is nourishing and nurturing and the specialty coffee, which contains two shots of vodka and one of rum, is just the tonic to arm a weary traveller against the bracing Polish weather. Keith and I, on separate days, visit Auschwitz as we planned. The museum is a harrowing and sensitively run Holocaust memorial, and after this long day we each count our blessings with renewed fervour. We don't take the children.

We eat pierogi at the Bar Mleczny Centrum, a communist-era cafeteria with original fittings and decor, and schnitzel at the deliciously kitsch Restaurant Szeroka12, paused in a 70s time warp complete with ruched curtains, fake flowers and statues of Lenin. In the local street market I buy 80s tea towels commemorating the wedding of Charles and Di, still in their plastic packaging. Outside the Polo Disco in Kraków I am admiring a poster of a pop star with the most luxurious forest of chest hair since 1978 when a gold Lamborghini nearly runs me down. It has a nefarious-looking character at the wheel, and I immediately worry for the safety of the highly decorated horses pulling carriages along the next street.

Everybody in Poland is grumpy, and we love it. Our budget Airbnb in the Old Town is full of character, with broken furniture, single beds pushed together to make doubles and old, smelly pillow inserts inside new cotton covers. Graffiti on the wall of the apartment building speaks directly to me: 'I write, but nobody listens.'

We play cards in restaurants while we eat cabbage and pickles and deposit lots of wonderful, hilarious memories in the family bank. The five of us decipher together the cultural mechanics – buses, money, food – of this new place. I am so grateful for the amazing experience. But two weeks of cabbage-farts are swiftly up. *Allons-y!* Back we go: to school, the Calade, Rue Canard, and to the Wormhole, which feels more like home every time we leave it.

The parenting cycle of failure and success

Tabitha and I are deep in conversation as we walk down Rue Canard. It's Wednesday, and the shops are just starting to wake up. Ponytail is yawning as he sets out his tables, and the baker is already clattering his long-handled shovel for the woodfired oven.

'*Coucou!*' says Franc as he swoops past on his bike.

The cobbles are a little slippery with the morning damp. No puffy doona for me today – there is a thin warming in the air, a hint that we may soon be able to extend our domain beyond the bottom room of our poorly insulated house. We may no longer need to pick our way around the laundry hanging off every piece of furniture and the 1000-piece kitten puzzle that has become Keith's life's work to solve. I'm wearing a brown woollen coat that I picked up at the Croix-Rouge. It's several sizes too big, but I've decided it has a sort of ragtag cool. Keith says it reminds him of the Artful Dodger, like I should be pulling a string of hankies out of the pocket or asking people if they want to buy a watch.

The subject of discussion: Amélie. Drama is afoot – again. Amélie is annoyed that Tab won't take her hand every morning for the entrance into school, when children line up in a two-by-two crocodile holding hands like in the comic *Madeline*. Tabitha wants to take Sabine's hand

215

sometimes, but Amélie has started throwing her exuberant tantrums if Tabitha walks in with another friend.

I tell Tabby that my advice is to try to leave it behind, like a fart in a hallway. Then I ask her plans.

'Can you set things up in the morning to sort of pre-empt her getting upset?' I ask.

'Well, I'm going to tell Amélie that she can have Monday, Wednesday and Friday, and on Tuesday and Thursday I'm going to walk in with Sabine,' Tabitha says. 'Except if somebody is sick – then I have a different system.'

I'm impressed.

'So do you know how to say all that in French?' I ask.

'Of course!' Tabitha says, and proceeds to rattle it all off, to my amazement. I don't understand half of what she is saying, but her accent sounds perfect.

Last night, as we lay in her little bed in the mezzanine, talking through the complications of friendship, I looked idly around Tab's domain. She had commandeered little stools and occasional tables from around the house, stuck her drawings on the brick walls and arranged her clothes in loose piles. There were discarded socks and suspicious lolly wrappers everywhere.

I've begun to insist on the occasional sheet change after finding Tabitha sleeping on a bare mattress one day.

'Where's all your bedding?' I asked her.

'Dunno,' Tabitha said. 'Who cares?'

Leaning against the wall, we dug deep into the psychology of friendship to try to work out what was going on with Amélie. Biggles's head appeared at the top of the ladder.

'Mum, I don't think Tabitha wants to talk about this anymore,' he said firmly.

Tabitha and I looked at each other in surprise.

'I'm okay, Biggles,' she said.

He looked unconvinced. 'I think she's had enough time talking about it, Mum, seriously,' he insisted.

'She's really okay, Bigsy,' I said. 'Some people like to figure out their problems by talking.'

Biggles gaped at me with incomprehension. He was feeling protective of his sister, I could see, and he was horrified by how long this chat has lasted. The idea of a lengthy, free-ranging discussion on interpersonal politics, to Tabitha a raging good time, is to Biggles a hellish torture.

His head disappeared. Tab and I wound it up.

'Goodnight, my little darling,' I said, squeezing her tight.

'Night, Mum,' she said. 'Love you.'

I climbed backwards down the ladder and switched the kitchen lights off, leaving Tabitha to her world. In the morning we revisit her Amélie plans. She's feeling capable and energised, and I am smug with parenting brilliance. Best-Guess Parent? GOAT, more like!

On Thursday morning the pendulum swings. I no longer feel like the GOAT, but like an actual goat. It has been a total shit fight getting everybody ready, and Tab and I silently fume on the way to school, running our own hot little internal arguments. But I never ...! But she always ...! Even yesterday's burst of sunshine seems to have been a cruel teaser of spring. The mercury dropped overnight. It's arctic again, and this morning has been one of those days where I feel as though I've done three rounds in the ring before 9am.

It is *such* hard work getting the children out of bed and upstairs for breakfast. I get up early to write but my back is aching, my mood is low and my muse is absent. I procrastinate half my morning time away, and then am furious at myself. I must dig deep to find the patience and compassion required to turn my attention to the children's needs.

The poached eggs and hot chocolate around the table are a reprieve, a sort of gathering of energies for the hard part that comes next: getting dressed, out of the door and through those gates. Keith and I trade drop-offs and pick-ups depending on our different schedules and capabilities.

Today the morning school run is mine.

Teeth! Hair! Bags! Scarves! Beanies! This part of the process is often painful, and it's at the root of today's contretemps with Tabitha. She has a letter for Amélie in her pocket and claims to be ready as she sits on the couch reading Harry Potter while I fight a brush through Mabey's hair.

Then, when we get out of the door into the icy air, she cries, 'My gloves!'

Mother and daughter take their places in the ring. My position: being gloveless is Tabitha's fault for saying she is 'ready' when she isn't. Tabitha's position: how is she to know that her gloves aren't in her coat pocket when she is positive that that is where she left them?

The unwinnable fight loops on and on until Tabitha rides angrily ahead on her scooter and enters the gates without saying goodbye. I go home with the sour belly of guilt. I've sent my child off discombobulated and elevated and uptight to manage a complicated day full of the emotional soap-opera stylings of her baby–Joan Collins bestie. I could have altered her mindset had I been the bigger person, able to rise above my own mood. And yet! The bloody gloves! My piss still boils.

Keith and I are always running that tricky line between strictness and permissiveness, trying to instil that mythical resilience in the kids by urging them to problem-solve and cope with some adversity, and intervening when the task is beyond them. When I get the line wrong, it eats away at my insides. Best-Guess Parenting: Where Sometimes Your Best Is Quite Shitty!

Motherhood is a game with ever-changing rules. From the full-service requirements of early childhood, we have entered this interim zone where I must transfer responsibility back to the children, bit by bit, as part of the overarching aim of making myself redundant.

Sleepless in the dungeon that night, my brain overfull with anxious worries, Keith and I talk about the children and listen to podcasts in the dark. Holding Keith's strong hand, I drift off, eventually.

It's a rough week, but we make it to Friday having made up – me with

Tab, and Tab with Amélie – and in the evening I cook with the kids. On Saturday we set off on a mission to deliver food about the town – a chicken pie to Mimi, who has been ill, and lemon cakes to Josephine, who has had sad news from home in Brazil. Tabitha has really taken to cooking, and she is learning the joy of cooking for others. We stop and kiss and greet people we know everywhere we go, calling *'Bisous!'* across the road to those too far away for kissing.

Keith and I walk behind the kids, who swerve their scooters around the crap on the cobblestones (bird? cat? dog?) as they dodge the Saturday marketgoers with their trolleys and cameras, and duck into the apartment buildings where our friends live. I watch the children weaving through the throng, neatly missing the pools of water near the oyster stall and the queues messily gathered in front of the rotisserie-chicken van, until they pull up to inspect the digital watches together, their sweet heads bent close as they show each other their favourites. Watching Tabitha joke with the stallholder, I'm filled with admiration for my small, brave girl.

Some days are up and some are down. We no longer have our 'newbie' passes. The novelty has worn off for our fellow school parents and teachers, our friends in the village and my classmates at the Calade. We are just folded into the crew now, and the donkey family must keep up with the stallions. Gallop or perish!

I've watched the children navigate playground dramas and work through problems. I hear the way they talk about the different lives of the children they know here, and the way they try to help each other, and I can see that they are growing as people. As for me, with every week that passes, I feel more rooted to Sommières. Life is not always easy, but it is magic: a story-book adventure in a fairytale setting.

A spasmodic Hercules

One day in late February, we finally dismantle the heavy blanket acting as an insulator between the kitchen and the sunroom, and move the kitchen table back up the three stone steps. The sun! The sun! Once again we can spread out and enjoy the spectacular vista below. It's like the Wormhole has doubled in size.

Early mornings on the stairwell are getting less bitter, but my writing schedule has become as soft and mushy as the gentle protuberance about my midsection that the children call Pillow Tummy. I've got into a terrible habit of checking my phone first thing from the dungeon bed, avoiding the moment of stepping into that icy stairwell. Pics and posts from home are full of late-summer barbecues and bare feet and sunrises, and my news feeds are all Trumpy dystopia. All of it leaves me feeling depressed, tense and twitchy from too much dopamine on an empty stomach.

I'm trying hard not to let my book get triaged downward in the face of more pressing everyday tasks, but I've become uninspired by this manuscript that will never end. I'm sick of myself, and it all seems pointless and desperate and humiliating. I try to remember that I am working towards that notion of 'vertical coherence': when short-term and long-term goals fit together, so that achieving small wins is part of a greater advance towards the big dreams. But currently my long-term goal of publishing my book is definitely hindered by my short-term goal of exploring how Kim Kardashian's former stepmum Caitlyn Jenner's ex-wife was once married to Elvis.

I remind myself of the Flaubert dictum: 'Be regular and orderly in your life, so that you may be violent and original in your work.' I vow to overhaul my morning routine. 'A small daily task, if it be really daily,' said Trollope, 'will beat the labours of a spasmodic Hercules.'

I have been grappling with *Mothering Heights* for a long time. I've written and deleted thousands of words. I cannot bear the thought of not completing this thing that I have poured so much time into – time that could have been spent working on paid journalism, or on exercising my pelvic floor, or conquering transcendental meditation or (God forbid) cleaning the windows. I've grappled with this unwieldy mess and written painfully through my old traumas. Now I feel stuck: I cannot bear the thought of how much work lies ahead in editing this manuscript into something decent that may ever sell, and yet I cannot bear the thought of abandoning it. The sunk cost of it all is terribly shaming.

I research. First I spend a long, delightful session exploring writers' routines. Benjamin Franklin, framer of the American constitution, said, 'I rise early every morning, and sit in my chamber, without any clothes whatever, half an hour or an hour, according to the season, either reading or writing', and Georgian diarist Samuel Pepys liked to 'caper about' for a time before getting down to work. Auden is comforting: 'Only the "Hitlers of the world" work at night; no honest artist does.' I feel seen: by evening I am toast.

Kafka, writing in 1912, possibly phrases it best: 'time is short, my strength is limited, the office is a horror, the apartment is noisy, and if a pleasant, straightforward life is not possible then one must try to wriggle through by subtle manoeuvres.'

Subtle manoeuvres it is! I employ many little tricks to get myself started. I put comfy socks in a basket, purchase a lovely candle in order to give the bare morning kitchen some Scandinavian hygge and take heart in the words of Steinbeck: 'Abandon the idea that you are ever going to finish ... Then when it gets finished, you are always surprised.'

I aim for 6am, when the sky is still navy blue. I don't always succeed in excavating myself from the tangle of bedclothes in my warm dungeon or the seductive siren call of the screen's blue light. But when I do, I find my day begins with a vitamin shot, a sense of achievement that lights a little flame within. I start to believe in myself – not in the merit of the book itself, but that I am capable of the work it demands – and it brings me a little flickering sense of momentum.

It's a bit cold to go full Nude Franklin. I stick with my fluffy socks. And while I am always a fan of capering about, doing it first thing in the morning is a bit extra for me. Where Mark Twain's family left him alone until they needed him (at which point they blew a horn) these quiet early hours are mine to focus on my own projects, before the day begins properly and my schedule is bound to the school run and the needs of the family.

'The repetition itself becomes the important thing,' says Japanese novelist Murakami. 'It's a form of mesmerism. I mesmerise myself to reach a deeper state of mind.' Day by day I train to manage this early-morning start. Every day it's a new battle against my lazy, distracted monkey-mind, but incrementally I make progress.

One morning my laptop belches, blinks and swoons like a Victorian lady before finally giving up the ghost. Keith manages to save my manuscripts but the process of fixing my computer gets complicated fast. We navigate repairs and warranties between French computer shops and Australian retailers before I'm forced to courier it to my dad in Australia for him to sort out. What could possibly go wrong?

In the meantime I'm stuck with the kids' computer, a machine they inherited from Keith when it became too slow, old and sticky for him. Helpfully, a day or so after I take ownership, Biggles drops the thing, leaving a massive crack bisecting the screen from end to end. This becomes rather a fitting metaphor for the way my head starts to feel after an hour or two working on it. See the lady laugh! Ha ha!

Next I borrow an old laptop from Momo and Andre, but instead of a headache-inducing crack this one has narcolepsy. Without warning, mid-sentence, the machine will suddenly go to sleep. It won't run unless plugged into the wall, and requires an external keyboard, so I can only work at home, putting an end to my wanderings about town.

The keyboard is French, with all the letters of the alphabet as well as the punctuation keys placed in quirky spots so that all my work looks as though I have been writing while simultaneously suffering a series of small strokes. It's the 'AZERTY' keyboard system I first encountered in my humiliating search for constipation medicine in the pharmacy, those many months ago. It also runs a French version of Word.

I spend long minutes toggling between my document and Google Translate trying to learn how to cut and save and paste. I find another portable keyboard at the shops. This one has a QWERTY system (hooray!) but symbols and shortcuts that look to be written in some Eastern European language (not so fast, lady). I save my work constantly, anxiously, worried that the computer will go to sleep. Every writing session reminds me of the way the philosopher Hobbes described the life of mankind: nasty, brutish and short.

But – somewhat surprisingly – my momentum is not entirely lost. As if my recent angst over the project was like the 'transition' stage of labour where a birthing mother feels that she cannot possibly complete the task, I am now crowning, and may actually give birth to this manuscript.

Up in the quiet kitchen, the sky outside fades from navy to cornflower blue, and by the time Keith starts carting our grumpy, blinking children up the stairs, I'm ready for the job of preparing them for their hard day with my arsenal of jokes and affection and hot buttered toast. The tasks of motherhood interrupt my writing, but they also inform and enrich my interior life.

Whether I will ever wrestle this epic elephant into shape enough for publication is a whole other thing. I'll deal with that on an as-needs basis. For me the great battle has always been the crippling inner critic who was sure I could never actually complete this project. But right now, in spite of the narcoleptic laptop and the mini-strokes and the Hobbesian brutality of the process, I am pushing through, and I can feel that the end is nigh – at least, the end of the beginning.

Beauty and art

We're not racing the bell this morning, so we take our time on the walk up to the carpark, cutting through the alleyway beside the old convent and walking the winding road past the tower. Spindly wildflowers are sprouting, and memories of winter are so recent that this mild morning feels like a gift. Mabel chats about the *Licorne* club on my left, Biggles talks about *Minecraft* on my right and Tabitha skips ahead, loving herself sick in her new knee-high brown leather boots.

'I feel like Katniss, Mum!' she says with excitement. Tabitha is all about The Hunger Games at the moment. She has taken to tucking a plastic arrow down the side of her boot.

I park in the carpark near the Calade and walk the children to the gate. There are triple-cheek kisses for Chloé, Gigi and Kat.

'*May-belle! May-belle!*' cries Clémentine through the fence. '*Le Club Licorne!*'

Mabey's face lights up. She hugs me quickly and runs inside to where Clémentine and the rest of the kindy gang are gathered by a tree in the courtyard. They start talking animatedly. Biggles and Tabitha linger till the final possible moment, when Madame Montagne is shooing in the last arrivals and closing the gate. They kiss me goodbye and walk in, resigned. Amélie runs to Tabitha, shouting in excited French, and I see Tabitha adjust her shoulders and put on her game face, digging deep to

227

find the social battery required to engage with her high-velocity friend. It's not fantastic, but I allow myself to feel relief and gratitude that the kids will not be desperately unhappy for the next few hours.

'*Toute à l'heure! Bonne journée!*' I call to the mums, and head off, exhaling the tension of the school gate farewell as I trek back through the streets to continue my day.

Back in the afternoon, I am talking to Chloé when the kids run out. 'Hi, Mum!' says Tabitha. I give her a hug and then my conversation with Chloé grinds to a halt as we watch a massive louse saunter out from her hairline and across her eyebrow. I don't have the French to parry this social faux pas and so I just farewell Chloé weakly and walk away. Ambassador Mode, activate!

That evening, I drench Tab's head with Marie Rose head-lice treatment. The hardcore chemicals of Marie Rose are where we have landed after softer approaches failed. These French nits have some sort of Gallic super-gene. They are big, strong and impervious to treatment. I try the natural method of combing conditioner through to smother them, but the French nits laugh in my face. On Vanessa's advice I attempt the oil-based treatment that not only leaves the nits alive but is itself impossible to wash out, leaving the children with lank greasy heads that they are *still* scratching. The atomic bomb of Marie Rose is the last resort.

I send Tab down to the bottom room, where the furniture is draped in protective towels, and the air is sharp with chemicals. Keith continues the task by removing all the tangles in Tab's hair and then dragging a metal fine-tooth comb through one small section at a time, before wiping the foamy residue off on a tissue to inspect it for tiny eggs. Tab is the last of the kids to tackle tonight in this hellish production line. Each one has hair thicker than the next; the miserable process takes hours and it must be repeated every seven days for three weeks. It's all just as we imagined in our South of France dreams!

It could be a psychological reaction to the horror of nits, but I decide to go for a leg and muff wax (the two do run together somewhat in my case) at a place in the village. In the six months we've lived here, it's the first time I've ventured into an actual beauty salon. I've been taking care of all my own business, too nervous to talk to a professional. But in the spring I decide it's time to face my fears and sort out my situation. Trim the hedges, as it were. Or, perhaps more accurately, log the rainforest.

I google some useful phrases and manage to make my bikini-wax wishes understood: a *maillot classique* (a hedge trim or bikini line) and not a *ticket de métro* (a little rectangle shape) or a *maillot entier* (the full kit and caboodle, leaving you plucked-chicken bald and susceptible to a nasty chill).

What do you call these fanny stylings in Australia? asks the beautician. Full Brazilian is easy enough to translate. 'Wax' as the product as well as the process is okay too. '*Et le ticket de Metro?*' she asks. I take a deep breath and launch in. On my back, in my undies, waving my arms about, I mime 'landing strip'. The plane. The earth. The road of the plane. It takes a while but we get there. And I am so thrilled that I have managed a full half-hour's conversation, as long as I don't deconstruct the content of it too deeply.

With legs smooth as an otter, I pass by Cédric's studio on the way home and stop for a chat. He is sitting on a stool, working on one of his Tupac portraits, limp rollie dangling from his bottom lip. I wander in to inspect an inside wall where he has hung a series of beautiful watercolours: buildings, flowers, streetscapes. In my halting French I ask him about the pictures.

'*Aquarelle,*' Cédric tells me. 'Watercolours.' That is his early training. He painted so much *aquarelle* that he is bored with it now. There's no money in it anyway. Cédric makes coin via young men buying his Tupacs and wives commissioning family portraits as anniversary presents for their husbands.

'Could we all come down for a lesson one day?' I ask Cédric. He is surprised but pleased. 'Of course,' he says, and so we find ourselves, a week later on a rainy Sunday afternoon, perched on low stools around

Cédric's large round coffee table. He has prepared carefully for the lesson, setting out glasses of water, paints and small thick sheets of paper, dense and promising under the hand.

In conversation, we realise that this studio is Cédric's whole home. We have always assumed that he lives upstairs. Today we learn that there is no upstairs, just an area behind a curtain at the back of the shop with a sink and a small fridge. Cédric sleeps on the sofa. Short and thin, Cédric suffers in the winter from a 'bad chest', wrapping himself in woollen scarves, drinking *tisanes*, or herbal teas, and watching action movies on the couch with Ponytail while the chill seeps through the stone walls.

The roof arches are close overhead, exhaling a musty damp as we work, shoulder to shoulder, around the coffee table. The rain falls steadily on Rue Canard, washing the cobbles clean, and the children are distracted by Cédric's fat black cat winding between our legs. Cédric pulls up an image of a poppy on his laptop and teaches us, patiently, the step-by-step process of watercolour painting. He speaks quickly and I have to ask him to repeat himself often.

'Start lightly,' Cédric says. 'Work in layers, building up intensity and depth. Begin with a gentle wash and *petit à petit* you grow your confidence: add a little, add a little, add a little more.'

It is a quiet, peaceful afternoon. Slowly we lay down our layers, learning how to manipulate the paper and the tools as we go. Our marks are stilted at first. Cédric shows us how to clean up our mistakes and the shapes on the page begin to emerge.

'Have patience,' Cédric says. 'Let it paint itself. The picture wants to show you.'

We tease the paint into unexpected patterns, each of our flowers with a different perspective. None of us experience the poppy the same, and the paint flows differently from the hand that holds each brush. The colours strengthen and bleed into each other. We need help, and Cédric gives it with that wonderful, pushy, gloriously French warmth and directness. He cannot quite bear our amateur efforts. Painting by painting, he goes around the table repairing our mistakes until all of them are beautiful.

We pay Cédric, give him a bottle of wine, bid him goodbye and run back up Rue Canard, tucking our paintings under our jumpers to protect them from the rain.

Je Critique

Sadly, school life is tricky for Tab right now. Luc has taken to teasing her, singing songs about what an idiot she is and sometimes kicking her. He is part of her friend gang, and so every day her happiness depends on how Luc decides he's dealing with her. A good day is a good day, but there's no predicting Luc's mood.

Keith is off to China for a few days. It's easier for me to cope with his occasional absences now, but I'm still hypervigilant when alone with the kids. Before Keith leaves, he and I discuss the Luc Problem at length. Up in the mezzanine, Keith explores it with Tabitha, and at the gate he talks to Madame Montagne. We both do our best, but in the end it's Tab's problem to solve.

Tabitha and I talk into the night. We look at things from different angles, discussing French culture, Luc's issues and why a 'frenemy' might run hot and cold. At home in Australia I would approach his parents, but that isn't an option here. I don't know who they are, for a start, and there's no way my French would be up to the complex interpersonal machinations of 'Your son and my daughter are mates, except for those times when he is an absolute little prick-monster – any thoughts?'

Sabine quietly sticks close to Tabitha, but Amélie is as likely to side with Luc as to shout at him. She's an unreliable ally. Alain draws Tabitha a picture in support. It shows Luc picking his nose with his pants down around his ankles, displaying an oddly rounded genital mound, coy as a G.I. Joe doll. Tabitha is a people-pleaser. She's very worried about upsetting others, far more likely to place herself in pain or stress than get somebody into trouble and quick to blame herself for any problem. She's very reluctant to talk to the teacher. I want to protect her, but at the same time I respect her agency. I reassure Tabitha that she's not at fault, and encourage her to talk to Madame Montagne.

Tab describes to me how Luc likes to run up to her, unleash a stream of fast French and then run away, laughing. 'You must be so interesting to him,' I say. 'Look at it from his perspective: this cute kangaroo has just landed in his small town out of nowhere. Can you imagine how funny it must be to a boy to say the most random things to a girl who can't understand them? "My bottom is almost entirely mechanical and made, in fact, of goat's cheese! Might yours be similar, sir?"'

Tabitha likes this. 'How was the rotten cabbage your mother made for dinner last night?' she suggests in rapid-fire English. 'I do hope it brought you the most incredible gastronomic pleasure!' She finishes with a wink. I am very proud. Comedy and resilience: what more could I ask? Calmed and armed with a plan, Tab goes to sleep, and I make my way backwards down the mezzanine ladder.

But in the morning she has a stomach-ache.

'I'm sorry, honey, you still need to go to school, but I really am sympathetic,' I say.

'You don't believe me!' she says hotly.

'I do, I do!' I reply, folding her into a hug. 'I don't think you're faking. Stress is real! People get cancer from stress!'

'WHAT?!' Tabitha shouts, with fresh tears forming.

On the walk I reach into my bag and accidentally smear the slimy contents of a forgotten cheese sandwich all over my hand. I yelp and then, off my guard, I slip on pigeon shit and land on the cobbles. Pain vibrates up my back. Biggles joyfully counts how many times I swear on the way to school. At the gate I crouch and look into Tabitha's face.

234

'Listen, my darling – you are a wonderful, interesting person doing a very hard thing,' I say. 'Do not let some little French wanker ruin your day. He is just a turd on the bottom of your shoe. He is a footnote in the story of your life.'

She shrugs off my consoling hand and trudges in the gate.

Mabel runs off to her friends without hesitation. They are gathered around a stunted tree, deep in a multi-day engineering project that involves carrying piles of dirt to the corner of the fence. Mabel is thriving.

Biggles ignores Franc's calls and heads to the pole he has taken to circling during lesson breaks. He holds on with one hand, bends his head towards the pole and swings around it, over and over. He can't really explain why he likes it, but he says that it feels like a good distraction and it pushes the thoughts out of his head.

It's unfolding for us how hard this school experience really is for Biggles. He hates to be the centre of attention, so being an interesting foreigner is painful. And a lack of facility with the language has required all of us to sharpen our senses, reading body language, context and tone to understand what's happening around us – skills that are very difficult for the wonderfully logical Biggles, even in Australia. Here, it's excruciating. Biggles withdraws further and further.

His teacher, Madame St Clare, is very kind. She doesn't put pressure on Biggles in class. Often my small boy comes home with a mark on his forehead from where he has spent the day resting on his desk. Biggles's school life is a test of endurance. At home he spends a lot of time glued to us physically, unable to articulate his feelings in words but drawing fierce comfort from the warm familiarity of Mummy and Daddy.

In their room, the children turn to each other. They invent ever-more complex kinship systems and cultural rituals for the Friendys. My favourite is Sausage Marriage. When two Friendys get sausage-married they eat a ceremonial sausage, *Lady and the Tramp* style, until their lips meet. Real marriage is romantic, but anybody can get sausage-married.

Even siblings. There's a Friendy anthem too – 'It All Revolves Around the Sausage' – which is sung in a deep, swinging baritone, reminiscent of 'Big Spender'. The Friendys, it seems, are getting a little ... French.

At the gate I speak briefly to Madame Montagne. I update her on Luc, making a point of the kicking, and ask her to keep an eye on Tabitha. Keith has spoken to the Directrice about the situation before. Things aren't changing. As I leave, Luc and I lock eyes. I point to him, to my eyes, and back. The international symbol: I am watching you. He looks nervous. I am pleased.

When I get to the Calade I head to the squalid loo to try to wash the cheese funk off my hand. Of course, there is no soap there. I try to deliver myself the Spanking of Privilege (Get a grip, lady! You chose to be here! Spank spank!) but it doesn't take and I burst into tears in class, surprising myself as well as my classmates.

I can't fix anything, is all I can explain. I can't fix anything. I am comforted by Fatima: we don't share a language but she hugs me warmly and pats me with her strong dry hands, and then she brings me a black instant coffee.

'The first year is really hard,' says Josephine in her deep, musical voice. 'But after that it gets easier.'

'But we're only here for a year!' I wail.

'Well, my love,' she says, 'you're fucked!'

We're all quiet and tired at lunch. I try to make especially delicious sandwiches for the children, and we watch a little Netflix comedy together before walking slowly back to school for the afternoon session. After class, I wait at the school gate and listen as Kat tells a funny story. Gigi pushes me gleefully, laughing at my bad accent every time I speak. I brace myself slightly so I don't fall over in the dust. Gigi used to be a rugby player. She's strong. Chloé asks how I am coping with Keith being in China. She can see it's been a long day.

Biggles runs out and wraps his arms around me tightly, burying his head in my stomach. Mabel walks out slowly, looking tired. I fold her into my side, making a mental note to check in with her privately about her day later. Tabitha is last to appear, with Alain and Amélie on either side. She looks pale but her head is high.

She cuts her eyes at me as soon as she spots me. Let's get out of here.

We extract ourselves from the crowd. Franc and Alain walk with us, chattering excitedly, but as we head up the alley the boys peel off and the kids and I are left alone.

'Let's walk to Lidl and grab what we need for an easy dinner,' I say. The kids nod. Tabitha starts to tell us about her afternoon.

'It was *Je Critique* today,' she says. 'The Luc thing was in it.'

'Oh my God,' I say.

Je Critique is the weekly tradition of Tabitha's classroom, a procedure with the full name '*Je Critique, Je Félicite, Je Propos*' – 'I criticise, I congratulate, I suggest'. During the week children write their thoughts on a piece of paper and add them to a bowl, and once a week, they discuss the issues. Children are allowed to speak only when they are holding the *bâton de parlant* – 'the speaker's stick'. It's democracy in action, and this week the force of the law rounded and landed on Luc.

'*Je critique Luc*,' began a girl who Tabitha doesn't know well. 'He was mean to Tabitha in sport and called her a *gros mot*.' (A swearword, literally 'a big word'.)

'*Je critique Luc*,' read the next slip of paper. 'He tripped Tabitha on her way to the bathroom and then he laughed.'

'*Je critique Luc*,' read the next slip, and the next, and the next.

Luc's face, Tabitha explains solemnly, got redder and redder, and then he cried. He was given the *bâton* and the chance to explain himself. He made a few excuses and sniffled, and then fell silent.

Alain held the baton. 'Our friendship is very important to me, Luc,' he said, 'but I cannot be friends with you if you keep being so mean to Tabitha.'

'Has anybody else seen Luc being mean to Tabitha?' Madame Montagne asked.

'*Oui, moi*,' the class chorused as one. Madame Montagne beckoned Luc up to the front. 'Bring me your *cahier de liaison*,' she said. This is the book that children bring home every night for their parents to inspect and sign. (We stopped bothering months ago, and our teachers don't care. They know they can speak to us every day at the gate if they need to.) In the book, Madame Montagne drew an angry face for him to explain to his parents.

'You are on a watchlist,' she said. 'If you step out of line in the next week you will be on sanctions. Do you understand?'

'*Oui*,' sniffled Luc.

Madame Montagne asked Tabitha if she had anything to say.

'I don't want Luc to get into trouble, but I do want him to stop,' she said. 'It's not all his fault and I don't want him to be upset.' Tabitha said all of this to Madame Montagne in English so that she could be sure the translation to the class was clear.

This is a huge moment for Tabitha. She has been navigating this problem by herself, using her barely blossoming interpersonal skills and communicating in her halting French, and she's shocked by what has transpired, still processing the invisible crowd of support that rose up around her today.

Together the kids and I walk the long way through town to get to the Lidl. We fill the schoolbags and my cheese-stinky backpack with sausages and apples and ketchup and comforting, sweet American bread. We spend some good quality time hovering over the ice-cream fridge choosing the luxury four-piece set we will have for dessert, going eventually for caramel ice-sticks dipped in nuts.

When we get home we shut the door of the Wormhole slightly harder than necessary, and we make our sausage sangers and eat them watching YouTube clips of news bloopers and funny animals, cuddled together under Big Bertha. It's been a day, but we're all okay – and Keith is home tomorrow, thank God.

The sexy pompiers

I'm trying to teach the girls the funny walk from *Laverne & Shirley* when a pair of firefighters cut in front of us and stride down the road.

'*Les sexy pompiers*,' we whisper to each other and giggle. French *pompiers*, in their tight black uniforms, are always referred to as the '*sexy pompiers*' by the family. It's not appropriate, but it is accurate.

I whisper a line from 'Baby Got Back' to Tabitha, referring to the contours of the *pompiers*' buttocks and how they might jiggle them. It's bad parenting but it makes us laugh.

But then one of them glances back at us, and Tabitha and I stare at each other in horror. We are so used to the freedom of speaking English that we don't always modify our voices.

'*Je suis désolée*,' I whisper to the *pompiers*' backs. '*Je suis une* sex pest.'

This school day starts and ends with the *sexy pompiers*, but the second time they appear it's significantly less lighthearted. Keith does the pick-up in the afternoon. I'm in the bottom room straightening up the lounges when he returns, and even before they open the door I can hear the girls crying. It takes a while for everybody to get the story out.

At the afternoon gate, Keith tells me, there was a crowd. An ambulance was leaving as he arrived, but blocking the road were the local police, a crew of *sexy pompiers* and parents in small, intense clutches.

When the gates opened the children swarmed out, wailing.

Tabitha ran to Keith in tears, and Biggles and Mabel followed, confused. On the way home, Tabitha filled Keith in, and now she retells the story to me. Léon, the boy in Tabitha's class who caused me such stress as excursion-parent, lost his rag entirely today.

The class had gathered for PE when Léon kicked Amélie in the back of the legs so hard that she fell over. The teacher cancelled the sports lesson and the children all rounded angrily on Léon. Back in the classroom Léon got more and more worked up. When Alain walked past his desk, Léon stuck out a foot so that Alain tripped. From the floor, Alain shouted at Léon, who leapt on him and started punching Alain hard, in the head.

The classroom erupted with screaming and shouting. Madame Montagne, who would have shut the situation down quickly, was away. A substitute teacher had the class, Tabitha says, and she managed to get Léon in an armlock before another teacher ran in and helped restrain him. When Alain tried to stand, he fell over.

Tabitha is distressed retelling this part of the story, tears flowing down her cheeks. Mabel listens, her face stricken.

'He lay there sort of twitching, Mum. He couldn't speak and he looked so weird. That's when they ran to call the ambulance.'

Head injury? It's a grim picture Tabitha is painting. At this point, the whole class was crying and shouting at Léon, who had curled into a ball on the floor.

Alain was able to walk to the ambulance, I ascertain. This makes me feel better, even though Tabitha says he walked supported, with a limping, strange gait. It seems reasonable that the school would call an ambulance. But the *sexy pompiers*? The police?

By the time the parents got to the gates the whole school was crying, the smaller children set off by the bigger ones, in a contagion of histrionics.

I know how dramatic Alain is. I hope he was just playing to the crowd. But I love this little boy and I am desperately worried about him.

Is he in hospital? Have they done a CAT scan? Eventually I manage to get hold of his father.

'What? Alain is fine!' he says. "E ees go to 'is circus class!'

Life in France is so hard for me to figure out at the best of times, but this one takes the cake. The next morning the gates run hot with gossip.

'Léon told a girl he would cut her head off!' Gigi tells me. 'He said he would kill everybody!'

I love the wild drama of it all, of course, but this is drama without subtitles and it is very confusing.

The next day a crisis psychology team visits to chat with the children.

'They said that if things get crazy, we should run,' says Biggles. 'Oh, and if there is acid, put your shirt over your nose.'

Léon never returns to École Albert Camus. I am told that he is sent to another school, but nobody seems to know or care. None of my school mums want to talk about what might be going on for this kid who, at nine, is careering off the rails.

'He is bad egg,' the school mums tell me with a shrug. I think again about the wildness of schoolyard life here, especially when I learn that the last time the *pompiers* were here, it was because a parent threatened to kill a teacher. I'm reminded of the terrorism protocols – the reason behind those imposing gates and no-visitor policy and advice on managing acid attacks. I wonder what is next in store for Léon.

I question again our decision to bring the kids here. Is this whole resilience-through-adversity theory just a notion I've picked up and then clung to, like when Tabitha was a baby and I worried desperately that she hadn't 'found her hands', like the milestone book told me she should have? Why had she not 'found her hands'? Would she never? Was she destined to travel through life trying desperately to clutch for bus poles, to smear nail polish with gay abandon, to fail at the noble art of masturbation?

At every stage of the children's development I look back on my past parenting efforts with a sort of rueful sadness, regarding Past Rachael as something of a well-meaning idiot. Is this whole France Experience another of those examples? Am I putting the children in real, present danger through my own desires to keep life interesting?

Farting above my own arse

Keith makes far fewer mistakes in French than I do, but there's always room for humiliation. Today, he is walking through Rue Canard with Kat when he pronounces the word 'neck' with a certain unfortunate flourish that makes it mean 'dick'.

'I hurt my dick last night,' he tells Kat.

She stops short. 'What?!' she barks, laughing so hard she is bent double at the waist. Keith and I are never sure what sets Kat off, so we usually just push through.

'I think I slept on it funny,' he continues.

Kat won't let this one go for weeks. It's right up her alley.

''Ow ees your dick?' she calls to Keith every time they see each other, and if I'm there too she adds, 'And you, Rachelle, you're horny?'

Keith, aside from the occasional comedy blunder, can converse with anybody, even if the news moves too fast for him to keep up with, and by this stage Mabel and Tabitha speak it pretty well too, including an eye-watering number of *gros mots*. Here's the deal, we tell the children: in France you can swear in English, and back in Australia you can swear in French, but you can't swear in the language of the country you are living in.

243

Biggles stubbornly insists on speaking as little French as possible, outside his *Boulangerie* French. As for me, I remain a dunce: queen of the accidental *gros mot* and the shameful faux pas. My Politician French and my Supermarket French are now fluent but my conversation still sucks. Parting ways with Kat, I mean to call '*À plus tard*' or 'See you later', but I accidentally shout '*À putain!*' This is 'whore' or 'fuck' depending on context. Either one is less than ideal in terms of polite intercourse. Kat will tease me about this for the next week.

Maurice teaches me the classic swear *putain de merde*, or 'fucking shit', which is a pleasing expostulation, the plosive beginning and lingering final vowel leaving room for various interpretations. It's a phrase for all occasions, and Maurice and I take great pleasure in communicating through it. I take every opportunity to make Maurice giggle. He is so dear to me, this septuagenarian in his wire-framed glasses and his fraying cardigans. '*Putain de merde, monsieur*,' I say to him in polite greeting as we kiss three times.

Whenever possible I throw in some of my favourite French words and phrases: *Tout de suite! Pas de tout! À table!* Momo teaches me the lovely *me ému*, which means 'I am moved' or 'I am emotional', and Nannette teaches me the phrase *dormir sur ses deux oreilles* or 'to sleep on one's two ears': to have a lovely night's sleep, as though everything is at peace with the world.

But my favourite French expression remains *Péter plus haut que son cul*, or 'To fart above your arse'. The spare, incisive Australian translation: to be 'up yourself'. Devastatingly, at this late stage I am yet to encounter a cross-eyed baby. *Putain de merde.*

With my English-speaking French friends, we communicate in Franglish whether they like it or not, as I pepper my conversation with French words as I learn them. I worry that this habit has become a little beyond my control. I am sure that once home, little Frenchisms will start popping out of me, at the pub for instance. '*Oui! Moi aussi! J'adore!*' I will say, farting above my own arse as my friend Sarah sinks to the ground weeping with laughter. Like Kat with Keith's dick, Sarah will never let me live it down.

~

The complexity of the lives of my Calade classmates is revealed over time. Josephine and I become close to Maryam and Mosel, a pair of glamorous Syrian lawyers. They are refugees from war who arrive in class shell-shocked at the reality of starting their lives over, having moved with their toddler son from a huge house in Damascus to a small flat in Rue Canard. I cook dinner in the top room for them and invite Maurice and Mimi, my Brazilian sausage Josephine and her partner Pierre, and a couple of the neighbours. We laugh and toast. Maurice and Madame Fanny swap stories of Sommières in the 60s (Larry Durrell features once again). Conversation is tricky but there are translators at the table and the warmth in the room transcends the language barrier. Mosel stretches his long, slender arm out to full wingspan to capture the whole table in a photo we all immediate dub a 'Moselfie'.

Shy, sweet Amal from Albania is denied asylum. I picture him in his AC/DC T-shirt, holding his small son's hand on the walk to school every day. When I hear his news, told through tears, I feel like a ridiculous dilettante enjoying my 'year of adventure'. I cannot imagine what will happen to Amal, who just wants a safe, ordinary life. Shirin from Iran, who likes to wear a T-shirt that reads 'Babe' in hot-pink script, stops wearing her hijab one day. We don't ask questions. We just show up to class, stay in our careful boundaries, make each other laugh and step into greater intimacy when required.

Sitting in that classroom I think about the quiet beachside bubble of home. I think about the safe and nurturing idyll of childhood there, the lazy freedom that comes with being born into a never-seriously-threatened democracy. When you don't know hunger you can give outsized value to the virtues and failings of varying kinds of nut milks. With access to universal health care you are free to object to childhood vaccination schedules. This kind of privilege can act as an insulating blanket against reality. It feels permanent. The safety of it feels immutable. But it is all a hugely privileged fiction.

We are a vibrant, diverse and multicultural society in Australia, but we squander our riches, failing to recognise how lucky we are. The experience and wisdom of migrants and asylum seekers are undervalued, and those born here have never suffered through a civil war, an invasion or a significant attack on our own soil. Our great tragedy is our failure to honour 60,000 plus years of Indigenous history and to cherish the treasure we hold of being guests of the oldest culture on Earth on their wide, brown lands. The treatment of First Nations citizens in Australia is a collective, continuing national shame.

Keith and I have been able to move our kids across the globe for the luxury of a personal adventure. We can practise our virtuous habits of frugality and sustainability with the breezy ease of hobbies because the safety nets of privilege stretch below us, invisible and strong. The basic needs of our existence – food, shelter, safety – are so easily met that we are free to dabble in the upper levels of self-actualisation: creativity, reflection, tinkering with dreams and desires. An accident of birth has placed us in this position. Pure dumb luck. With a roll of the cosmic dice, this could all change.

Here at the Calade, we untangle the intricacies of French bureaucracy as fellow students navigate their way through tax paperwork, *cartes de séjour* (residence permits) and documents asserting the right to work. The world goes on outside – war, Trump, global politics – but we hardly discuss these things at all. We talk about children and food, shopping and skin care. We take excursions to the snow, the Roquefort cheese factory, a discount store, a famous bridge. Our Calade bubble is a sort of other-worldly place, a liminal land where our superficial conversations are infused with shimmering, untold backstories of war and social breakdown and heartbreak and families far away. Outside the classroom there are noisy bigots and fundamentalists, their hateful views fanned by the hot breath of a diabolical media machine. But inside that room we are just everyday schmucks, doing our best to cope with – as the Buddhist proverb has it – our ten thousand joys and ten thousand sorrows. We lean into our similarities, which are far more common than our differences. Democracy is not debated but lived in this room.

My experiences at the Calade are perhaps the most enriching of my lucky, safe life. Around this ordinary table, our mélange of accents and ideas merge into something idiosyncratic, unrepeatable and precious. I may not have learned how to speak French so well (mime skills notwithstanding) but the lessons I take here will infuse the rest of my life. What more could I ask of a classroom?

Life goes on at home in Australia. One day Mum admits on the phone that Dad is in hospital. He's having a stent put in after he had a 'bad turn' and the doctor found a massive blockage in an artery. She's cagey, too, about her own health. I can tell that there are details she is hiding from me. Sitting at my battered dining table, bare feet on the cool stone floor, I imagine Mum on her tiny Coledale deck, anxiously crossed legs in some random op-shop chair. I feel very far away.

People come to stay

The dining table, both extendable leaves attached, is outstretched to its most generous capacity. Tonight the restaurant is full. Two sets of friends are visiting at the same time and the house is happily bursting at the seams.

Our friend Lucy from Australia sits across from me peeling potatoes. Biggles has drawn his chair up close to mine, and he's happily buried in his Minecraft book. I decide it's a good moment for a little Person Practice.

'Three questions, Biggles,' I say. He looks at me desperately, but I nod firmly and squeeze his knee. 'Why don't you have a chat with Lucy?'

I've been talking to Biggles about the Three Questions theory, a concept I read about recently. This listening hack is supposed to help you drop deeper into conversation with another. It goes like this: you ask a person a question, and then without replying about yourself, or using their remarks as a jumping-off point for your own opinion, you ask another question about what they have just told you. And then you do it once more. I think Biggles, who finds socialising so challenging, may like the clear structure of this theory, and warm, kind Lucy is a very safe person to practise on.

'What do you do for a job?' Biggles asks in his quiet voice.

'I'm a doctor,' Lucy replies.

'What kind of doctor?' he parries. All good so far. Lucy shoots me a glance and I give her a reassuring smile.

'Sexual health and drugs, mostly,' she says.

'What kind of drugs?' Biggles asks.

Lucy looks panicked. Keith and I nod encouragingly.

'Well,' she says valiantly, 'ice, and some heroin and also ... cocaine, I guess.'

'That's three questions!' Biggles says with triumph.

I congratulate him before he scampers away to read in a safer location. Keith and I share a quick pleased nod. Life is good! Biggles just had a conversation with an adult and there are roasted potatoes in our near future! Lucy looks a little uneasy, but she'll recover.

Spring is in her full plumage, and from now into the summer, we will have a steady stream of visitors. We've got into the swing of running the Wormhole as a little bed and breakfast. All our systems are in place, the menus and Intermarché shopping lists adjusted to their new requirements. One of the great benefits of being so far away is that when friends come, we really spend time together, deep-diving into shared meals and long walks and late nights. In comparison with so many of our relationships here the communication is effortless.

We take our visitors on our favourite hike to the castle at Pic St Loup, on daytrips to nearby Avignon and Nîmes, and to eat fresh oysters and drink rosé at the Saturday market. We take them along on the school run and introduce them to our friends, who inspect the Australians with fascination, like they are exotic bugs under a scope. The children thunder together up and down the spiral stairs, and we all walk Rue Canard, exploring the *brocantes* and boutiques. My girlfriends buy vintage sheets from Juliette and art from Cédric. We all give the full Withering Parisian to Scary Cool Guy.

Mostly we eat and play cards and drink wine and laugh around the kitchen table. I construct cheese platters and serve aperitifs and sling out the tried and true horde-feeding favourites: lasagne, casseroles and quiche, with fancy salads and lots of greens. Always there are mountains of potatoes. Mabel makes her Caprese sticks and Tabitha her Eton mess. Biggles clears plates and stacks the dishwasher.

Mabel makes a poster for the visitors:

Rules in France

- Don't do a poo while somebody is in the bath
- Don't get in someone's bed without permission
- Ask Mum if you're hungry
- Make a joke if you've got one
- Don't get angry when people are singing and dancing

Mabel and a friend's daughter, Isla, both six, fashion themselves as 'cleaning ladies' and spend three days sweeping the house. The children take Dan, another visiting friend, along to a chess tournament. I upset Tabitha one night asking her to explain Sausage Marriage to the group around the table. She's embarrassed, and I feel terrible that I have stepped outside the boundaries of what is okay to share. I apologise. Tabitha is growing and changing. I must readjust.

Ross and his daughter Élodie are staying in the house, while our friends Dim, Lucy and Quentin, with twelve-year-old Dan, have rented an apartment nearby. They are introduced to Bad Sommières on the day that Dim decides to let Dan walk alone to our house from theirs. It's a short distance, just one street away, and Dim decides to thrill Dan with a little independence. Unfortunately she chooses the day that our street is shut down by the police.

A man is hiding out in a Rue Canard apartment after shooting another man dead in Nîmes. He's connected by some degree to Bad Fonzie, and to the brother who stabbed another brother outside the post office a few years back. A rough crowd. The police track him back to Rue Canard, where the man refuses to leave the apartment, and the resulting siege shuts the street down for hours. We've only just found out about this when Dim calls.

'*Bonjour!*' she says. 'I've just sent Dan up to your place on his own!'

'Now?' I squeak, and run downstairs to intercept. Dan is safe, luckily, but he's stuck with us for a few hours before the police get their man and Rue Canard returns to business as usual. All's well that ends with a great story for Dan to tell his friends back in Australia.

Keith sees Juliette, who knows the backstory. A crime of passion, she explains. An affair, a jealous guy. '*C'est la vie!*' She shrugs. 'It's life, you know?'

When friends go home we take the leaves out of the battered dining table and readjust the Wormhole routines to our gang of five. We all fall into a bit of a slump after each of our visitors leaves. The work of hosting and socialising is hectic, so there's a relief to calming the system down again, but losing the easy connection of beloved friends is sad.

Pichets and dreams

The arm of my back-up spectacles has fallen off. Both my proper pairs of reading glasses have been crunched underfoot on the cobblestones, and with only a couple of months before we get home so I can get new health-fund prescription glasses, I'm dealing with these magnifying readers from a rack at the Intermarché. But now even my back-ups are buggered, like the rest of me.

When I make it up the stairs to work at 6am, on the Bulgarian keyboard of my borrowed laptop with the sleep disorder, I have to hold my head very still so my glasses don't fall off. Go to France, they said! You'll be sophisticated, etc, etc!

As we draw towards the end of the final school term, a glorious thing happens. Keith and I finally get all three kids to go to the *cantine* for lunch. This means they will be spending the full day at school. Originally I had imagined that the children would go to *cantine* every day, enjoying the full three-course lunch and allowing me the freedom of the day for my own schedule – trips by bus into Montpellier or Nîmes, perhaps, or lunches alone with Keith in nearby towns. Ha ha! See the children smile! See the lady laugh and tear the notebook called 'Plans' into tiny pieces! See the scraps flutter down over the pavement like teardrops!

It has never worked out like that. School has been such an intense experience that there has rarely been a time when at least one of the three kids hasn't needed those two hours in the middle of the day to regroup and cope with the afternoon. And if one was coming home for lunch, the others would be desperate to come too, and why not? The day is lost for any alternative purpose anyway.

But then: a Tuesday when all three are in robust enough form for a full school day, including lunch. The menu for the day, posted on the board outside the gates, is as follows:

Salade verte (green salad)
Escalope de poulet au jus (chicken with gravy)
Légumes aïoli (vegetables in aioli)
Montboissié (cheese)
Flan au chocolat (chocolate tart)

Keith and I go for a date for lunch at Chez Tibère on the river. We scan the water for Charles and Camilla but can't find them. We order a large *pichet* of icy sauvignon blanc from the waiters. There's a narrow road hugging the Vidourle, and the restaurant's tables are on the river side while the kitchens are across the road in the restaurant building. To serve us, the waiters must cross the road. They are nimble, practised at dodging traffic, and they put on quite a show as Keith and I dip prawns into sauce and trade dreams about the future.

We entertain each other a little with notions of how we might stay in Sommières. Where would we live? How would it work? We can feel a shift in the children, especially Tabitha. In these last few weeks she is speaking so much French, and given a little more time, she would be absolutely fluent. Mabel too is very settled, and although Biggles hates school, we take this with a grain of salt. He hates school in Australia too, and in the Wormhole he is happy and relaxed with his books and his games and his Friendys.

The teachers, despite the shouting and the foghorns, are very kind. By this stage there is no homework pressure. Tabitha gets her work done at school, Mabel is too small to have any and Biggles's teacher handles him with a very light touch. We assume that she feels that just coping with the language is enough hard work, and we agree. He's not yet ten, after all.

The dreams slip away with the *pichet*, and soon it's time to return to school for pick-up. There's no way, we know, of staying here in Sommières. Even if we could manage the visa process again and negotiate agreement from the children, Mum is still not well, Dad is recovering from his heart scare and Keith's mum, although strong as an ox, loves and misses her grandchildren too. Another year is off the table.

'This is what life will be like when we retire, Cakes,' I say to Keith. 'Dinner at four-thirty. I'll order you a prune cocktail to keep things regular.'

'Waiter! Your finest back cushion for my wife!' Keith says. 'We'll rent a one-bedroom with a view of the river and drink gin looking out the window, Chops. Can't wait.'

With the last of the wine, Keith and I clink glasses and promise to come back when the children grow up and scatter to their own adventures. We've needed this moment of leisurely indulgence together. This last few weeks, anxiety has been sitting, like a damp and heavy animal, on my chest. I have felt overwhelmed with the tasks before me, unable to drop any balls but incapable of juggling them with skill. I feel that I am kicking hard, but still drowning, and I feel a disconnection from Keith, who is so full up with tasks of his own that he has no room for my worries.

Along with his busy work life, he's been fitting in the extra tasks of entertaining our visitors. Since they're on holiday, our friends are looking to pack experiences into every moment, and so Keith must do double duty, hosting and socialising while also facing the normal schedules and demands of his growing business. We've been retreating into our own solutions rather than leaning into each other. The Dungeon is a little cold.

While I manage the ups and downs of daily life with the kids, I battle through my manuscript, switching between my two broken laptops and adjusting my one-armed spectacles. I soak my sore back in the bath and send my energy into the menu, kneading dough at lunchtime for evening pizzas with fresh mozzarella and basil, slowly simmered tomato sauce and Ligurian olives.

Our lunch date is so restorative. Keith and I head back to school, ducking down the stone stairs to follow the river along the small path below street level.

'Bingo!' I say, pointing out Charles and Camilla in the reeds. Keith gives me a high five and then helpfully pushes my bum back up the steps, before we before we walk, hand-in-hand and slightly wine-buzzed, past Momo's house and through the square to school.

We're pleased to have squeezed in a romantic meal. Keith and I trade off nights at the Sisters' Bar so we can each blow off steam with friends, and we love to be home together pottering about, but time one on one, experiencing France, is rare. This year has been a period of intense growth for all of us, and the romance of the experience has been inextricably embedded in the difficulties of it. We built this rich and lovely life together, and it's taken both of our different skill sets to manage it. I can't imagine how I could have navigated this year without Keith at my side: his steady counsel, his easy jokes and his ability to see the big picture when I am caught, stuck and floundering in the weeds of the moment; and I know that he sees the work on my part that runs the complicated machinery of our lives.

The weeks slip away with increasing speed. Time has the wind at its back. *Brocante*, drug house, *boulangerie*; *bonjour, coucou, salut* – the rituals and routines of our France life so second-nature that almost before we know it, it is June, and we are coming to the end of our final term at École Albert Camus.

The school play

I don't always have the energy for parent-socialising in these last weeks of term, nor for the antics of Franc and Alain. I arrive for school pick-up last-minute, lurk at the corner and signal to the children when they appear. On the walks to school and back, we usually have my bonus sons. Franc tenderly settles Mabel on the foot pegs of his bicycle and races her home, while Alain loves to talk to me in his animated way. One day, telling a story, Alain kicks his foot in the air so hard that his shoe flies off and lands in a backyard on the other side of a high wall with a wire sleeve running atop it. We try and fail to retrieve the shoe. Alain is distraught. In the end Biggles runs to fetch Keith, who leaves work to come down, climb the wall and retrieve Alain's sneaker, while bystanders watch from below, arms folded, giving advice. Scaling a wall, solving a puzzle, chatting in French, helping the kids: it's the kind of work interruption that Keith adores.

On hot afternoons the children and I take the back path to the Lidl supermarket, cutting through the swamplands behind the school. A bushy, overgrown path winds through marshy scrub and pops out, unexpectedly, at the carpark edge. We pop in and grab ice-cream to eat lazily on the long-way-round walk back to the Wormhole.

In the last week of term Mabel complains of feeling sick on the walk to school, and then vomits a copious puddle at the gates. I'm so used to

257

treating all complaints of illness as a somatised psychological state that I am momentarily taken aback.

'I guess we'd better go home, Mabey,' I say as children stare, bug-eyed, through the gates. Back at the house Mabel hands me a set of crumpled pages as she clutches her bucket on the couch.

'I have to learn all my lines,' she says, 'for the school play. It's on tomorrow night.'

I stop in my tracks. No words come out of my open mouth. Mabel, bucket in hand, is grinning like a loon.

'I'm the lead!' she announces.

By the evening Mabel has rallied. I get the story from her: after another child dropped out of the lead role, the teacher asked Mabel to do it. She is playing a lizard. It's more than likely that notes were sent home with Mabel about the play. They may never have made it out of her school bag, or they might have gone straight into the bin or joined the sea of papers, Friendys and books that carpet the floor of the kids' room. But unlike a similar event at home, which would rope in parents to manage costumes, rehearsal schedules and tickets, this show has come together with no input from us at all.

Together we run lines with our little star. It's hard to believe, but Mabel seems ready to do this. From within the audience on the following evening we watch with wonder as our small girl, all recovered from her random illness, pipes away in French, spiky plaits peeping out below her *papier-mâché* lizard mask.

The play is acted by Mabel's class and the Big Sexies. They are four, five and six years old, shy in the spotlight, sweeter than stolen honey. The stage is a makeshift collection of tables and step stools arranged in the play area in front of rows of chairs. The children clutch each other's hands for comfort and whisper behind their masks. Many deliver their lines with their backs to the audience, unable to face all the eyes upon them, and teachers prompt and encourage from the wings.

I cannot follow the plot at all. Animals seem to wander about having problems, which Mabel and another lizard are trying to solve. But I'm overcome with pride to watch my little girl stand before the group and deliver lines in French. Her speech is fluent and laced with the particular accent of the area. Though she is so tiny she has travelled beyond me in this moment. I can only sit back, applaud and marvel. The thought of the children understanding this second language, which I have never managed to grasp past the basics, is amazing to me. It is one of so many examples of them growing up and away, into a place that transcends our ministrations, making us redundant, in that wonderful, bittersweet way: the aim of all Best-Guess Parenting.

Mabel may never remember much of this afternoon. Her capacity with the language will drop away, and so much of this experience will be like a strange dream. But I hope fervently that something will lodge deep inside her growing sense of self and place so that she is a little wiser, a little more compassionate, because of what she learned about being an outsider and relying on others. And perhaps one day when she travels the world and lands in France, some latent part of her language brain will turn a dusty key, and she will find herself rattling away in the French she never realised she had stored.

The evening is lowering. Mabey's play is coming to an end. The École Albert Camus kids, so familiar to me now, are forming a messy line, holding hands and taking their bows before the cheering, applauding audience. I look across the room to Gigi and Kat and Momo, and to Chloé and her sister Liesl, along with a clutch of their Rwandan family who have travelled from Belgium and Italy to see their beloved young Clémentine's performance. We grin at each other as we wipe our tears, united in the particular, heart-clutching magic of being a spectator to the wondrous unfolding of a child. My French might be terrible but my school mums and I understand each other perfectly.

Sommières summer

Heading towards the square I can hear shouting in the street. I pull Mabel closer and keep Biggles and Tabitha behind me as we approach. It's Juliette, arguing vociferously with Bad Fonzie's wife outside her shop. Oh no. Again? They are yelling so fast that I can't understand a word, while neighbours up and down the street stand on stoops and lean out of windows, smoking cigarettes and enjoying the show.

I give the action a wide berth but catch Juliette's eye.

'*Ça va?*' I ask.

'*Oui!*' she shouts, and rolls her eyes at me, with a hand gesture at Fonzie's wife that reads clearly, in the international language of frustration, This bitch! Fonzie's wife is outraged and raises the decibel in her response.

I keep on moving. It looks pretty intense, but I have faith that Juliette can handle herself. Very soon the noise is swallowed up by the square, where Ponytail is dragging chairs across the stone to set up for the day and an *aquarelle* artist has set up her stool and easel in an irritating place. I tut and purse my lips at her like a native as we rush past, late as usual.

Summer is in full swing, and Sommières is vibrating with joie de vivre. Every Monday night the Place du Marché under the clock tower hosts the glorious *Les Estivales*, where stalls sell fries and oysters and burgers, vineyards flog wine by the glass, children run everywhere and couples slow-dance to live music in the square. The Saturday market extends out into the street and then starts running on Wednesday night too as Sommières expands and spreads to its full high-season wingspan.

Life is lived outside. In the evenings the heat is deliciously estivating, and the residents of Rue Canard meet to drink and chat on the street. The snake guy hangs out on his stoop, sunning his python, and the senior tour groups in their unflattering shorts clog the streets with their elephantine pace. Children on their scooters are a hip-fracturing threat.

'Biggles!' I shriek, as he swoops especially close to one woman. She tuts at me and I roll my eyes at her – this is *our* town, lady – but out of her earshot I lecture Biggles on being more careful. Franc, with Mabel perched on his bike, skirts the seniors with graceful ease. In the street we run into Maryam and Mosel, who are walking with a tall, striking man in flowing brown robes. He has a long beard, a complicated hat and a heavy gilded cross that swings above his cassock. This is their Syrian Orthodox priest. We all beam as we are introduced.

One night we join the lantern festival, where every child in town carries a lighted candle in a procession across the bridge. This is a brilliantly loose event, featuring naked flames everywhere and a good amount of drinking. Biggles is in disgrace after he accidentally sets Tabitha's hair on fire outside the Bar du Nord. We head home, but our friends go on to L'Esplanade for the drinking and dancing.

The *arène* (arena) at the edge of town hosts much-loved bull events. The bull tradition of Sommières dates from the nineteenth century. Unlike the Spanish tradition the bull is not harmed, but for generations local young men have tested their mettle every summer in the ring. Watching the scene I start to grasp another layer of our wild little town.

The *raseteurs*, dressed in white, use a claw-like metal instrument called a *raset* to snatch rosettes, strings and ribbons tied to the animal's horns. The black Camargue bulls, nimble and lively, gallop about the ring with their heads down and their sweeping horns pointed up.

The small amphitheatre features a dusty circular centre ringed by stone benches, which are packed full of ebullient spectators. The pungent tang of weed wafts past my nose. Mabel sticks close to Keith, but Tabitha and Biggles eat churros on the first-row bench with the other kids, lifting their feet out of the way of the bulls, who frequently leap the guardrails and run along the passageways in front of the bleachers.

One day we go to watch the *toro piscine*, a crazy bull-fighting event for kids in which a small, rectangular pool is set up in the middle of the dusty arena and children compete to run and jump in the water before the mini-bull can catch them. Tabitha begs to be allowed to run in and tease the bull, but Keith and I draw the line. A teenage boy trips while running away, rolling under the hooves of the massive animal for a horrifying moment before he leaps the gate, a little bloodied but essentially unharmed. He sheepishly hangs his head as his mother berates him loudly, before she laughs and pulls him into a rough hug.

From Momo and Andre's window above the road we watch the *bandido*, a tradition where the bulls are released to run from one end of the street to the other and herded onto a flatbed truck by *gardians* on horseback. There is no *encierro* this year, where bulls are released into the barricaded streets, in a 'running of the bulls' scenario, but it often features in the Sommières summer calendar. Momo tells me with delight how the bulls sometimes escape the barricades and run through the crowd.

With Alex and Manuel, we have a wonderful dinner in Momo's backyard after we watch the *bandido*. I'm really happy to bring Mosel and Maryam and introduce them to these kind friends. We attend to the gang of children, eat pork with prunes and apples and drink red wine. Alex and I sing 90s classics while she plays her ukelele, and sneak away from Tabitha to smoke rollies on the stoop. Mosel captures a Moselfie of the whole gang.

Now in full summer, the sun is hot and sharp. It bounces off the stone, unrelieved by any greenery, and clothes dry in an hour on the baking terrace. The Château Gonflable, a pop-up jumping-castle park, has appeared on the far side of town. Under some patchy trees there are half a dozen temporary waterslides, a few picnic tables and a kiosk selling cheap ice-creams and wretched coffee. We visit after school on especially hot days, but more often we swim off the footbridge in the shallow Vidourle. We find a hidden staircase to the river and take to popping down in the long evenings to throw stones and splash in the water. Charles and Camilla occasionally join us.

We leave town on the weekends too, packing picnics of baguettes and cheese and fruit and visiting museums and cafes in Avignon and Arles and small, quaint towns around Provence. We attend the Great Roman Games, a re-enactment festival, at the Arena of Nîmes, one of the best-preserved Roman coliseums in the world. Across thirty-four terraces, a crowd of twenty thousand perches on the same stone benches as those ancient Romans did, waving handkerchiefs to tell the MC to 'Kill!' or 'Spare!' the gladiators, as they did two thousand years ago. The crowd roars. It is dizzying.

Hiking up the spectacular Pic Saint-Loup, we crawl around the ruins of a twelfth-century castle and eat our baguettes on rocks overlooking a scrubby hillside. At night we lie around together in the bottom room watching our shows, playing *Monopoly* and reading out loud. We've finished *Death on the Nile* and started *Murder on the Orient Express*.

Late on the night of Juliette's argument, we've been eating margarita pizza and playing cribbage at the joint by the river. Walking home, we encounter Juliette carrying chairs across the road with the deft ease of the fleet-footed riverside waiters. I didn't know Juliette had picked up a second job, but this is common among our friends here. The town is so dead in the winter that everybody makes a bit of extra bank in the summertime.

'Hello!' we call. 'Are you okay?'

'But of course!' she smiles, drawing me into a hug. 'Ze neighbour? Don't worry, please, my God.'

She ruffles Biggles's hair before he can shrink away.

'It is fine, I 'ad to finish zis stupid problem. On and on, you know, for months, zis woman give me trouble. I 'ave zis,' she says, gesturing to her eye. It is purpling into a deep bruise.

'Eek,' I say. 'Looks painful.'

''Eet's nothing,' Juliette says. She smiles wickedly. 'She look much, much worse. Ze talking, you know, I 'ad enough. I swing' – she demonstrates – 'and *voilà*! Ze talking stop.'

I can't help but be sorry I missed it. I love all of this madness: the heat, the sweat, the gossip, the action. It's exhausting but it's so exciting. These kinds of fiery arguments don't happen in Coledale. It could be that the veganism makes for general muscle weakness, but fights take the form of snarky commentary on Facebook or perhaps a snub at the P & C trivia night. It's only in Sommières that I could face the possibility of being in an actual fistfight, and only in Sommières that I would have my flashing-eyed Celtic sidekick to back me up. I'm very glad that Juliette is with me and not against me.

The centre will hold

One incredible day, I finish the first draft of *Mothering Heights*. I sit for a moment looking at the words 'The end' and trying to take them in. I can't quite believe it. It's not a book in the hand, or even a manuscript with a publisher, and this first draft needs, I know, a huge amount of work. It may never take the form of an actual book-shaped object in an actual shop-shaped bookstore. But the deep and powerful sense of achievement I feel is real. I have never really believed that I had the focus or the grit to make it to the end of this project, but here I am. I ate this elephant, one bite at a time, and whatever happens from here, I know I have that capacity.

Keith and the kids are down at L'Esplanade having a drink with Mosel and Maryam, Josephine and Pierre, and Kat. I head there with a bounce in my step. At the bar I confer with the owner to establish the second-cheapest bottle of champagne, and then I carry it out with a tray of glasses to where our friends are gathered around a wooden table under the spreading green umbrella of a huge tree. This is a moment worth celebrating, I think to myself, and this is a tradition I am starting, and maybe it will not be the only time I celebrate a finished first draft with a bottle of sparkling, because I now know I can write a book. I wrote a book!

We toast, all my friends delighted for me, and then I notice the red, blue and white bunting hung over the peach stone building of the bar, the tree branches and the wooden furniture.

'*C'est quoi?*' I ask. I really should get this phrase on a hat.

'*La Coupe du Monde!*' the group shouts at me.

Oh, the World Cup. Of course!

It's quite a day for France – they have made it to the grand final and everybody is pumped for the match tonight. As the evening wears on L'Esplanade fills with people dressed in French colours. Flags are waving everywhere. The energy builds to a fever pitch through the game and then explodes with joy when France wins. A hundred French men, women, children and small dogs go nuts as a DJ plays 'I Will Survive'. They dance in messy, euphoric conga lines, do the cancan, make limbo cords out of the bunting and proudly bellow the national anthem, 'La Marseillaise'. The streets are ringing with honking horns and I am really proud because, just quietly, I think it might all be because of me. I've been at this party before.

In 1998 I was backpacking with my sister and we landed in Paris on the night that France won the World Cup for the first (and so far only other) time. Sam and I were not into sport. We barely knew that the World Cup was a thing (I haven't improved much in this regard, twenty years on). But we loved the night-life and we liked to boogie, and that night Paris erupted into the biggest party we'd ever seen.

The streets were surging. A man lifted me off my feet, swung me through the air and planted a huge kiss on me, and then Sam and I spent the next hours in a dancing, singing procession up the Champs-Élysées. It was a sterling introduction to the concept of joie de vivre.

I needed the help. In 1998 I was struggling with chronic pain after my speedboat accident and the resulting year in bed recovering. By the time I landed in Paris I was both chronically depressed and expert at avoiding thoughts of the future, and after that World Cup party I spent two years in London running away from myself, desperately scared of what the rest of my life would look like.

From L'Esplanade, champagne in hand, I remember that ghost of myself, a young woman who was so afraid that she would never have a pain-free or productive life. Time folds like an envelope. There I am, fresh-faced and dancing up the Champs-Élysées, most likely wearing a vintage nightie over a tight T-shirt washed poorly in a hostel bathroom, and shrouding the quiet, stinky shame of my chronic pain in a cocktail of alcohol and euphoria.

Kat throws her arms around me, and the past dissolves: here I am, back in France twenty years later, surrounded by friends as the streets ring with honking horns and shouts of *'Allez les bleus!'* – 'Go the blues!'

Our experiences write our stories. I am here now, whole and healed, but that broken version of me remains, in shadow. I think of Keith and me, in what now feels like the distant past, sharing with each other all those articles and ideas about the impact of living overseas on the 'creative brain' of children, so ignorant of how life would truly unfold.

'Cognitive flexibility,' I breathed into his ear all those months ago. 'Depth and integration of thought,' he moaned. 'Neural pathways! Neural pathways!' we cried together, before settling back to light a smug cigarillo.

I wonder. Has it been a positive experience for Biggles to spend half his school year asleep on his desk? Certainly watching him circle the pole did not make us think that he was thriving. What about Tabitha and her friendship struggles? Her ability to manage the schoolyard bully in a second language was remarkable. But at what cost? As for Mabel, so small, would her nascent brain have fared better with the safety and security of a known universe, as opposed to the forced new shoots of growth she developed when thrust into such an unfamiliar environment?

Keith and I have always comforted ourselves with the idea that this gamble will fall, overall, on the positive side of the scales. But perhaps the experience is lodging itself in a different place, a place of confusion and anxiety, where the sand is shaky beneath a child's feet. The thing about Best-Guess Parenting is that there is no clear answer.

One aspect of life is sacrificed for another, one child's need weighed against the others', all this work a fiction, really – a pointless shield against the inevitable pain of life faced by each child differently. My miserable time spent running away from my chronic pain saw me circle and return to myself in this wild little town, surrounded by friends, with a drink in my hand. Would I have found the pleasure without the struggle? Would I have planted my feet in it with such gratitude? Is that shadow self – the flaw, the crack – perhaps the most important mechanism?

I don't know what meaning this year will hold for the children. Ultimately, it will be up to them to tell us. (Hopefully not across a family-therapy couch with an earnest woman in statement jewellery.)

Will their experience seed some notions of compassion and social justice? Foster their resilience? Give a profound jolt to their imaginations? If nothing else, this crew can swear in French to a degree that would make a sailor clutch their pearls, a skill that will surely come in handy someday. *Putain de merde!*

These three children we are soon taking home are not the same three children we brought with us. This epic, rich adventure has not always been pleasant. We have blown the wind beneath their wings, but we have also singed their lovely feathers. Parenting is all change and course-correction. The sea does not force the fish. Adaptability is the constant requirement. For me, this year in France has been joyous and wonderful, but it's also required some painful evolution as a parent and a human. I've wobbled, but the centre will hold.

I don't crack on tonight, down in the dusty square by the river with the dogs and the cavorting middle-aged men in party wigs. I stay for the football; I shout and hoot and hug at the win. I even do a little cancan, a little conga and some *Fortnite* moves, to Tabitha's dismay, although I don't limbo (my back is a hundred times better than it was twenty years ago, but I'm still glued together with screws and bolts and my limbo days are long past).

Then I go home, happily leaving Keith to kick that party can down the road, because I have three children at my feet waiting for me to dish up the spag bol that's been simmering all afternoon so we can slurp it back on the couch with too much cheese, an episode of *Friends* and a fizzy lemon *sirop*. This is my treasure, my epic win: this everyday domestic bliss that I believed, for such a long sad time, was out of my grasp. It's a thrilling night for France but just as momentous for me too. We are, perhaps, each other's lucky charm.

The pack-up, in reverse

The outline of Mabey's spew at the school gate is visible for a couple of weeks. We point it out daily, in our glamorous way. A little touch of the homeland, perhaps. 'Hooroo! The Australians were here.' Ambassador Mode, activate!

Our days of doing the school run are nearly over. It's not a minute too soon for my feet, which become more painful every day, the cobblestones driving themselves deep into my flesh like a trauma memory. Traipsing these stone streets has become so normal that it's hard to believe that soon I'll be back home in Australia where life is navigated in the car, driving to school and play dates and classes. I'll miss the cobblestones, even if my feet won't.

In the last week at school, things are loose. The whole kindy class seems to have left already, including the teacher. Did we miss a memo? It's possible. All of our school admin has gone to smoke. Mabel just hangs out in the big kids' classroom, playing board games with her siblings and Franc and Alain. She could just stay home, but I gladly pack her off to school because I need the space. I'm running around like a chook with my head cut off.

Every morning I drop the kids off and race home to tackle the house, where I'm facing down two weeks to dismantle our lives, pack up and clean the whole place. There are no more visitors booked and my hosting days around the old wooden dining table are over. It's all about the bump-out now. Alongside the everyday mundane details of school snacks and lost socks, and the social whirl of summer, we're orchestrating our exit.

But before we get back to Australia: one last hurrah. We have a final month left to travel around before our flight home. What should we do with this incredible gift? It will be a long, long time before the five of us return to Europe. The cost of flights from Australia makes that an impossibility, let alone the pandemic we can't yet conceive of that will envelop the globe not long from now.

I dream of a barefoot month on Hydra, the Greek island where Leonard Cohen and his gang of artistic friends lived in the 60s, but Hydra is way out of our price range. I explore the idea of the Trans-Siberian Railway. We consider a month in Iceland. Corsica? Sardinia? I plug our dates into 'I'm Feeling Lucky' on Google Flights, and the internet delivers the specials: Tunisia! Wales! The Outer Hebrides! Nowhere is off the table. My sessions on the sofa researching options are luxurious and fantastical, and I am aware of the wonderful madness of this moment in time.

In the end we decide to make the most of this final time in Europe and take an old-fashioned road trip. We'll finish strong and go hard before we go home: four weeks, ten countries, one hatchback. We have a few friends to visit and Keith has a work stop to make, so we plan our first couple of days on the continent and leave the rest empty in order for the road to lead us.

Job portability is the key to the whole thing. We'll just take our normal work-from-home setup on the road and Keith will scramble all kinds of makeshift offices, from ironing boards to bathrooms. There are no Insta-worthy hotels and restaurants on our itinerary; rather, my accommodation-hunting involves careful screening of bottom-end Airbnb reviews. (One sample: 'Flat smelt weird and toilet contained a large unflushed poo.')

During our last two weeks in Sommières, Keith beavers away to clear space so that he can work only half-days for our big trip. He's caning it with work, and the pack-up of our France house is my job. It's a daunting task.

I am transported back to those long six months of prep before our arrival: the posters down the hallway of the house and that epic Master List. It's all happening in reverse now, with those six months truncated into two weeks. I must empty and sort out the house, pack all our stuff for home, prepare us for four weeks on the road and enact the end-of-lease clean – the mother of all cleans.

I set up my systems.

In the sunroom I start organising the road-trip gear. It's summer, so the kids need only a school backpack's worth of clothes. There's a Fun Bag for the car with books and toys and games, a suitcase for my gear and Keith's, and the Bathroom Bag for us all. The Swim Bag contains towels and goggles and costumes and sunscreen, and the Food Bag totes all the essentials for a travelling kitchen: the coffeepot, Tupperware containers, salt and pepper, coffee, tea, honey, vinegar, olive oil, garlic, emergency pasta, tinned tomatoes, crackers and nuts. A Car Bag for the front seat holds maps and papers and documents and chargers.

In the downstairs bedroom I gather a towering pile of all the gear that will be coming home with us. I must shrink our belongings to fit only what we can carry. Thankfully, visiting friends took a suitcase of our stuff home with them to Australia last month, but it's a hectic job trying to cull life down to the minimum, considering all the random bits and pieces we've added to our belongings over the last year. Using socks, I wrap Keith's coloured water glasses, my vintage butter dish and the two or three ornaments the children have bought, and I insert all my little packages into various boots. I pack the vintage linen sheets from the *vide-greniers*, and the old candlesticks that I bought in the Museum of Poland under the Communist Regime. I pull out the good old plastic space-saving bags and shrink-pack all the winter woollies.

275

Cracking my knuckles, I tackle the tall desk in the bottom room that holds all our documents. This job alone takes two days: when unloaded, it's a paper mountain containing everything from schoolbooks to formal paperwork, every souvenir menu and postcard collected this year, every story written by the children, every card received from home and every receipt I have shoved in a drawer. I sort and file, sort and file, keeping samples of maths work and essays, cards and notes for posterity, storing important papers for travel, and ditching the rest. I pack all the papers we are taking home into manila folders and zip them into the big suitcases.

When we return from our road trip, we'll have three days in Sommières to say our final farewells and finish cleaning the house. It's not enough time by far, so I scramble to clean as much as I can before we leave. Starting at the top of the house, I scrub the floors and wash all the cushion covers in the sunroom, and then I dismantle the kitchen from top to bottom. With my podcasts to keep me company, I go in hard, emptying cupboards and drawers and scrubbing them spotless, getting down on my knees to scour the flagstones. I empty and wash the fridge and dust the bookshelves, and then I remove our identity from the walls. I take down Mabel's list of Rules in France and the Morning Schedule, and then one by one I peel off the limp, lopsided post-it notes of French vocabulary that dot the room. I pack a few more sauces and vinegars and condiments in the Food Bag for the road trip and put the rest in a box for Kat.

I empty and clean the bathrooms and then I deep-dive into the children's bedrooms. One object at a time, I dismantle their France lives.

Up in Tabitha's mezzanine cave, I excavate lost socks and illicit sweet wrappers. I cart her random furniture pieces back down the ladder and into their places in the main house. Unable to stand upright in the small space, I awkwardly crouch to sweep and wash the floorboards. I pause for a moment when finished, contemplating this bare, empty space that was, for a while, such a strange and rich and deliciously private world for our tiny, funny girl. Tabby will sleep downstairs in the kids' room for these last days.

I sort that room next, starting by dismantling Mabey's ILoveYou.com business from the top bunk. Her fur 'business lady' coat is here, as well as a handful of desiccated garlic cloves, courtesy of the Friendys. Copies of Harry Potter lie about, read so many times that they are frayed and tattered. This room is a Hogarthian scene of chaos and disorder after hosting a year of energetic games. I think of the children piping away in the Friendys' falsettos, and then dropping into deep baritones to sing 'It All Revolves Around the Sausage'. I remember the Friendy Olympics, when each animal had three specialities and the debate over how to rate and score their efforts was a complex, endless conversation.

I think of Alain giggling and Franc wailing and Amélie throwing sudden, inexplicable fits of rage. I picture them all dancing to the pre-programmed demos of elevator muzak on the electronic piano. I remember the fireworks being set off on that notorious play date, and the acrobats bouncing along outside the window on our first astonishing morning.

Lying on my stomach I excavate books and toys and papers from deep under the beds. I vacuum the floor and then I get on my knees to scrub the flagstones. I pack sheets and towels and pillowcases into the road-trip piles and wash all the bedding to dry quickly in the searing midday sun. I edit clothes until only the road-trip essentials remain and take everything else downstairs to the give-away pile.

This pile is on the couch in the bottom room. Everything not coming on holidays or going back to Australia lands here, and I send the message out to my school-mum friends: *Sell-out Sale Saturday! Everything is Crap! Everything Must Go! Everything Free!* I make a plate of cakes for the friends who turn up all through the morning to inspect the high pile of toys and books and clothes on the couch. Anything left over I donate to the Croix-Rouge. Half of it came from there anyway. There's something of a lovely symmetry to that.

In the background of all this industry, the children start school holidays. Half the time Alain and Franc are over to play. I'm aware that soon we'll be gone, and that losing their Australian playmates will be a wrench for my little bonus sons. My three will miss their company, but they are also elated to be returning to friends at home.

The children rattle up and down the stairs playing *Loup Touche-Touche* and messing up my packing piles while I yell at them to stay out of the kitchen. In his office Keith tries to work through the noise. Outside his door our army of children thunder about, and outside his window the next-door TV blasts soap operas at high volume. If Keith shuts the window the noise is muted a little, but then he loses the breeze that makes the high summer bearable. He pushes through, a trooper, steady as she goes.

There's a final task for the children: the farewelling of the French Friendys. With Muscles, the giant leopard, in pride of place, the kids line Friendys in a row along the chaise longue: the cousins, aunts, estranged husbands and long-lost children of the Australian Friendys. Ms Chanandler Bong is there, the penguin Tabitha won at the bingo, along with Alivia Dog's mother, Spotty, and Bear Bear's twin sister, Alexandra (there was another sister, but she died in a gruesome house fire).

The kids try to angle for an extra plane ticket for Muscles ('We can save up, Mummy!') but eventually they accept that all the French Friendys cannot come home with us. Lined up patiently, the French Friendys sit and wait with Big Bertha, ready to greet the next children who might be lucky enough to love them. Alivia Dog, Pandora and Doo Doo are coming along on the road trip. For the rest of the crew, it's time for the undignified ordeal of the space-sucking bags.

When we need a break I make long, mozzarella-filled baguettes and Keith and I shepherd the flock up the road to the footbridge over the river. There is a rusty old chair in the shallows and I sit in that, cooling my feet and watching the children leap off the bridge into the murky green water.

In the evening we often head out to enjoy a wine at the *Estivales*, or a pizza in the square, or a drink with some friend or other. Usually I must drag myself out the door for these evening events. More often than not I am absolutely wrecked by this point, my back sore and my brain fried.

But our year is nearly over and there's no time for the hermit life. We want to squeeze the last drops from our adventure. There is also no avoiding the farewell parties, which are like bizarre bookends to the identical versions we had a year ago on the other side of the globe. We were buggered then too, frazzled from packing up our lives, dragging ourselves out to farewell beloved friends. The invisible hand of time is at our back again, pushing us forward, the future clamouring for space even as we try to sit for a second and rest in the present. Things are over, it seems, before we are quite ready.

Farewell to all that

We organise a goodbye party at the Château Gonflable for the École Albert Camus gang: Franc and Alain, Amélie, Sabine, Luc and our three. On a wooden picnic table under a tree I lay out fruit and sandwiches and biscuits and olives. I've made a chocolate cake and studded it with candles. At the kiosk I buy a terrible coffee, and Keith and I settle back to watch the kids play games on the waterslides. It doesn't take long before the party drama begins.

'Alain is crying,' Tabitha says. 'And Franc is upset too.'

I follow her to a giant purple elephant where the two boys, wearing their tiny speedos, are looking fraught and gesticulating. Alain is dramatically slapping his own legs.

'Stop!' Franc is screaming. 'Please stop hurting yourself! When you hurt yourself, you hurt me!'

Alain braces himself to get a better angle. He starts slapping his face.

'Whoa, whoa, whoa,' I say, stepping between them.

'Enough!' shrieks Franc, before running and crawling into the far corner of a nearby jumping castle. Keith follows the wailing noises to crawl awkwardly after him while I try to look after Alain, who has stopped slapping himself and now weeps, shoulders heaving theatrically.

'What's the matter?' I ask. 'Did you have a fight?'

Alain launches into a stream of angry French. I make soothing noises, but I can't understand a word. As Franc emerges, Alain slings his satchel over his shoulder and stalks off wearing only his black brief speedos.

'Goodbye forever!' he shouts over his shoulder. Keith hands off Franc to me and goes after Alain. We are in charge of these children and having them walking home half-naked and crying seems to me like a dereliction of duty.

I feed Franc some cake and wipe his nose while making non-specific clucking noises. He responds well to these ministrations and soon he is restored, running off with Mabel, to whom he is such a sweet bonus big brother. Keith returns with a slightly shamefaced Alain. He is soon becalmed with cake too, and joins the others. Keith and I sit back down and return to our conversation about Trump, neither of us much better enlightened about what happened, but both of us used enough to these boys by now to take their histrionics in stride.

After lengthy farewells to kids and parents, there's just enough time back home for a bath and a rest. We scatter to our separate hidey-holes, books in hand, to regroup before we must leave for a Calade farewell party that Josephine, Maurice and Mimi are throwing for us in the backyard of their apartment building.

Poor Biggles is hitting his introvert limit.

'It's alright, Bigsy,' I say. 'You don't even have to talk. You can just say hello and then go and read your book in a corner while you eat chips.'

'Urgh,' he groans.

'You know, Biggles,' I say, 'in Victorian times, there was no concept of childhood as we know it today. As soon as you were old enough to work, they'd send you down the mines.'

'Well, in the old days they had to watch black-and-white television and hunt dinosaurs,' Biggles replies.

'That is incorrect on so many levels, sir,' I say. 'Buck up. The kittens are there, and there will be food. For now, you've got an hour to chill.'

We grin at each other.

'Do you want a new fact, Bigsy?' I ask.

'Yes, Mummy!' he says, big blue eyes beaming.

'There's a giant squid called the colossal squid that not only has massive tentacles but on each tentacle, a giant, swivelling hook.'

'Great!' says Biggles. 'Thank you!'

Like Biggs, I wish desperately that I could go to bed, but I need instead to head to the kitchen and heat the lamb curry that I made yesterday so that it can be packed up and carted across town.

In Josephine's backyard we drink wine from plastic cups under the spreading wisteria. Maurice and I grip each other's forearms and yell *'Putain de merde!'* with glee. Maryam pulls me aside to give me a small wooden religious painting and a tiny jar of Syrian honey, both of which she has carried from Damascus. We hug hard to make up for the words we don't have.

Nanette makes a beautiful speech (I catch half of it) in which she thanks me for bringing some 'Australian charm' to her classroom. (Ambassador Mode, activate!) She presents me with a gift of engraved Calade glasses and a wonderful tote bag printed with a photo of the class, along with a card containing messages from all the other students.

I stand and gibber nonsense for a few minutes before I call on Keith to finish our speech. The children are having a wonderful time upstairs playing with the kittens, Tik and Tak, and I snaffle the chance to sneak out the front for a cigarette with Josephine. Tabitha engages her sneak-alarm and comes to find me.

'Busted, custard!' she says, and I gird myself for a lecture or tears, but she merely shakes her head with exasperation.

'You should charge her, Tabitha,' says Josephine. 'One euro for every cigarette.'

Tabitha perks up. 'How many euros do you owe me?' she says excitedly.

'Well,' I say, 'just the one.'

She peers at me and then nods and returns to the party.

It's been nearly a year since I sat in Tabitha's bed with the ceiling close over my head while she railed at me for an hour about the horrors of cigarettes. Has she become inured to the evils of tobacco after a year in this smoky town? Or is she growing a better ability to cope with the idea of Mum as a flawed human? Paying your child a forfeit when they catch you smoking a party ciggie is perhaps not optimum mothering. It may end in her encouraging me to have 'just one more' so she can save up for a set of Hunger Games novelty arrows. Still, I'm not lying to her and she's not crying her eyes out. Best-Guess Parenting?

It's midnight. There is a series of final Moselfies in the foyer and a round of deep and tearful hugs, and then the Calade crew sends us on our way. Elevated and buzzing with exhaustion, the five of us wind our way home through the deserted streets. We sing 'It All Revolves Around the Sausage', our baritones rolling and reverberating off the locked shop-fronts encircling us. The children play leapfrog and swing around poles. I hold my arms wide and breathe deeply, luxuriating in the silent, familiar darkness and inhaling the dusty-stone tang of the sultry summer air.

The night before we leave, there's a wonderful farewell party for us at the Sisters' Bar. Around the table are Alex, Momo, Kat, Josephine and Juliette, my beloved lady gang. We are a few glasses of Yin Yang in when, for no clear reason, a woman at the next table begins to paint our faces with glitter. We laugh and tell stories. Alex delights in telling me about an early night out when I told the table, 'I love cock!' Although we try, none of us can imagine what I thought was saying.

Stonemason appears to deliver a barrel-chested hug. We all cry, tears dissolving tracks through the glitter on our cheeks. I make my friends promise to look after each other when I am gone.

My heart feels too large for my chest. No more drinking wine with Momo and Alex on a Friday night at the Sisters' Bar; no more dancing, whirling and sweaty, to Irish music with Stonemason and his Harpo Marx curls. No more talking to Bastien the glamorous winemaker and groaning at the approach of ageing punk Scotsman Terry, always drunk. If Terry isn't winking, he is negging; both are tiresome, but I now know how to handle him.

No more stories of ancient Mesopotamia from brilliant Alex. No more of Kat's wicked grin. No more rapid-fire gags and gossip with Chloé and Esmé and Gigi at the gates of École Albert Camus. No more three-cheek kisses. No more trading jokes under my breath with Josephine like schoolgirls in class at the Calade, throwing spitballs at darling Mosel's head and giggling at his bespectacled bemusement. No more deflecting advice from the wonderful Vanessa. No more walking arm in arm, midnight-drunk, up Rue Canard with beloved, fierce Juliette. No more wandering the markets with Australian Nell, relaxing with relief into stupid jokes and loose, slangy mumbling. No more trading greetings with shopkeepers down the length and breadth of the street, and no more giving the Withering Parisian to Scary Cool Guy. No more cobblestones (Thank God for that, say my poor sore feet).

What an odd thing to build a whole, full life and then leave it just as you are starting to figure out the rules. The transition seems so sudden, so final, made even more so by the geographical distance of France. It will be ten years, if we're lucky, before we see these friends again. Keith and I racked up endless kilometres on these cobblestones, but these twelve magical months borrowed from the normal run of life are over. It's time for us to hand the Wormhole over to the next inhabitants of its long history.

Grand tour

I love Keith very much. He is capable and hardy, with the practical, poetic mind of an engineer who can play 'Total Eclipse of the Heart' on the piano. He will rule the shit out of the zombie apocalypse, and we have a very happy marriage. But our union is tested whenever we hit the road, because although I am clinically incapable of reading maps, if Keith's driving I must navigate. And on this trip we face changes of language, road rules and toll currencies, as well as crazy European drivers.

I see the talking map-robot lady as a boon for humanity on par with the discovery of the clitoris (the late 60s, I believe). I adore that ever-calm voice, awkwardly accenting the wrong syllables of street names (so adorable!) with no hint of judgment in her tone. Keith, however, sees GPS as a tool de-skilling a generation into hopeless babies. The problem is that he is a wizard who can always orient himself in space while I am prone to mixing up my left and right.

When I'm in the passenger seat and Keith asks me to open up the map on my phone, my heart starts to beat a little faster. I plug in our destination and hover my fingers over the 'start route' button, hoping that this time Keith will concede to its powerful magic.

'Shall I switch on the voice thing?' I ask, a slight quaver betraying my faux cheeriness.

'Just tell me the way,' he says.

'Why don't I get the directions?' I say. 'So much easier, yes? Okay then?'

'Nah, just give me the general run.'

My heart sinks, my IQ drops and I start poking the screen ineffectually with my sweaty paws. I zoom in and out. I start over. Does that say F1 or F7? Which bit are we at now? Which direction are we pointing in? What kind of a monster did I marry?

The next few weeks are a whirlwind of road-trip madness. We book accommodation as we go, wash clothes with soap in the sink and eat picnics made of random foreign-supermarket fare. We shrink family life to fit into our little hatchback, splitting tasks into portfolios of specialty and preference. Nobody's completely happy, of course – I'd rather not manage every scrambled meal and Keith is very much over European drivers, but I'd prefer to cook than eat what Keith might dish up and rather than sit next to me panicking on a German autobahn, Keith would do ... almost anything, I expect.

We make our way through northern France and Switzerland and Germany, visiting friends and exploring swimming pools. In Germany we marvel at the 'display shelf' toilets and learn the complimentary phrase *'Das ist eine schöne Scheiße'*, or 'That is a beautiful shit'. In Austria we twirl on the actual *Sound of Music* meadow where Maria taught 'Do-Re-Mi' to the children, and make the Best-Guess Parenting decision to visit the Hohenwerfen Castle and explore their collection of medieval torture implements, which includes a scold's bridle, a Spanish boot and a full-sized stretching rack. Kid's nightmares sorted for the next decade, then. Thanks, Austria!

Travel life wears a little. Across the Alps, the hills are alive with the sound of children armpit-farting and my back hurts for days after riding a terrifying German roller-coaster we called the Trouser-Soiler. Constant, minor physical discomfort of various kinds is a hallmark of life on the road, but there is no way to skulk off and indulge a black mood on a low-budget hatchback-based adventure. It's all about the togetherness, you see. Dear God. The togetherness.

In Slovenia we take a rickety train down into the ancient Postojna Cave, home of the strange and wonderful species of salamander called an olm, also known as the 'human fish', which can live for a hundred years. We jostle and hurtle for an hour, shivering, through an incredible subterranean landscape featuring mountains, rivers, stalactites, stalagmites and formations called 'curtains', all formed over millions of years. It feels as though we are surrounded by chilly, intricate lacework, the embroidery of a primordial grandmother.

We emerge from that cold, dim Slovenian cave system into the roasting heat of the day. We are slightly discombobulated, our skin prickling with the strange shock as we eat a makeshift picnic of apples and olives and crackers under a generously shady beech tree. Biggles lies with his head on the grass next to Keith as they quietly discuss some point of mathematics. They are wearing matching beige shorts made from trousers that have lost their knees, the edges fraying and the legs uneven from my inexpert measurements. Mabel leaps about gathering leaves.

In deserted, scrubby rural Croatia, the children invent a game called Hug-Bombing, and a large wasp stings me in the beautiful, white-walled Kotli Falls. Mabel learns to swim in a rickety above-ground pool in a leafy thicket. I toss a bottle of olive oil into the Food Bag, which shatters, seeding glass through the nuts, crackers and random bags of herbs and snacks, which by this stage include food from several countries. Far from shops, we eat spaghetti with unadorned tinned tomatoes, drink black coffee and snack on handfuls of salt crackers.

In Italy we stay in a super-cheap apartment in the industrial outskirts of Verona. The wi-fi works here, but only in the bathroom. Keith, unfazed as always, carries in a little table and sets up next to the toilet. Unfortunately I am wrestling with a low-to-medium-level case of the affliction I believe the British royal family refer to as 'the squits', an indignity compounded by an encounter with an Italian bidet that shoots boiling-hot water. The 'togetherness' factor means I must keep going to Keith's office to sit on the toilet next to his desk. It's not what you might picture in a remote-worker's 'Living the Dream' brochure.

In Verona we eat creamy burrata, zesty pesto and soft, salty bresaola; in Venice we explore palazzos and dangle our feet in the canals; and in Monaco we stroll among the facelifts and superyachts before we drive home in one last intense push. My straw hat is so bent out of shape that I look like Worzel Gummidge, the children are dazed and exhausted, and Keith has holes in the bum of the shorts that once were pants. I think it's time to call last drinks.

Back in the Wormhole at 5am, Keith and I collapse in our familiar dungeon, our minds a scattered gibberish casserole of Airbnb beds and languages.

It seems like only minutes later that we are woken by Alain, who has been checking in at the house every day to see if we are back. I lie in bed, loosely holding Keith's hand and listening to the children chat to Alain upstairs. I think about the idea of memory and a concept I read recently about the importance of the 'end' of things for how we frame the whole. Memories are so porous and unreliable, so fickle, easily influenced. We are likely to judge everything based on the last part of proceedings, even if this is merely a fraction of the full picture. We'll remember the party as wonderful, for instance, if we had a goodbye kiss from a handsome sex idiot, and terrible if we tripped over and showed our undies on the way out the door, regardless of how much we enjoyed the entire night.

Ending our France adventure with this rollicking road trip has been a brilliant cap on proceedings, I realise. It tightened that family bond, the greatest gift of my life, and reinforced for me the idea that 'home' is wherever we are, safe and comfortable in our shared jokes and immense affection for each other.

In less than two years, the world will be irrevocably altered by the COVID-19 pandemic and family life will be equally reshaped as the kids enter adolescence and assert their independence in the most unexpected ways. The big kids will be all about teaching me how to 'ship' and 'stan' things. No longer grappling with French, I'll be learning a different vernacular. The children will present me with astonishing versions of themselves and I will receive these gifts with delight. Nothing is permanent, either inside or outside these walls. The present, this moment in time, with all its complications and irritations, is such a gleaming gift. I am suffused with gratitude, but I can't lie here any longer having Wonderful Thoughts. Franc has arrived and he is crying.

Cuddles and snacks are required, and time is ticking. We only have two days left to pack up the house completely before our final week of travel: a few days in London, a few in Dubai and the long, curving flight home to Australia.

Home at last

Our Coledale house is stranger-smelling and thickly silent, as though it has been put on pause. The air is wrong, the light excessively brilliant. Our bodies must adjust from the full sweaty glory of a European summer to the damp chill of a coastal winter after a long day's immersion in the canned, recycled air of a plane. We drop our bags and wander around, reacquainting ourselves with all our objects. I stand and stare at the bookshelves, where all my old friends live. Keith immediately sits at the piano. The familiar soundtrack of Chopin fills the air.

'My wheelchair!' Mabel cries. She leaps into her cherished object and wheels about the house. It's been an age, I suddenly realise, since Mabel has wanted to discuss surgery or intestines. Tabitha and Biggles open and close the cupboard doors, inspecting the pantry, the bathroom and the games shelves. We all make our acquaintance, once again, with the good old composting dunny.

We're home, surrounded by clear, constant language: irreverent gags, easy small talk, upward inflections and politicians bickering. I'm struck with the strange normality of Australian news, where on the hour, our national broadcaster updates the staff changes, match results and varying scandals of our (almost exclusively male) teams of varying codes of football.

Home, where my brain is out of storage space, stuck in a caps-lock

293

cortisol overload. Where is the hot water bottle? The slow cooker? What side of the road am I on? What money do I need? Our suitcase mountain from France is joined by crates and boxes from the shed to form an unholy mess in the middle of the lounge room that daily grows more epic as the children comb through the pile for their special long-lost bits and pieces and I hunt for school uniforms and lunch boxes.

Home, where Keith is delighted to return to his lovely calm office in the old cowshed at the bottom of the backyard, where instead of the blaring next-door TV he is visited by the occasional wallaby or the nocturnal possum that has taking to creeping in the window and pissing on his paperwork.

Home, where Keith starts giving piano lessons to the kids every night, who have taken a year's break from their tuition. Thundering Rachmaninoff chords replace thundering feet on the ancient staircase.

Home, where the house jumps with a sea of Australian kids over to play on the trampoline and the rope swing. The big girls conduct a ceremony in the bush opposite the house, where they sacrifice each other to the gods of the underworld and then hold a lemon-eating contest, their peals of giggles giving away their location in the scrub. The boys play a wedgie-based game on the rope swing and then settle to *Dungeons & Dragons*. Biggles has brought this obsession home from France and now proceeds to indoctrinate his two besties, Henry and Saxon, into the game that will capture their imaginations.

Mabel arranges her small objects and treasures in her bedroom. She is quiet. The swirling dust from the sudden reversal of her world is taking time to settle.

Soon after our return, the pump that runs the water tanks breaks down. Until we can replace it, we must wash out of buckets and boil water on the stove to do the dishes. Biggles brings home a new friend from school, and I explain the composting toilet to him.

'Don't be freaked out – it's just like a normal toilet except that you don't flush it. So, you just go like normal, and then you wash your hands in the … Oh. That's right. Okay, little buddy, you go to the tank out the back and use the tap underneath …' Amélie and Alain may not be setting off fireworks here, but life is still full of surprises.

Home, where I languish in my bathtub, the bench behind my head held together with gaffer tape. I gaze at the timber ceiling where the light fitting traps scores of tiny dead insects, and a lacy petticoat of mould creeps inward from the corners. I think about the tiny, mysterious medieval window I used to stare at every day from this very position, in this same body.

Tabitha crashes in.

'Mum! Where's my shoe bag from Barcelona?'

'On the back of your door, I think,' I answer and then, hopelessly, 'Shut the door!'

I sigh a little, remembering how peaceful it was when children had other toilets to visit – three! Jesus take the wheel, the luxury! – and left me to soak with my thoughts. Here, the bathroom is like Grand Central Station, right next door to the toilet, and serves as a general thoroughfare for the entire family.

Dinner and a show

Down at Earthwalker, the local cafe, the decor is a feast of earth-toned neutrals, cane-woven chairs and exuberant bouquets of grevillea, kangaroo paw and bottlebrush, so calming to the Australian eye. Wooden boards display battered pastries dusted with icing sugar, and the menu offers ingredients I haven't seen for a year: kimchi, kelp flakes, nutritional yeast, mushroom dust and bush honey. Handmade ceramics, wobbly with wabi-sabi imperfections, are on display on raw timber shelves, and the staff wear Birkenstocks and hemp T-shirts belted into high-waisted jeans. They take my order, blinking through extreme eyelashes like strange birds.

The coffee is nutty and smooth, delivered with a perfect crema. Scary Cool Guy would shit his nappy if he tasted this, I think. Around the table, my wonderful, funny, smart and sassy girlfriends are discussing the diets of their dogs. I left them deep in conversation a year ago about the 'gut brain'. Time folds. It's like I never left.

'Tell us everything, Rach!' says Sarzy, but I don't know where to start. When Bad Fonzie shagged his mistress in the laundrette? When my makeup melted off at the Halloween party and left me looking like I'd just fallen off a cocaine-addled party bus in front of all the school parents? When Madame Montagne locked us out of school? When Keith told Kat he'd hurt his dick by sleeping on it funny? When Biggles set Tabitha's hair on fire at the lantern festival? When I injured myself falling off the detachable toilet seat?

In any case, the conversation has moved on. I can't quite access my Coledale vibe. I cradle my superb coffee and let the conversation flow around me. Like a magic switch has been flicked, I am suddenly hyper-aware of my surroundings. Understanding everything that is said, from the body language to the side eye, feels like adjusting from black-and-white TV to full technicolour. I realise that while my lack of French was a barrier to so much of what was happening, it also insulated me from the full, flooding experience of social interaction. Some of that outsider status was a gift.

We adjust, with some awkwardness, to social life at home. Kat and Alex and Franc and all the rest have become Facebook friends experienced at a distance, rather than in the everyday rough and tumble of life. It's hard to interact online using only my awful French. I've lost all the ancillary body language that used to smooth my lack of facility with the language. Kat and I can't communicate through physical comedy, Gigi can't just kick out my knees with affection, and I can't just mumble sympathetic noises and make appropriate faces when I understand what people are talking about on an emotional level, even though I cannot catch their words.

Kat and I rely a lot on the phrase '*Je suis excitée*', but even though I am a lowbrow-comedy queen, even 'Me so horny' gets tired after a while. I use good old Google Translate to describe what's going on at home to my Calade message chat, but even though this makes my French comprehensible, I feel fake, like I'm pretending to be something I'm not. Distance grows.

A long message arrives from Alain, who rather disconcertingly opens his missive with the all-caps greeting '**SLUT!**' I'm taken aback until I realise that poor Alain, spelling never his strong suit, has meant to write '*salut*'. Even from the other side of the globe he still makes me laugh.

~

A key reason that staying longer in France was never an option was the health of my mum and dad. As soon as we get back we go to dinner at their place down the hill from us in Coledale.

'Finally,' Dad says, 'you've finished fart-arsing about Europe!'

I think immediately of Kat. How she would have loved this phrase.

There are signs that things are not quite okay. Mum's lungs aren't good. She coughs constantly throughout our visit and she is very thin. While we were away she had a deep skin cancer cut from her face and treated with a topical chemotherapy cream that eats deep into the dermis. These kinds of skin-cancer procedures are a rite of passage for the pre-sunscreen generations of Australians. The slow and painful treatment has left Mum anxious and worried about leaving the house. Her response is entirely understandable, but it is part of a shadowy, deeper change I am starting to notice.

A year later, Covid will arrive to scatter-bomb us all. Mum's illness will grow teeth, her symptoms becoming stranger and more inexplicable until she is eventually hospitalised. Mum will recover from this illness but she won't return to live at home again. My sandwich-generation responsibilities will grow.

Inspired by my beloved Calade I will start volunteering on a crisis line and then take up a new professional role in suicide prevention and education. A dog will enter our lives, capturing all of our hearts, and adolescence will hit our house with the delicacy of a wrecking ball. Keeping my balls in the air will take all the hard-won wisdom of middle age.

But all this still lies ahead, although the hints of it swirl about us now like settling dust. Mum and Dad are delighted to have their grand-children home again, close enough to touch and cuddle. Mabel sits at Nanna's feet with a tray. She's fossicked through her grandparents' familiar cupboards to find her special tiny ceramic cups and bowls and saucers, which she fills with milk and sultanas.

On their little front deck, with the sea at the bottom of the hill and the escarpment at the top, we drink tea and tell stories of France: the food, the school, the cobblestones. Tabitha, my darling comedian, re-en-acts Madame Montagne for Nanna and Pop. They watch with glee and pride as she rails in French.

'Where is your geography assignment? In your bedroom at home? How dare you! What kind of an excuse for a student do I have before me? Would your mother be proud of this? Go! Sit! Detention for you! Detention for everybody!'

Re-entry, petit à petit

Smallest buddy Mabel and I are struggling to adjust. My sweet little one refuses to speak a word of French, her time horizon the most disturbed by the emotional whiplash of the whole experience. She reconnects with her old friends, but the systems and the routines of school are all stressful. She does not, like her older siblings, 'return' to these things, but rather must learn them all over again. It's her third time acclimatising to a new school environment, and she only just turned seven. It's a lot for a little brain. There are tears, headaches and stomach-aches, and the school-gate drop-off is fraught. I sympathise. *La rentrée* is bumpy for me too.

I try one night to soothe Mabel. Curled up with her Friendys on a camping mattress, she is full of thoughts and cannot sleep. Her half-sized toddler bed was turfed before France, and we haven't replaced it yet. I shift uncomfortably on the floor beside her and reach for an old favourite.

'Do you want a secret dream, Mabey?' I ask. She nods, clutching my spare hand close with damp fingers.

'You're in the hospital,' I begin, 'and you've just been diagnosed with diabetes ...'

Mabel sits up sharply.

'No! I don't want to be in hospital!'

'It's not helping you to ...?'

'No, Mummy! Do a new one!'

I'm stumped. If she doesn't want diabetes, she likely won't be interested in splenectomy, or renal failure, or liver resection. If I can't describe a Whipple procedure, how am I supposed to comfort this child?

Eventually we come up with a secret dream incorporating one of her new obsessions: quadruplets.

'You are big sister to four quadruplets,' I say softly, 'and you must help to get them all up and ready in the morning.'

Mabel relaxes back onto her pink-spotted flannel pillowcase, clutching Alivia Dog.

'They need you to give them a bath and put them in their special seats around the table. It's hard to feed them all at once so you have to be a really good helper to Mummy and Daddy.'

I ask Mabel the names of her quadruplet sisters. She sighs with contentment and thinks hard.

'Marigold,' she starts, 'and Button, and Fairy Feather and Plingus.'

'Beautiful,' I say reverentially. We spend a few minutes discussing the details of the quadruplets' diet (spoiler: it contains no mushroom dust) and then I leave Mabel to her secret dream.

We buy a new bed frame for Mabel, and an old bomb of a car, and I fill in scores of forms to sort out schools and health funds and insurance and house stuff, winding up tenancy agreements both here and in France. I drag my raggedy road-trip children into respectability, taking them shoe-shopping and sifting through crates from the shed for long-lost uniforms and lunch boxes.

At Just Cuts, Mabel is in the chair and I am making small talk about our European summer when the hairdresser turns to me in disgust.

'I will finish this cut because it's half-done,' she says, 'but there are nits all through this child's hair.'

'Oh, those are just dead eggs,' I say weakly. 'There're no actual live lice. It's just that French eggs are really hard to get out. They have, like, superglue on them. You just kill the lice and the eggs fall off eventually.'

She shudders. Our chat fizzles. Was ever a boastful expatriate cut more neatly down to size? 'French lice are incredibly hardy' is hardly aspirational south-of-France conversational content. What about the cockroaches? Tell me more! The rats – are they special? Do they wear stripey shirts?

Our Coledale school, perched at the edge of a cliff that overlooks the Pacific, is small. The children sit cross-legged under the heat-glimmering aluminium roof of the outdoor area in their baby-blue uniforms, a sea of fidgeting surf rats with salt-crusted hairstyles. Parts of the grassy oval are roped off to protect the plovers who have taking to laying eggs there, and in the far corner of the field is a small wooden whale-watching platform. When humpback whales pass on their long journey from Antarctica to Northern Australia, the office rings a bell so the children can run and watch their graceful passage.

The colours of home are the sharp peacock hues of the water, the expansive blue canopy above and the thousand greens of the bush escarpment. It's taking me a moment to recalibrate myself in space. In Sommières the light was filtered through the low-squatting sky, a worn-in bowler rather than an airy sunhat, and the colour palette was a muted watercolour box of grey and beige and brown, infused with the dusty patina of age and history.

Before I can blink our Australian life is in the full and fecund flowering of spring, expanding under the weight of play dates and sports and extended family visits. Aside from the practical tasks, I'm trying to help the children feel securely rooted home. My mental load feels overwhelming, and my brain doesn't quite know how to categorise my feelings. I need a new word, probably in Franglish, something like *fuffoir*: 'the combined emotions of nostalgia, gratitude and sadness, felt most strongly when managing the psychological wellbeing of small children while keeping to a punishing snack schedule and being unable to find one's bra, coffee maker or Medicare card.'

It's coming at me from all angles (as the actress said to the bishop).

But *petit à petit*, I start constructing a new life for us – one that absorbs the growth of the year we just spent and adjusts to the changing needs of the children. I find a moment of silence in the local library. Away from the Master List and the accusatory Box Mountain in the middle of the living room, I drop in to that quiet place of work and feel an internal settling. I get a coffee from the cart outside, boot up my laptop and turn again to *Mothering Heights*. The zinc countertop of the Bar du Nord flashes into my mind and then dissolves.

I find my routine, writing around tumbling and taekwondo and drama classes, grabbing moments around pick-me-up-here and drop-me-off-there and if-I-just-grab-milk-and-bread-and-apples-I-can-hold-off-on-the-big-shop-till-Friday. I sit with my laptop in the backs of community halls and in carparks and in glorious Australian cafes (which I will never take for granted again). I wake early and sit with the boxes in the quiet lounge. Just me and my sore back, thinking.

Our year in France, gone like a puff of smoke, already has the shimmery, half-real quality of a weird dream. I spoke French every day, and drove a little car across a Roman bridge, and then a giant cat taught my Pilates class and … wait. Did that happen?

Walking to school along our dirt road, the muscular surf booms gently in the background, like constant, soothing white noise. The children and I pause to greet the miniature donkeys Chocolate, Harry and Marshmallow, who race across their paddock to insert insistent noses into our hands. The occasional lyrebird runs with its awkward, comedic gait into the bush. Rainbow lorikeets swoop, frogs bellow their nightly soundtrack and Kevin Rudd the kookaburra is back on the clothesline, perching calmly and letting us creep close enough to marvel at the beautiful blue markings on his wing. I peg out the laundry surrounded by trees whose lush green is as thick and insulating as Sommières stone.

On a bushwalk through the nearby national park we nearly step on two brown snakes fighting. They are eastern browns, the second-deadliest land snake on Earth, and when I do a little research later on the very Australian Facebook page 'What Snake Is That?', I learn that when browns fight, there are often other browns lurking nearby to join the fray.

Another day I have to get out the tick kit to extract a big specimen from Mabey's head, first using scabies cream on it as per the protocol against the Mammalian Meat Allergy tick that can be found in our area. This particular tick gives the victim a serious anaphylactic allergy to meat that cannot be cured, turning them instantly into vegetarians. If anything could strike fear into the heart of your average French citizen, it would be this tick. An allergy to *boeuf bourguignon?* Permanent? *Putain de merde!*

We're definitely not in the south of France anymore. But this place is paradise too. How joyful to have lived that temporary life and then come back to one as lovely as this, even if the toilet requires turning, the ticks can make you allergic to roast lamb and venomous snakes fight right under your nose. It is a full six months before my feet stop hurting. The bruises fade as slowly as my memories: from sharp pain to shadowy ache, from bright colours to watercolour wash. But they leave a permanent, beautiful etching somewhere deep below my skin, an imprint of those faraway fairytale cobblestones.

Acknowledgements

This book is a love letter to Keith, the best wedding pash I ever had and my partner in shenanigans for the last twenty years. Thank you for putting up with my nonsense, scaffolding my dreams, holding my hand through 4am anxiety insomnia, finding badly filed documents, rescuing lost work, gently informing me that I am editing the wrong copy ... Wow, I really am a pain in the arse. What would I do without you, Cakes? You deserve all the roast lamb in all of the lands. Next: the sailing years!

It's also a love letter to my three magical children, Ivy, Teddie and George, all of whom have read, signed off on and helped me with this book. Kids, I feel you chose me from some universal catalogue, and that is a gift I will never take for granted. I feel so lucky to be your mum, and I am incredibly proud of your kind, funny and generous spirits. I must also acknowledge our fourth child, Biggles: the fluffiest, sleepiest and naughtiest of them all. We love you Bibby Wibby. You're a very good boy.

My mum and dad, Christine and Frank Mogan, have always been wholly and unconditionally supportive of me and for that I thank you from the bottom of my heart. Love and gratitude to my sister, Sam Doorey, one of my life's greatest blessings. Everybody should have a person they can rely on to tell them when to pull their head in, and with whom they can draw on five decades of bad shared gags. What, this hat?

To my wonderful in-laws: McIntosh family, I love you dearly. A special mention must go to my beautiful mother-in-law Liz McIntosh, lover of all things French. Thanks to Deb, Jen, Adrian and Brendan for all your support.

Admiration, love and gratitude to our French friends, who showed us what true generosity looked like. Elizabetta, Steph, Caro, Pedro, Manon, Andrew, Julia, Pablo, Nathanaëlle, Basel, Michelin, Tony, Martine, Michel, Naomi, Julian, Clémence, Emelie, Ghislaine: the way you cared for us during our Sommières year taught me lessons about compassion and community that I will never forget. Thank you to the wonderful Virginie, and to the brilliant teachers of La Condamine primary school. I have teased you a lot in these pages! But we admire and appreciate you very much. A special hug and thank you to the gorgeous children of Sommières, who will always hold a place in my heart.

The older I get, the less I want to leave the house, but despite this my friends are the joy of my life. Love and acknowledgements must go to my entourage in Coledale, the C-Words: Jen Stone, Sarah Goss, Priscilla Neilsen, Lizzie Buckmaster, Charlotte Reid, Raylee Golding, Chantal Banyard, Jane Fullerton-Smith, Al Merceria, Megan Badham, Al Battestini and more. Bless your kale-forward smoothies and your cold-water-swimming. May we always cackle so hard there is light bladder leakage. Huge love to my school crew: Lisa Grimmond, Nikki Marriot and Katie Orsini. Our WhatsApp was a lifesaver over the last few years in particular. And my darling Pink Ladies: Lucy Cho, Dimi Rayner, Emma-Jane Watson, Bianca Martin, Sonia Komeravalli and Shirin Town. You are my ride-or-dies and I love youse all. My writer friends from the Hardcoven have always been a support and an inspiration, in particular the wonderful Nigel Featherstone, gentle mentor to so many. Thanks to Simon Lockhurst, an early reader and generous champion. A special mention to Tori Haschka, Jodi Wilson and Jayne Tuttle, brilliant writers themselves as well as generous, funny friends, always there to receive and parry a rant, a vent or a sweary diatribe. Our French visitors: Cill, Mark, Elke, Sabine, Bron, Mick, Ross, Élodie, Lucy, Dim, Quentin, Dan, Rich, Bianca, Isla, Xavier, Mal, Lyndel, Elizabeth, Ernie and Louis. Thanks for sharing so many wonderful moments with us at that table.

Deep gratitude goes to my exceptionally supportive agent Jane Novak, who took a chance on me when she first read my work at the brilliant program Hardcopy with the ACT Writers Centre, and to my publisher Kelly Doust, who's been a joy to work with from our earliest meeting. My editor Armelle caught all the places where I repeated my gags and said wildly idiotic things, and I'm only devastated she cannot follow me around in life performing this function. The Varuna Writers' House in Katoomba gave me the gift of a two-week fellowship, which enabled me to centre my writing for the first time – an incredible opportunity for which I am hugely grateful. Thank you to the wonderful magazine editors I have worked with, where some of these France tales took their first form. And my workmates at Lifeline keep me grounded and laughing with every tea-room conversation.

Thank you to France for allowing us to spend a year setting down roots in your wonderful country, and specifically to Sommières for the chance to be temporary misfits and *marginaux* in your storied, wicked, raunchy, joyful streets.

Finally, to books themselves: since my first library card at three, you have always been my best friends. At any given time, I have one foot inside some other land in my mind, and I am so delighted to have been given the chance to create a land of the mind for others. It's like my very own Faraway Tree. To the readers who have bought and read this book: thank you. *Merci! Putain de merde!*